A LIFE LIKE NO OTHER

A Compilation of Short Stories
From My Early Years in East London
1951-1975

Paul Lucas

Copyright © 2024 by Paul Lucas

All rights reserved. No part of this publication may be reproduced, distributed, or transmitted in any form or by any means, including photocopying, recording, or other electronic or mechanical methods, without the prior written permission of the author, except in the case of brief quotations embodied in critical reviews and certain other noncommercial uses permitted by copyright la

About the Author

I thought long and hard about exactly what I should say about myself, I then realised that I need not say anything, as the pages of this book will reveal everything there is to know.

What I can tell you is that I had no intention of ever writing about my early life in the East End of London, it came about because of writing the story of a period much later in my life, which is in fact volume three of my life story.

I shall say no more, enjoy.

1 - Birth

Thursday 22nd March 1951 at 9.50 am, just another moment in time, for many, however it was a monumental day in my life, as it was the day that I came into this World, all 8 lbs 3 ounces of me. I was the second son of Rose and Stanley (Slim) Lucas. There would be two more sons born to our parents, completing a set of four brothers. The number 1 record when I was born was, "The Tennessee Waltz" by Patti Page. In the bed next to my mum, at St. Andrew's Hospital, Bromley by Bow, London E3, was a lady of Scottish descent, wonderfully named as Dorothy Winterflood, but forever known as 'Dorrie.' She had given birth to a daughter, Janice, at almost the same time as myself and my mum and Dorrie would spend the next 21 years trying to get, "the twins", Janice and myself together. That of course was never going to happen given the fact that Janice came out of her mother's womb with looks akin to the elephant man, she grew up to become the understudy to Olive, that 'pin-up' girl from on the buses.

Dorrie was the only lady that we knew that did not have a cockney accent. She was married to a giant of a man, Ted Winterflood. My brother's, and myself would be in awe of this man until the day he died, suddenly, in his late forties. Ted was, for a while, the leader of Tower Hamlets Council. His sheer size put the fear of God into my brothers and me. Dorrie remained a family friend throughout my mum's life.

St. Andrew's Hospital had opened in 1871, as the Poplar and Stepney Sick Asylum and was positioned directly opposite the Stepney Workhouse. This itself epitomised just how far down the wealth ladder we really were. My brother's and I would visit St. Andrew's on many occasions, it was to become almost a second home to Graham, the youngest of the four brothers.

For seventeen and a half years I was to live in an old, Victorian, bay windowed house with my parents, three brothers and our paternal grandparents, Ted, and Lilly Lucas. The house consisted of four upstairs and four downstairs rooms. Us four boys shared one upstairs bedroom until our grandparents let us have one of their rooms downstairs, a room which, until handed over to my eldest brother Peter and the third in line John, was only ever used on Christmas day and for funerals. Grandad Ted never stopped moaning about the fact that he had released this room to two of his grandchildren. Ted was a miserable old git, he never really did anything other than to moan all day from the comfort of his cushion less armchair which he rested in from eight in the morning until ten

A Life Like No Other

at night, when Lily would carry him to his bed. We had a back yard it contained an outside toilet, a coal bunker, and a very large shed. I knew from a very early age exactly what 'freezing my bollocks off' meant. Also in the yard was a five-foot galvanised bath, every Sunday two of us would have to carry the tin bath, upstairs to the scullery (kitchen) whereupon all six of us would bathe in the same water. My father would always be last, there was no doubt in my mind that he got out of his bath a lot less clean then when he got in. To my recollection my grandparents never had a bath, God knows how my grandfather's arse must have smelt, as his breath was bad enough.

Thus far, there is nothing remarkable about this story, as thousands of post war families in the East End of London lived in much the same way as we did. We were poor, make no mistake, but there were families on our street, around the corner, and up the road, whom were much, much, worse off than us.

Our dad was never out of work. It seemed to me that he could do anything if it involved using his hands. Following in his own father's footsteps, my dad, "Slim" (his nickname derived from the fact that he never stopped eating, but was always the same weight, throughout his life) had taken an apprenticeship as a carpenter and could literally build anything from wood, however my earliest memories of my dad's work, was as a mechanic, or "fitter" as they called them back in the day. Dad normally worked six days a week. On Saturday's two or three of his sons would accompany him to his workshop in Marsh Gate Lane, Stratford, London E15. It was a run down, decrepit area back in the 1950's and remained so until someone came up with the bright idea of building an Olympic Park there. If you leave the immediate area of the park, even today, you will see parts of, "pre-war" Marsh Gate Lane still standing. Saturdays were great fun for my brother's and myself. We would all jump into whatever lorry my dad had brought home the previous evening, neither of us ever wanted to get in first, as the first in would have to sit on the cover of the engine and after a mile or so, both your backside and undercarriage would be toasted. This was not so bad in the winter but in the summer months it was torture. Upon arrival at, Laurier's Sack & Bag Company, the lorry would stop outside the imposing wooden gates and our dad would get out and open a small side door, he would then unlock the main gates and drive the lorry into the yard. My brother's and myself would then sit very quietly in the lorry until our dad had unlocked the kennel that contained, Wolf, the gigantic, pure white Alsatian dog. Having gained his freedom, Wolf would then almost always knock our dad over with the excitement of being let out of his kennel. This excitement would lead to him having a dump, which through the eyes of a nine-year old would be as huge as the mess left behind by the horses pulling the dust cart that collected our rubbish every Friday. I remember asking my dad many times as to why a guard dog would need to be locked in his kennel all night. My dad told me that if he did not lock him up then he would probably kill someone. He would throw Wolf half a sheep, this was when we knew it would be OK for us to leave the safety of the lorry. Once Wolf had been fed, watered, and chained up for the day we were all free to create whatever mischief took our fancy. There was one drawback from going to work with our father on Saturday's, we never got to visit Upton Park or Brisbane Road with our mates. My dad's brother, uncle Ted (Ticker), once a very bad amateur boxer, had a nose that covered the width of his face, underneath it he had a pencil moustache. His ugliness was matched only by that of his three offspring. Ticker and his family lived in a house not unlike ours, in Hackney Wick, just a ten-minute walk from the home of football, Brisbane Road. Uncle Ted Lucas, uglier than Plug, of the Bash Street Kids fame, later condemned my brother and myself to a lifetime of supporting a team, Leyton Orient, that would, apart from one season, only ever languish in the lower divisions of the football league.

2 - Queen Elizabeth 11 Coronation

My earliest childhood recollection is that of June 2nd, 1953, the day of the Queen's Coronation, I was 2 years and 3 months old. My mum and dad, never Royalists, had gone to Greenwich Park for the day, taking younger brother John with them. My eldest brother, nearly 5, had gone off with some of his older friends, their task for the day was to nick some lead from the roof of St. Michaels Church. This left me to spend the day with my grandparents.

My nan found an old an old army blanket and a broomstick and I became Friar Tuck (see front cover). Grandad Ted gave me a farthing to get some sweets but told me to bring the change straight back to him. Behind the makeshift fence was just one of our playgrounds, a bombsite that we called the dirty park. On the other side of the park was Poplar Library. I was to receive the gift of a balloon for taking part in the fancy dress competition. Big brother, always malicious to me, burst the balloon seconds after he was returned home by an officer of the law. Visits to our house by the boys in blue were so frequent that in my very young days I believed them to be part of our family. Our Coronation Street party took place in Venue Street, Poplar, London E14. Ena Sharples and Hild Ogden were the guest of honours. The miserable old git that was my grandfather remained in his chair in the corner of his tiny downstairs living throughout. He hated people, especially small boys. When he slept John and I would tie his shoelaces together, he had several hospital visits because of him falling over.

3 - The Wheelbarrow

On the 1st, September 2022 my youngest brother, Graham celebrated his 65th birthday, all alone. He had decided that by having only himself for company that no misdemeanours could befall him.

Just weeks before his birthday I had discovered a photo that rekindled a memory that otherwise was long forgotten. The photo itself, taken by brother Peter's friend, Ronnie Green, is the only one that I have of all four brothers together. We are pictured with the wheelbarrow that Graham was given for his second birthday in 1959. I apologise for the poor quality of the photo.

Our dad had helped us in the making of the wheelbarrow that we presented to the birthday boy on his big day. The back wheels were slightly bigger than those at the front, having been taken from a pushchair that had been conveniently left outside a house in Spey Street. The front wheels were lifted from the trolly that carried grandad Ted's large, brown oxygen bottle, whilst the miserable old sod was snoring one afternoon. How we smiled when watching him struggle to lift the bottle when he needed to go to the outside loo. The wood came from dad's shed and the front mudguards were taken from a child's bike in exchange for an orange jubbly and a bottle of King Fling. The barrow had no steering, we tied some rope to the front axle in order that we could pull our little brother from our house to Greenwich Park.

It was the last week of the school summer holidays and we set off at just after 9.00am, our parents had already left for work. John and I had made the journey several times previously. We knew that it would take us about 90 minutes to reach the Greenwich foot tunnel and a further 20 minutes or so to enter the park. Graham had received one pound and five shillings for his birthday, enough money to see us all through the day. As we were leaving home nannie Lil gave us each a slab of bread pudding, this was ditched as soon as we were out of sight of the house. At 10.30am we arrived at the tunnel entrance and slowly carried the wheelbarrow, with the two-year-old birthday boy still onboard, down the wide spiral staircase and into the coldness of the 1215 foot long, fully tiled tube that lay under the river Thames. The tunnel had opened in 1902.

As anyone that has ever walked through the tunnel will tell you, it slopes downwards until it reaches the midway point and from there it is all uphill. We positioned the barrow dead centre, untied the pulling rope, and gave it an almighty shove. There was not another soul in sight. Halfway down the slope the barrow decided to mount the white tiled curved wall before levelling up and hitting the shins of an old couple, who were brought down upon the damp paved floor. God knows where they had come from. Graham was buried underneath the barrow. Holding back the laughter we helped the elderly couple to their feet, they seemed to be OK but were concerned for the welfare of the little boy that had almost ended their lives. I saw an opportunity.

With the elderly lady snuggling our little treasure to her bosom, I turned to the man, that looked to be about the same age as the senile old git that masqueraded as our grandad, and said –

'We had to run down here to get away from some older boys that wanted to take the barrow from us,' (tears streamed down my cheeks as I continued) 'they tried to pull our baby brother from the barrow by his feet, but he held on to the sides but lost his shoes.'

The man reached into his jacket pocket and took out a brown leather wallet, that he must have had since the Crimean war, and said –

'Here, take this and get yourselves some ice-cream when you get up top.'

He then handed me a ten-bob note.

We checked the barrow, all seemed to be OK. The lady gently returned Graham to it, and we bid our generous new friends goodbye. Once outside the tunnel entrance on the South side of the river, we once again tied the rope to the barrow and pulled our slightly traumatised brother along.

Five minutes later we entered the first sweet shop after passing the Cutty Sark and bought 5 cornets, with flakes and spent the rest of the ten shillings on chocolate and drink. By the time we reached the entrance to the park Graham was already covered from head to toe by a mixture of all three.

Big brother Peter and Ronnie Green pulled the barrow up the incline until we reached the highest point of the park. From our vantage point there was a great view of the Thames and the many ships that frequented the Royal London Docks. There was not a hint that one day all of that would be gone, replaced by Canary Wharf and apartments for the learned gentry.

It was now time to test the wheelbarrow. We positioned it, with Graham inside, at the midway point of a wide, tarmacked path and gave it a gentle nudge. Graham and his new mode of transport quickly gathered pace. As it disappeared, out of sight and into a cluster of trees we heard the screams and saw people at the bottom of the hill running, we knew that all had not gone to plan. When we arrived on the scene Graham was being comforted by a small crowd, he had been thrown clear moments before the speeding birthday present had crashed into the massive oak tree, however the barrow, on the road for just a few hours, was a write off. Ronnie quelled the baby Graham's sobbing by handing him a half-eaten mars bar, he was then put onto big brother's back and carried back to the foot tunnel. Ronnie then piggy-backed him to the

North side and we collectively waited for the 277 bus to take us back to East India Dock Road.

We were back home and eating fish fingers and chips, that our nan had cooked for us long before mum and dad arrived home from work. We told our dad that some boys from Bow had taken the barrow from us. Graham fell asleep in our grandad's arms; this was the only time in his entire life that the miserable old bastard ever cuddled one of his grandchildren. John, and I went out to play football in the road, which was a lot less dangerous than going to Greenwich for the day.

Left: John – Middle Back: Peter – Right: Me – Middle Front: Graham

4 - Our first records

Just before Christmas, 1959, Slim, our father, brought home a Dansette record player, with it came a matchable and detachable speaker. This was a true Stereo sound system and was, for many a year, the envy of our close neighbours, family, and friends.

On boxing day, our dad took me, aged eight years and nine months and brother John, seven years, and five months to Brick Lane, just off Whitechapel High Road in Stepney, London E1. Our older brother, aged eleven, was not interested in music, he excelled in petty crime and had a different agenda to us. Graham being just two and a bit, spent most of his time in his second-hand pram, parked, most of the time, outside the front door. John and I did try to get him into our music, by placing the extension speaker under the army blanket that pinned him down. We would turn the speaker on full blast, but it just made him cry. He was at his happiest when buried under the stacks of kindling that we would steal from Bobbing's, the local wood factory.

The purpose of our trip to Brick Lane, was simple. In a shop, half-way along this street, there was a record store and it opened on boxing day. It was owned by a member of the Jewish Community, as was every other shop in this area of London. Even in 1959 the interior was, as it had been before the first world war, Victorian in appearance. On the counter of this shop, under a sheet of glass, was a copy of the latest New Musical Express, (NME) Top 40. We had, neither seen this magazine nor knew of any of the records that it listed. From that day on, brother John or I would purchase a copy of this music rag every Friday morning. I say purchased, however we would get Geoffrey Salter, a boy with a paper round and three years older than us, to nick one from the paper shop for us.

We studied the glass encased chart, Mr Cohen, the shop owner, studied us.

Brother John asked the long-nosed brother of the owner of Tesco's to show him -

'Rawhide' by Frankie Lane.

'Mack the Knife' by Bobby Darin and –

'Deck of Cards' a spoken ditty by that world-renowned crooner, Wink Martindale.

Mr Cohen, dressed from head to toe in black and sporting a long, matted grey beard, drooled as he took the eight-year-old boys entire Christmas money of exactly £1.00.

Asking my younger brother as to why he had selected those three songs, John explained that he liked the theme tune from the TV cowboy series of the same name. He would sit, cross legged in front of our six-inch black and white TV and shout 'get em up, move em out' whilst whipping himself on the thigh with a belt that he had removed from our grandad's forty-year-old trousers. Although he had never heard 'Mack the Knife' or knew of Bobby Darin, he was always playing with knives. He would pin the ace of spades onto the kitchen door and throw knives at it. Hence his third choice of records.

It was now my turn. I selected three records, two of which I had never heard. They were,

'Oh Carol' by Neil Sedaka.

'Red River Rock' an instrumental played by Johnny and the Hurricanes.

And for my mum, I purchased, 'Living Doll'" by Cliff Richard, a song that she was always singing to herself as she ran the washing through the 100-year-old mangle that had been given to her, by her own Grandmother. The mangle had made the journey from Yorkshire to London in the sidecar of uncle "Tickers" motorbike. His wife, the third 'Lil' in our family, had somehow managed to fit herself in beside the mangle and stay in the same position, without moving, for over 250 miles. 'Living Doll' had been in the charts a few months earlier and I knew that my mum would be pleased to get it. I handed over my pound. Mr Cohen took it from me as if it were a hot potato, he dropped it into his till and locked it as though it was a vault in the Bank of England. I was now skint. The record for my mum turned out to be a good investment, as not only did I get extra chicken on my boxing day dinner, but I also received the largest piece of Christmas Pudding.

My Dad wanted to buy more record's whilst in Brick Lane, however he was under the threat of losing his undercarriage, had he done so. He spent his money in the next-door baker's, which belonged to Mr Cohen's brother. He bought my mum a very lovely looking seedy bloomer. I think he made the right choice, as that night, he was back to making the kind of noises, in his bedroom, that we had come to expect, whenever our mum was pleased with him.

Whilst my three brothers and I were eating the leftovers from our Christmas dinner in the upstairs of our palatial abode, my nan and grandad were entertaining Aunt Lil and Uncle Harry, our father's sister, and brother-in-law, in the room directly underneath. After Graham, who had been lifted onto a chair, in order, to reach the sink, had finished the washing up, Lil and Harry made their way upstairs. We were each presented with a present, neatly wrapped in thick brown paper, that Harry Roberts, a postman until he gained notoriety a few years later, had undoubtedly lifted from work. I was elated to find that I had been given a 1960 diary, resplendent with its pink outer cover. I would later find out that Harry had given this to Aunt Lil for Christmas and the black eye that he was sporting was a direct result of her thanks. From the beginning of 1960 I was to make entries into my feminine diary. Aunt Lil was so pleased, I would be provided with, exactly, the same present until I was sixteen.

On New Year's Eve, 1959 our parents hosted a party for about forty people. I still do not understand exactly how they all fitted into our minute living room. What I do know, is that our record collection now stood at twelve 45's and a large stack of 78's. The latter of which were given to us by Wally Smith, a man that, in appearance, resembled Mr Magoo. Wally did not have a record player. God knows why he had nearly one hundred 78's?

And so, the joint record collection of Paul, John and Slim Lucas had begun. In the ensuing years, the purchase of certain records would allow us to retain, in our memory banks, both personal, and public events.

The 'Dansette' Stereo Record Player that was the envy of friends and family.

5 - Back to School

Christmas 1959 had come and gone. My dad returned to his work, he was now a long-distance lorry driver, and my mum clocked into her job on the sweet counter of Woolworth's, near to Crisp Street Market. Brother John and I were left to fend for ourselves, whilst also having the responsibility of looking after our baby brother, Graham, aged just 2 years and a few months. We spent most of our time in the road, playing football. Traffic was almost non-existent in the side streets where we resided. Graham's large, third-hand Silver Cross Pram, that our dad had found, without a baby inside, outside of a house in Hackney, was used as a sizeable goalpost. One of our classmate's, eight-year-old Eden Aylet was used as the other one. At noon, Lily Lucas our paternal grandmother would call us in for lunch. For ten minutes we would tuck into, bread and dripping, sugar sandwiches or toast. Toast was given at the end of each week as the bread was just too stale to make sandwiches out of. Our grandad sometimes cut the bread with a saw. We normally left Graham, and his pram, in the middle of the road until we resumed our game. After all, who would want to steal a continually screaming, shit ridden boy with two different coloured eyes?

On January 11th,1960, John and I returned to school. We attended Manor Field Primary. It was just a two-minute walk from the house. No one ever took us to the gates or collected us at lunch or at throwing out time. I do not recall ever seeing a single 4x4 parked up, awaiting the arrival of snotty nosed girls and boys. Our nan would have our young brother in the mornings however he would have to wait patiently outside the school gates for the whole of the afternoon as nan and grandad would be away with the fairies after lunch. Our little brother would be given various leftovers by the more conscientious of the passing mothers. That was, until a sixteen-year-old mum of three decided that she would share her gobstoppers with the child, that appeared to have no parents. The result of that act of kindness was that Mr Richards the assistant headmaster, was summoned from the school. He took baby Grahan from his pram, held him upside down, by his legs, and whacked him firmly on the back. Out came the gobstopper, his tonsils, and a good portion of his right lung. Even today, Graham cowers at the sight of anything that resembles one of those yesteryear sweets. He never took up golf as a direct result of that experience. During that, first week back at school, all pupils were subjected to a search for head-lice. Of those that were found to be infected, which included both John and me, the offending heads were shaved, and a large purple cross

A Life Like No Other

was painted onto the tops of our skull. Had we been given striped pyjamas, a yellow star and put onto the last train out of Kings Cross then we may never had been seen again.

John and I, ever mindful of the fact that we needed to raise money, in order, for us to add to our record collection, came up with the idea of selling young Graham's Silver Cross. We wrote the words, FOR SALE, ONLY 12 PREVIOUS OWNERS on some Izal toilet paper, just before our grandad could wipe his hairy arse upon it. In big bold writing we added £2.00 at the bottom of the third sheet. We carefully painted over the skid marks that had been left by the many previous occupants of this 1941 baby carrier.

Our nan sent us to Hedge's, the butcher, to get some offal for her dinner. We wheeled our young brother the mile or so to the shop and joined the queue inside. Five minutes later we placed the newspaper containing the offal at the foot of the pram. It was only then that we realised that our darling baby brother was not there. We lifted the tarpaulin that kept him dry, he was still missing. However, there were two, screwed up, one pound, notes under the elephant that doubled as both a cuddly toy and a pillow. We looked at each other in sheer jubilation. We could not only buy six brand new singles, but we also still had a pram to sell.

Graham was handed in at Poplar Police Station three days later. A lady, dressed as a man and answering to the name of Norman had taken him. Our mum had not even asked as to his whereabouts. The Seargent, a man of over twenty-five stone handed him to my nan and told her,

'Of all the many children that we have had at the station, this little cherub is the best behaved of them all.'

We took £1.50 for the pram from a 12-year-old girl that had given birth to a son that she had conceived via a brief fondle with the local Vicar. We stole it back two days later.

My brother and I were just too young to be doing a paper-round although our eldest brother was doing just that. I noted in my pink diary that he was fired after just a few weeks, for not actually delivering the papers.

John and I ran errands for our grandparents and a few neighbours. Our nan would give us twopence, less than 1p in today's money. Our Grandad, who was as tight as a ducks-arse, never gave us cash, he would say,

"I'll settle with you boys on Friday."

However, when Friday arrived, he always, without exception, would have his head buried under a tea-towel that covered the bowl that was full of Vick's Nasal Vapour. We would stand either side of him as he breathed in the menthol air, but he never surfaced. On Saturday mornings, we would pressurise him by standing at his feet as he sat in the one armchair that our grandparents owned. John would slowly turn off his oxygen supply. He knew why we were there, however he would feign death, in order, for us to leave. He was, without doubt, a miserable old git and when we stopped running around after him, he simply got our nan to get us to do *his* errands.

When collecting his weekly tobacco order, two ounces of Old Holborn, we would nick about a quarter of it. We would replace what we had taken by mixing in some sawdust from the floor of our dad's shed. The old git, whose nose seemed to be constantly dripping, never seemed to notice. This allowed us to sell one ounce to a neighbour, Brian Smith, every fortnight. With this money, plus what we earnt from the stealing of kindling from the local wood factory, we managed to purchase one single, every week. John would choose one week, and I would pick the next.

6 - Eden Aylet

By the time March 1960 arrived we had been playing music on our prized Dansette for a little over ten weeks. We then came up with another revenue stream. We would invite our friends and neighbours in to listen to our collection. The invitation would be from 4-6pm on weekdays. Our mum finished work at 6pm and dad was never home before 6.30. We would charge sixpence (2 and a half pence today). We told our guests that they were quite welcome to bring their own records.

During the first week, only Eden Aylet, the posh boy, who always wore a white shirt, a blue tie, and pullovers of varying colours, took up our offer. He brought his own 78's, all were scratched, he remarked as to how much better the sound that emanated from our twin speakers was, in comparison to his Carnival Toy Record Player which played only 78's and had a stylus (needle) as thick as a 3-inch nail.

It was painful to listen to Max Bygrave's singing "You're a pink toothbrush, I'm a blue toothbrush" as it was scratched, way beyond salvation. We persuaded young Eden, named simply because his mum had conceived him whilst on a school visit to Kew Gardens, to give up his stack of 78's and listen instead to our collection of 45's. He duly obliged and after he had left on that first visit to our humble abode, John and I put several of his records into boiling hot water and made cones out of them. During the second week, Eden, now looking even more resplendent in his newly acquired, bright red, bow tie was to visit four times, this added two shillings (10 pence) to our coffers. Jimmy Conroy who lived round the corner, also paid his sixpence, and joined us. Jimmy lived, with his nine brothers and sisters in a house that had no running water or electricity. Both had been cut off. His mum was just too frail to work, and his dad, Herbert, was simply a lazy sod that never did a day's work for as long as we knew him. He would shout out obscenities at anyone that got in his way. It was no surprise for us to learn that Herbert Conway was banged up for flashing his private parts at women whilst walking around Crisp Street market. We had no idea where, or how, Jimmy had managed to conjure up the shilling that he paid us for his twice weekly visits.

By the third week of March, we were selling cups of orange juice and a penguin to our patrons for a shiny thrupenny bit. The orange juice was provided by Ernie, the milkman, and the penguins came to us courtesy of Mr. Lloyd, a man that owned four of the local shops. Neither of these men were aware of their

A Life Like No Other

donations to our cause. We were never caught when removing a whole crate of orange juice from the back of the electric milk cart or whilst sliding the penguins down the front of our well-worn shorts. By the end of the month there were up to nine boys and girls of our age group in our tiny living room. There was also the strange man from Zetland Street. He used to wander in, sit on the floor for an hour or so, and then fart loudly before he left. He never paid us, and we were too scared to ask. Just before my eleventh birthday he set fire to his mum's house and was locked away. He was, Ernie Lighten. Shortly after his release the pyrotechnic died, in bizarre circumstances after setting himself alight on the upper deck of a 108 bus.

Our money-making scenario came, to an abrupt end, when my mum began to realise that twice a week, when she came home to prepare dinner, all the food was gone. Yes, it was Jimmy Conway. He was stuffing everything he could lay his hands on, into his dad's oversize demob army overcoat. He even nicked my nan's chicken giblets, (which were resting under the tin bath in the back yard), whilst on his way to the toilet.

April brought slightly warmer weather, which was good news for John and me as we never had "winter" coats. The holes in the soles of our shoes were blocked by putting cardboard on the inside, which was perfectly fine until the first sign of rain. During the winter, our feet were continually cold and wet. Even the wearing of three pairs of our dad's army issue socks did nothing to help this situation. At any formal family gathering only one of us could attend as we had just the one pair of "best" shoes between us. Some people would have you believe that these were the best days of our lives. Forget that, at times life was just horrendous.

Eden Hallet takes centre stage in this school photo from 1960. There he is - white shirt, blue tie, and a new pullover.
I am stood directly next to him (on the left as you look at the photo). Mr Richards, who saved baby Graham's life, is on the extreme right.

7 - Wonky Albert

In May 1960, we met, for the first, and last time, a man that was known as Wonky Albert. Albert Schindler, a man of Jewish decent, had been born with a left leg that did not quite touch the ground. In fact, the outside of his left foot was the only part of it that reached the floor. Many years later John and I decided that John Cleese had based his silly walk upon Wonky Albert. Hundreds of thousands of disabled people in the UK were classed as being Spastics and growing up, children of all ages would taunt even normal people with phrases like 'you, big spastic' whenever they did something wrong or were cack-handed. Our dad was a person without bias; however, he had pre-warned us that Wonky was coming to the house and that he was a spastic. It was explained to us that Wonky had contracted Polio as a baby, forever afterwards John and I would refer to him as "Trebor." Bowing to pressure from society, in 1994 the Spastics Association changed its name to Scope.

Before telling you all about Wonky, I should give over a few lines in respect of another character that it was our pleasure to have met during our growing-up years. Tony Dumpling, whose real name we never knew, was a 15-year-old, rotund boy, of limited sense. He hailed from the Devon's Road area of Bow, although he was well known around the railway arches that held up the district line between Bromley-by-Bow and Bow Road. He would only be seen in Poplar under the cover of darkness. Dumpling had somehow attached a go-cart to his push-bike, the cart had a 5ft steel frame, which was covered by dark green tarpaulin and inside this little house he kept a bull-nosed jack, capable of lifting 10 ton, in addition, he had many other tools of his trade. His trade being the stealing of wheels from vehicles.

Getting back to Wonky, he arrived outside our house at 8.00pm, he was an hour late. He was wearing one of those army issue trench coats, which was the same colour as his motorbike. He had on those long leather gloves that stretched up to the elbows, a pair of motor racing goggles and a black leather hat. The purpose of his visit was to hand over to Slim (our dad), over 200, 78's. We helped unload the records, which were much heavier than 45's, from the sidecar of a motorbike that our dad had told us Wonky had taken, single handily from a group of six German's somewhere in Belgium, which is where our dad had first met him. Wonky had lovingly restored the vehicle to its former glory. I still have the picture in my mind, of Wonky standing next to his motorbike and sidecar as John and I first exited our front door. His left side was so far down, in comparison to his right that we thought he might collapse. We knew that we would be unable to help him to his feet for fear of laughing at his unfortunate predicament. John and I lifted about 20 records each from the inside of his sidecar. Our dad managed double that. Wonky stood, motionless, left leg on the pavement, right leg in the road. This, it seemed, somehow balanced him up. On the second journey from the street to our upstairs living room, our dad invited Wonky in for a cup of tea. He was reluctant, at first, then John said,

"Come on Uncle Wonky, come and see our record player."

Wonky led the way, John and I were close behind him. He was carrying a small pile of records. He entered the hall and clunked his way to the bottom of the stairs. Our nan appeared from her tiny living room and asked,

"Who are you and what are you doing in my house?"

Before the unsteady man could answer, John interjected.

"He is Uncle Wonky, nan. He has brought us a load of records."

Looking him up and down, before replying, she said –

"Well, you behave yourself with my boy's. I've heard about your type before."

At this point, Slim, who had been talking to Mrs Eisel, our next-door neighbour, came into the hall.

"It's alright Mum, this is Albert, he works with me, I have told you about him before."

"Well, just make sure he behaves himself around these boys."

Wonky placed his records onto the floor of the hall. He then lifted his left leg with his hands and let it drop onto the first step. There were twelve steps to climb. John and I put our records down, turned, and went out into the street. We found our friends playing football in the road and joined in. After half an hour or so, during which time John had managed to render two opponents, incapable of playing on, we wheeled brother Graham, whom had been one of the goalposts, back to his position outside our front door.

By this time, Wonky had just reached the top of the stairs and was about to climb onto the step that took us into our living room. Unfortunately, at that very moment our mum had decided to open the door, the door that opened outwards, onto the first-floor landing. A door, that our dad had altered, to open outwards, instead of inwards, just a few weeks earlier.

The door hit the unsuspecting Wonky Albert at the precise moment that he was lifting his left leg onto the step. John and I looked on as Wonky hit our dad on his way down, felling him like a ninepin in a bowling alley. Slim's, hand-held pile of records flew up into the air and made an almighty thud as they hit the wooden floorboards of the hall beneath. This commotion had prompted grandad Ted to get out of his chair, a chair that he had sat in, religiously, for the best part of six years, ever since retiring from his job as an apprentice carpenter. Ted, severely hampered by the large steel oxygen tank that he carried around whenever leaving his chair, said something. Quite what he had said, we did not know as his full-face mask stifled whatever was coming out of his mouth. Leaning against the door of the understairs cupboard, in order, to get his breath, he simply disappeared inside when his weight, combined with that of the oxygen bottle was simply too much for the door, that, for some reason, opened inwards after our dad had changed it a few weeks back. My nan entered the fray, she looked down at her forlorn husband of fifty years and mumbled,

"Get up. You, silly old git can't you see we have guests?"

By now, our dad had helped wonky to his feet, John and I had scarpered. From our vantage point, behind Ray Puxley's dad's Morris Minor van we saw Wonky mount his bike. A few seconds later he dismounted and slid his bruised torso around to the nearside of his sidecar. He then saw what we already knew. The wheel of the passenger part of his motorbike, was gone, courtesy of Tony Dumpling, who had seen the unattended vehicle earlier and had returned when there was no one about. After our dad had left, to take Wonky home to Bow, in his lorry, John and I set about looking through the 180 records that had survived the melee that had ensued just a short while before.

What we found was a real eyeopener to us. Most of the songs were of Big Bands, Opera, or singers that we had never heard of. Some were as old as the 1940's, whilst there were others that were recently in the charts. We put to one side, the following as they were the only ones that we had heard of.

Guy Mitchell – "Singing the Blues"
Frankie Vaughan – "The Green Door"
Frankie Laine – "Hey Joe"
Frankie Laine – "The gang that sang Heart of my Heart."
Mel Torme – "Blue Moon"
Elvis Presley – "Teddy Bear"
Tommy Steel – "A handful of Songs"
Danny Kaye – "The ugly Duckling"
Frank Sinatra – "Goodnight Irene"
Billy Cotton – "What a Referee"
Pat Boone – "Ain't that a Shame"
Bing Crosby – "Deep in the heart of Texas"
Guy Mitchell – "Call Rosie on the Phone"

The following evening, when returning with a new wheel for his sidecar, Albert (Wonky) Shindler knocked on our door and handed our dad a slip of paper. He said –

A Life Like No Other

"Here is a list of what I have given to you. You can pay me ten shillings per week, until you have paid me off."

Our dad was a very passive man. He never lost his temper, even when he was on the receiving end of either one of mum's verbal bashings or her direct hits upon his manhood. We never heard him swear, a rarity amongst men that had been brought up in the sheer desperation that was, East London. He calmly took the list from Mr Shindler and shut the door. Wonky mounted his bike and was gone. Back upstairs, Slim piled all the 78's into neat piles and secured them with masking tape. He then asked John and I to help him take them downstairs and put them into the Bedford TK that he was driving at that time. Our mum asked him what he was doing. He told her that he thought he was being given the records and as they were a load of rubbish, he was taking them back. For us, this was the end of the story. Two days later when returning from work our dad told our mum that Wonky Albert had been killed on Old Ford Road. The wheel of his sidecar had come off and he had ploughed, head-on into a heavily laden lorry. The police believed that the wheel had not been secured properly. The Sergeant mentioned that Wonky had reported the theft of his wheel and had asked my dad if he had seen anyone near the sidecar when Wonky had visited us. Our dad's response was negative.

Tony Dumpling was arrested as he was taking off the last of the wheels from a black maria, that had broken down in Coventry Cross. When they raided his uncle's tyre repair shop under the arches, they found over 200 other, stolen wheels. It was only when the film of the same name came out that we realised the significance of 'Schindler's List.'

8 - Flickers

In addition to our dream of collecting more records than the Decca Record Company could produce, we were also avid collectors of the new schoolboy craze. That was, owning more "flicker" cards than anyone else. Flicker cards were given away by the likes of the **"Brooke Bond Tea Company"** who included about 3 cards inside a bag of tea. **"W D and H O Wills"** included them in their packs of cigarettes and a few other companies gave them away. They were, we were told, a way in which to promote children's education. Brooke Bond was by far, the largest promotor of these cards and schoolboys everywhere (girls had no interest, they just got on with their knitting) collected them. A wide range of topics were covered. It was normal for a picture of the subject to be shown on the face of the card, with a description on the reverse. There were quite a few series of footballers, cricketers, and other sports. Educational wise, we learnt about, Wild Birds, Butterflies, Native Animals and Asian and African varieties as well. Some cards were thinner than others, however all of them were suitable for the game.

Our collection began when we trapped Jimmy Conway against the outside wall of his house and took from him about 200 cards. They were mainly of Birds and Butterflies. Jimmy had been taunted by the other children for not having any masculine samples amongst his small collection. John and I had singled out Jimmy, firstly because he was a wimp and was not likely to put up any resistance to our manhandling of him. Secondly, he had stolen our dinner on several occasions, and this was pay-back time for him. And so, to the game itself.

The contests mainly took place at school. Boys that had a collection of cards would stuff them into their pockets and wait for both the morning and lunch time breaks. Two boys, normally those with the most cards in their pockets, would compete, whilst the onlookers would gather around, behind them. The contestants would kneel, about eight feet from a wall, cards at the ready. There were two, slightly different games. One was that each boy would "flick" his cards towards the wall until it landed on top of another. That boy would then pick up all the cards on the ground. The other game, which was the one that was played at our school, was that two or more cards would be stood-up against the wall and each player would take it in turns to knock them over. The player that knocked over the last card standing, was deemed to be the winner. The amount, of cards in the kitty would depend on the accuracy of the players. There could be as few as four cards to be won if both players were good. However, it was not unusual to scoop up over a hundred if the cards against the wall refused to surrender.

When it was known that a contest was going to take place between two of the heavyweights of the flicker game, half of the school would be in attendance. Even the girls would watch, although this proved to be quite dangerous as their knitting needles seemed to be attracted to the eyes of the boys.

Inevitably the game, whilst peaceful to begin with, almost always lead to a fight, or a "bundle" as we used to call them. There was, of course, an amount of cheating. Friends of the players would get very, close to the wall and blow down the cards when their mate would be flicking. Almost every day a teacher would have to intervene. Sometimes both, of the fighting boys would have their cards confiscated. No parent ever came to the school to complain about this. Teachers, back in the day, were never challenged. We had one teacher, a small, bent over nasty bloke by the name of Mr Bell, we of course called him Quasimodo. Quasi would confiscate our cards at any given opportunity and then sell them back to us. Even at the age of nine most of us were taller than him. He could look us in the eye without bending. We would taunt him whenever he was on playground duty by shouting out 'the bells, the bells' and whilst he took no immediate action, he would know whom the ringleaders of the chanting were. Back in class he would come up behind us and flick the back of our ears with his twelve-inch ruler. Well, we thought, and hoped that it was his ruler.

One day, after school, brother John took on Ronnie Watson, the recognised hard man of the neighbourhood. He was eleven, however he had already done six months in a young offender's institution for biting off the ear of Billy Gripp and punching out all of Gerald Horrabin's front teeth. Ronnie had thousands of cards, mainly took by force, from the more sedate of his fellow pupils. John and I had devised a way of making some cards stronger, these would fly, through the air in a straight line. What we did was to get two duplicates and glue them together. We called them our 'snide cards.' We only used these when there was just one card left standing. John was accurate and his wrist action was second to none. He nearly always knocked over the last card standing. In the very first game, with about sixty cards on the ground, John utilised the snide which I had slipped into his hand, unnoticed by the others. Ronnie was incensed, he dived on top of John. I then dived on top of him. Several others joined the melee, until there was a mountain of bodies, piled up in the alleyway of the block of flats where the contest had taken place. Ronnie managed to free himself from pile and stood up, he was in a rage, his ears, which resembled the FA Cup were bright red. He turned to me and shouted, but before he could finish his sentence, which would have been, you are cheating bastards, or words to that effect, our big brother felled him, with one savage blow from a cricket bat. Ronnie Watson never bothered us again. In fact, two weeks after this rather brutal episode of our young lives, he was locked up for dropping a full bottle of milk from the fourth-floor landing of Hilary House. The bottle of milk hit Richard Head on his shoulder, breaking it into many small pieces. 'Dick' Head wore his right arm in a sling for the rest of his life, however he still managed to open the bowling for the Poplar and District Cricket Club. He also played in goal for the local football team. He claimed Social Security and a disability allowance. He never worked again. Most days he could be found in one of the local pubs.

We continued collecting cards and playing games until leaving our primary school. No such tomfoolery would take place once I was ensconced into the Grammar School education system, with its much stricter learning regime.

9 - Brother John's 8th Birthday

On the 10th, July 1960, our mum got up an hour after our dad had left for work. This was John's cue to present himself as a willing party for the acceptance of birthday cards and presents. I followed him into our tiny living room just minutes later.

Back in the living room, there were to be no surprise presents for John. Whilst our mum got on with preparing the Sunday dinner, I helped him search the entire upstairs of the house, we found nothing, not even a card. Thinking that his birthday goodies might just be waiting for him downstairs in our grandparents living quarters, we descended the stairs in anticipation. Grandad Ted was sat in his armchair in the corner of the room. His greeting was not,

'Hello boys, happy birthday John.'

It was,

'What do you little sods want?'

We carried on, past him, John was spot on with the kick to his ankle. The kick that made the old git wreathe in agony. We entered the scullery, today we call them kitchens, or family rooms. We both looked, into the large steel pot that was simmering its contents on the gas stove. Inside, all that could be seen were a pair of our nan's dark blue bloomers. Hidden in the bloomers was the massive piece of flour and suet that nan had earlier kneaded on grandad's lap, well we thought that was what she was doing. We knew that later that day, we would be enjoying, suet pudding with custard and jam. We stepped out into the backyard. Our nan was in the yard, using the mangle. She was wringing out grandad's long johns, vests, and Y-fronts. Most of them were of a slightly light brown colour, despite the fact, that they had been boiled for over forty-eight hours.

There was not a word from our nan in respect of it being Johns eighth birthday. We checked the large shed that divided our back yard from that of the first house in the neighboring street. There was not a single shred of evidence that anything appertaining to a birthday gift was or had been hidden there. Nan let on that we could have some suet pudding, after we had eaten our dinner and that she had managed to get a tin of syrup, that big brother had lifted from Lloydie's shop, which we could have instead of jam, if we so wished.

By now, John was beginning to become agitated. He could not believe that everyone had forgotten his birthday. We decided to go out and play football.

Harry Redknapp was one of the older boys playing that morning. John kicked him hard and then scarpered. Harry was a few years older than us.

At just after 2.00pm our dad returned home from work. At 2.30 four of us sat around the dinner table. When I say "dinner table" I mean the hard boarded door that our dad had removed from the kitchen and would place on top of two sets of carpenter's trestles. This would be covered with a sheet of Lino, that was once laid on the kitchen floor. The dansette was fired up and we listened to alternate sets of six records whilst we ate. After dinner, which mum had only slightly burnt, on this occasion, Slim, John and I headed downstairs and did our best to consume the contents of nannie's bloomers.

After our desert, we climbed the stairs, our nan followed us, this was completely out of the norm. Old misery guts had been tied up and had no choice but to remain in his armchair. I realized after he died, that he had never once washed up or emptied the chamber pot that he kept under his bed. He was one lazy old sod.

We entered our upstairs living room to a cacophony of sound. In the room there were so many people that I thought the upstairs would become the downstairs. Momentarily I prayed for this to happen, as surely, this would once and for all rid us of the miserable old git that posed as a loving grandad. Unfortunately, it was not to be. Through the smoke, I could see dads' elder brother, Uncle Ticker, his wife, Lilly and their two sons and a daughter. We never found out why Uncle Ted was known as "Ticker" he had an uncanny resemblance to Sid James. There was Dad's sister, Aunt Lil, Uncle Harry and their three sons, Tom, Dick, and Harry. Our parents' friends, Wally, and Connie Smith were there, as were Ted and Dorrie Winterflood and their two daughters. That day it dawned on me as to how many females within the family were named 'Lil or Lilly.'

On the table, which mum had cleared after dinner, and which took up over half of the available floor space, was a stack of birthday cards, cakes, jelly, soft drinks, booze, and our nans teeth. John was called over by each visitor and was given a brown bag, each bag contained a 45rpm record. No one had taken the trouble to disguise the fact that all of John's presents were records. In his haste to get the records onto the dansette as quickly as he could, he knocked over the bottle of single malt that Wally Smith had brought with him. As the whiskey trickled along the table and cascaded, like a waterfall, at the far end of the door, baby Graham laid on his back and let some of Scotland's finest fall into his mouth, minutes later there was a loud yell as he hit every step on his way downstairs. John had been given seven records for his birthday. He would not tell us what they were. We all had to listen, as they fell, one by one, onto the deck of one of the few, genuine stereo record players in Poplar. For his eighth birthday John added these to the record collection. In July 2022, at his 70th birthday party, brother John would play those 7 records on his imported jukebox. 62 years may have lapsed but that music has never waned. The 7 records were –

Cliff Richard and the Shadows – "Please don't Tease."
Everly Brothers – "When will I be Loved."
Brian Hyland – "Itsy Bitsy Teeny Weeny Yellow Polka Dot Bikini"
Shadows – "Apache"
Sam Cooke – "Wonderful World"
Rolf Harris – "Tie me Kangaroo down Sport"
Duane Eddy – "Because they're Young."

10 - Home Alone – Part 1:

Due to his new position at work, our dad was unable to take us all to Yorkshire during the school holidays of 1960. Mum had decided that she would return to her place of birth, alone, leaving us four boys, at home and fending for ourselves. There had been a lot of rowing going on between our parents prior to our mum's departure. After our dad had departed for work on the first Saturday in August, brother John and I helped our mum put her bags onto the platform of the 108 bus. She would alight at Bromley-by-Bow underground station and take the tube to Kings Cross Station. From there she would make the journey to Hull and then onto Beverley. John and I had been given instructions by our mum on how to behave whilst she was away. Our nan, had agreed to keep a close eye on us during the day, making sure that we looked after our little brother Graham. We were told not to go out before 9.00am, to be back for lunch at 12.30 and tea at 6.00pm. We never had a watch between us, but we knew that when the sun was directly above the library it was mid-day, which was fine unless it was cloudy. Five minutes after mum had boarded the bus, John, and I, with Graham still sleeping in his pram, were out of the door and within minutes we were playing on the nearby railway line. Graham was oblivious to the fact that his mum had gone and left him. After a three-hour stint of football, which started out as six a-side, but finished with over thirty young boys taking part John and I headed home for lunch. Our nan asked as to where Graham was, John returned to the football pitch, unfortunately he was still there.

 As it was a Saturday we were in for a treat. The smell of kippers cooking in nannie Lil's six-foot by six-foot scullery was, overpowering. We could almost taste them as we entered the front door. A front door that was always open. Leaving Graham in his pram just outside the front porch, John, and I, now caked in mud from having played through the football, on a pitch with no visible grass, whist the summer storm rained down upon us, sat, expectantly at the small square table. Grandad Ted, whom we believed to have been somehow fixed into his armchair in the corner of the room, snarled at us. Nannie Lil placed a plate of toast, some butter and a few of those small jars of jam, that our mum had nicked from Woolworths, onto the table. A few minutes later our nan returned from the cookhouse with a stack of kippers, that she handed to the grumpy old sod. That was my cue to leave. I hated kippers almost as much as I hated the man that was about to eat them. Lilly had sat herself down on a

A Life Like No Other

stall on the other side of the room and was sucking on a bone, that days earlier, had contained some meat. Our nan had no teeth at all. She never chewed, she only sucked (which may have had some advantages for Ted) or swallowed food, whole. I had once asked her why she had no teeth, she replied, 'ask your grandad.' I never did. Nannie Lil won many prizes for being the best "gurning" face in the East End.

John and I had discussed how we were going to make some money whilst our mum was away. We took hold of Graham's pram, which had wheeled itself half into the road, mainly because it had no brake and John had parked it incorrectly. We headed for Coventry Cross, an area that, geographically, was just before Bromley-by-Bow underground station. Coventry Cross was adjacent to our place of birth, St. Andrews Hospital. All the properties were new, in comparison to where we lived. It always seemed strange to me, that less than a mile from what we called home, everything looked nice and clean and even had grass and trees. The row of shops along the bottom of a low-rise block of flats were positioned at the top of a steep incline. I would wheel the pram to the top whilst John stood at the bottom, I would then let the pram, with baby brother inside it, freewheel down the slope and hope that John would be able to stop it before it crashed into the steel railings. When it did crash Graham would yell out in agony as his head would be crushed against the inside framework of the pram. Once Graham was hysterical, we would stand the pram outside the chemist and start crying ourselves. As we sobbed, people, mainly women, would ask us what was wrong. Through our tears we would tell them that our baby brother needed medicine, and that our mum had left us, with only our gran to look after us and she had no money. In nine out of ten cases, it worked. We would be given varying amounts, from a shilling (5p) to five-bob (25p). There were six chemists within walking distance, and we would systematically use our, well-rehearsed act at each of them. Given that the lunches provided by our nan were sparse and completely void of any nutrition, we would spend some of our earnings at the local bakers. We would treat Graham, who never seemed to get any breakfast or lunch, to a chocolate éclair. He, the pram, and his clothes would be plastered in melted chocolate and cream. He was left like that until Friday's, the day that nan did the washing in the tin bath that spent most of its time, upside down in the back yard. On Friday's Graham wore no clothes at all. We never knew if this affected him or not as he virtually cried all the time.

Most Saturday mornings John and I would push the pram, with Graham on board, to "Bobbins" the local wood factory. We had worked out that at 10.00am, each, and every Saturday, the few workers present would be allowed inside to take their tea-break. With no one policing the yard, it was easy for us to collect a pram load of kindling, which was normally stacked just inside the large green gates, which were, for some reason, always open at that time of day. The kindling was tied, in bundles, with wire. We would fill the pram, taking great care not to suffocate our precious little sibling. We then placed an old army blanket on top and slowly disappeared around the corner. It would be nearly two-years until we were rumbled. Whilst it was the middle of summer, every door that we knocked at gave us a shilling (5p) for a bundle of the wood burning material that would cost them treble that once the autumn arrived. One week after mum had legged it, we had made over £3.00, and our dad never had a clue.

11 – Home Alone – Part 2

On Sunday, our dad, possibly feeling guilty that no one was looking after us, informed his three youngest offspring that he was taking us to Brick Lane. He did ask if we knew where Peter was, we knew, of course, but in the East End you never grassed anyone up. We simply acted dumb when he raised the question. We knew full well that our older brother was up to no good with some of his undesirable mates.

The £3.00 that we had accumulated during the week was to be spent, in full. For the first time since boxing day, we visited the antiquated record shop that belonged to the Cohen Brothers. Manny, the eldest of the brothers had a constant 'dewdrop' hanging from the right side of his substantial nostril. He was dressed, just as he was several months before, from head to toe, in black. Hymy, who also ran Cohen Bakeries the shop next door, which had now had the wall that once separated them, removed, was a replica of the man that fronted every bag of Home Pride Flour. He was dressed entirely in white. Manny and Hymy Cohen were forever known to us as "The Flour Graders."

John and I hogged the left-hand side of the counter. This is where this week's copy of the NME top 40 chart rested, under the sheet of glass that prevented anyone from stealing it. We knew every record that we already had; we needed only to buy those that were new to the charts that week. We began calling out the records that we wished to buy. When we reached nine, two burly Jewish wrestlers stood in front of the black painted doors. Our dad looked puzzled, he asked –

"How are you going to buy nine records, I can afford only two this week."

"Don't worry Dad, Grandad Ted gave us some money." John replied.

Our dad knew that there was no way on this earth that his tight-fisted, miserable old bastard of a father would have parted with such a large amount of dosh, especially on two boys that he hated. Slim let it go. I handed Manny three one-pound notes. The bells rang out from 59 Brick Lane, the nearby Synagogue and church of the Jewish faith. Six young flute playing flour graders appeared from a hole in the wall. Mrs. Cohen brought in a plate of salt-beef sandwiches and an 'elder' with the longest beard I have ever seen, wailed at the plate glass window.

John stuffed the nine singles into his duffle bag, a duffle bag that he had stolen from Victor Hardy, a boy so small that we were able to push him through his letterbox on the day that his entire family had been wiped out by

A Life Like No Other

scurvy. Victor had been relieved when John had taken his bag, as even when empty, it was too much of a burden for his tiny frame to carry. Dad handed John *his* two records. They also went into Victor's duffle bag.

Before leaving, dad stepped sideways into Cohen's Bakery and bought us all two cakes each.

Once safely back in the lorry and after untying Graham, we tucked into the cakes and before we moved off Graham was covered from head to foot in cream and chocolate.

John took out the records and slowly thumbed through them. We had bought the following –

Elvis Presly – "Mess of Blues"
Jimmy Jones – "Good Timing"
Shirley Bassey – "As long as he needs Me."
Connie Francis – "Everybody's somebody's Fool."
Roy Orbison – "Only the Lonely"
Johnny Preston – "Feel so Fine."
Ricky Valance – "Tell Laura I love Her."
Hollywood Argyles – "Alley Oop"
Hank Locklin – "Please help me I'm Falling."

12 - Mums Back

Our mum arrived back from Yorkshire on Monday 29th August, a bank holiday, she had been away for four weeks. It appeared that our parents had made their peace as Slim had had a long telephone conversation with Rose the previous Sunday afternoon. The phone call had taken place in the Puxley's house, which was directly next door to us. At that time the Puxley's were the only people in the street to have such a facility. We did suspect that the Saint's, who lived on the other side of the street, had a dog and bone, however they were almost "god like" to us. We did ask to use their phone once, when grandad Ted lay on the floor, pinned down by a very large oxygen bottle, however, Jimmy Saint denied owning such a thing. When our dad knocked on his door and pointed out that a wire ran from the telegraph pole to the top of his house, Mr Saint shut the door in his face. In the dead of night, big brother scaled the pole and cut the wire. The next day, a GPO van arrived and re-instated the service. For a long time after this incident, the Saint's gleaming black Austin A35 always seemed to have flat tyres. Out of interest, the miserable and ugly old bastard that posed as our loving grandad, screamed the house down when the ambulance crew informed him that he would have to go to hospital. He did not want to go, he clung on to the six-foot, dark brown, steel bottle that contained the oxygen that kept him alive, it took two medical staff and two neighbours to lift him into the ambulance. He was adamant that if he went into hospital, he would never come out. How I prayed that night. After a week in the London Chest Hospital, he went into reverse gear. Now he did not want to come home. He told the ward sister that 'those two little sods' were trying to kill him. He spent three weeks in the care of the National Health Service, he was not any more cordial upon his return home.

When mum arrived, at 7.25pm on that Monday night, her younger sister, Carol, had come back with her. Carol was otherwise known to all and sundry as "Auntie" a title that she retains to this very day. The story goes that when big brother, Peter, was born, in 1948, some of the Yorkies came to visit us. When Carol, just thirteen-years-old, held aloft, the boy that should have been called Damien, for the first time, the nappy less little devil emptied the contents of his bowels down the front of her pristine white dress. Slim, taking his first born from his sister-in-law, commented,

'Well, you will always remember the first time you held him, won't you Auntie'?

A Life Like No Other

The name stuck.

On this occasion, Auntie, now twenty-five, had been brought back to London to help our mum look after her four boys. This unexpected addition to the family that occupied four small rooms on the first floor of a house that had no hot water, no bathroom and no indoor toilet further complicated our day to day living conditions. It was at this time that Slim negotiated with Ted, his father, the possible use of one of the downstairs rooms, that his parents never used. An agreement was reached, whereby, in lieu of rent, John and I would become our grand-parent's carers. Amongst the endless amount, of jobs that we had to undertake on their behalf, were –

The clearing out of the previous days coal fire and the preparation of the new one.

The scrubbing of the floorboards throughout the downstairs.

Putting the washing through the mangle.

Cleaning the front, sides, and back windows. Inside and out.

Stripping grandad down to his long johns on Fridays, so that nannie Lil could wash his clothes.

Carry the large steel dustbins from the backyard to the front of the house and then back when emptied.

Run all errands to and from the shops.

I even had to pick out the numbered pegs from a bag that Ted used when doing the pools every Thursday.

On the 1st, September 1960, young brother Graham was three-years old. When our parents left for work that morning, John, and I were told that we were not to take him out in his pram as Auntie was going to look after him. We were not in any way, disappointed at being told this. We were going to enjoy the day, without the burden of having to worry about where we had left our young sibling. We were still on our school holidays and were now free to do whatever we wanted. There was to be no party for Graham, he did not get taken to McDonald's, KFC, or Nando's. He did not have scores of friends, visiting the house. What he did have, after dinner that evening, was a yellow Rowntree's jelly, a bowl of ice cream and a cake. The cake had been given to him by nannie Lil, and was, strangely enough, known as a "Grannie Cake." Nannie Lil had a constant supply of Grannie Cakes as they were made at the Far-Famed Cake Company, which was just under half a mile from our house. This factory was also John's favourite window smashing building, over the years he perfected his stone throwing abilities, using the large stones that supported the railway line that ran along the length of the factory. I distinctly remember this Grannie Cake as it dismantled one of my back teeth. Had "sell by dates" existed back in the day, then our nan would have been executed. She had several friends that worked in the Far-Famed Factory, and she would accept payment, in cake, from those women unfortunate enough to have had their corns and other foot infections treated by nurse Lil. Although not qualified, in any medical way, whatsoever, she was held in high regard by the locals.

By the second week of being our Grandparents slaves John and I had had enough. We had little or no time in which to play football, play records, steal, or terrorise our little brother. We paid grandad Ted an official visit. We stood, side by side, shoulder to shoulder, in front of the ugly old git, that was now subjecting us to so much grief. We asked him exactly how much he was going to charge our dad for the rent of his room, that was now occupied by John and big brother, Peter. We began to walk away when he replied,

'A pound a week.'

'The whole house is only £3.15 shillings a month.' I replied.

'We will give you eight shillings (40p) a month Grandad and still go to the shops, but we won't be doing anything else, unless you pay us.' Said John.

The most miserable grandad in Poplar agreed. He then dropped his snout deep into a bowl of Vick's Vapor Rub that Lil had placed on the table. Later that evening, we informed our dad that Ted had asked us for money for the rent of the room. Slim was incensed, he flew downstairs. John and I had our ears to the door when he told his dad that his sons were not going to pay him a penny. He further pointed out that as *he* was already paying two-thirds of the rent each week, he was entitled to a bit more space. That was how we managed to not only get out of doing all the chores, we, also avoided having to pay old scrooge anything at all.

Auntie was taken to King's Cross Station, by our dad, on Saturday 10th September and she returned to Beverley. She was starting a new job, as a "glue sniffer" in a newly established adhesive factory that had been set up on the banks of the river beck, just yards from the family home. Her departure meant that I no longer had to sleep on the floor in the living room, on the other hand, Graham had been given his marching orders by our dad. He would no longer be sharing the bed with him and mum. He would now be sleeping with me, in the double bed. I deemed this to be totally unfair, as Peter and John had single beds in the room downstairs.

On the 12th, September, Rose returned to her job at Woolworths, she was transferred from the haberdashery section to the newly opened record counter. This was "music" to our ears. John and I danced to the tune of "What a wonderful World" by Sam Cooke, which just happened to be playing at the time. Slim was oblivious as to the reason for our utter joy. Mum, on the other hand, knew exactly why we were so happy.

The following day, after school, John and I walked the mile or so to Crisp Street and entered the large double doors at the front of the store. We walked past the kitchen utensils, the bathroom accessories and the sweet counter. In

A Life Like No Other

our excitement we failed to nick anything. We descended the five steps that took us to the lower level, and there, to the left of bedding and toweling, was the newly established record counter. Rose was serving a rather dapper old gentleman. He tipped his hat at her once he was finished. By now we had seen and squeezed into one of the two listening booths at the far, right hand side of the counter. At the time we had no idea as to what they were. Mum was now free, she called us over. She explained that if we both occupied one of the booths, she would put on a record, and we would be able to listen to it. We easily maneuvered our young frames into booth number 1. John picked up the earphones, listened for a while and then handed them to me. Mum had chosen "Nine times out of Ten" which was Cliff Richards latest single. It was 4.30pm, there were not that many other shoppers around. I moved to the other booth and listened to "Lucille" by the Everly Brothers, I had no idea what my brother was moving his hips too. Woolworths closed at 5.00pm and we escorted our mum home.

The following day, again after school had finished, John and I were back in Woolworth's record department. Whilst we had not discussed anything with our mum, we knew that she was on the same wavelength as us. We studied the Melody Maker chart, that was both on the counter and pinned to the wall next to the listening booths and asked Rose to play six songs that we did not have. After we had listened, we confirmed that we would like to buy them. Mum put three records into a brown paper bag and handed them to John. She then repeated this for me. We each gave her a £1.00 note and then marched through the store and out into the street. Once outside we peered into our respective bags and discovered that as well as the three records, we each had a £1.00 note.

This bit of skullduggery carried on until January 1961, when a dedicated manager was brought in, from HMV, to run the ever-expanding record department. Mum was transferred to the sweet counter, which, in its own way, was even more beneficial to John and me.

We added the following nine singles to the collection during September 1960. We did not even like most of them, however they were "free", and we were still trying to achieve our aim of having every one of the top 40. Rose told Slim not to buy any records as she received a good staff discount. Dad never did get to know of our little scam.

Lonnie Donegan – "Lorelei"
Ventures – "Walk don't Run."
Cliff Richard – "Nine times out of Ten"
Adam Faith – "How about That"
Mike Preston – "I'd do Anything."
Everly Brothers – "Lucille"

Emile Ford – "Them there, Eyes"
Fats Domino – "Walking to New Orleans"
Wanda Jackson – "Let's have a Party."

It was only after playing our new records to our dad that we learnt that none of them were by the real artists, they were all fakes. All of Woolworth's records were on the Embassy label and they contracted little-known singers and groups to make copies of current hits. Over time we would replace most of those woolie's records with the kosher versions.

13 - The big boy's

Growing up in the East End of London, in the 1950's & 60's was, as countless writers have written previously, fraught with poverty, crime, grief, sadness and sometimes a complete sense of not belonging. Even allowing for all this negative stuff, children, especially boys, were able to deal with day-to-day life, in a way that those born during the next generation would never be able to.

Try to imagine a child today not having access to i-phones, i-pads, electronic games, Netflix, sky sports, x-box's, overseas holidays, Macdonald's, KFC, designer clothes, fancy footwear or even a football to kick around. Well, we had none of the aforementioned. Strangely however, we still managed to grow up, buy houses, cars, and other materialistic clobber that our kids and their offspring now take for granted. Our parents did not have a bank account. There would have been no point anyhow, as there was never any money to put into one.

We were brought up in a world whereby we had to fend for ourselves. Those children that could not turn their hand to committing the occasional felony, would fall by the wayside. We lived on our wits. In the main, we followed the lead of our parents. In our case, it was our mum that tended to lead us astray, as our dad was too busy trying to earn a living, a living that had to support six of us. By the standards of other families in our street and around the corner, we were angels. That is not to say that we stayed out of trouble, indeed we got up to a lot of mischief. Our elder brother was, by far, the worst of us when it came to being in trouble, but he was only top of that, league table, because he seemed to get caught more often than those that appeared to be, more savvy, than he was. Big brother's school year was three ahead of me and four in front of brother John. He had his own group of friends, some of whom would congregate in our tiny living room whenever our parents were, out. Of all his mates, Ronnie Green, Tony Brazil, Bobby Bedfont and Johnny Darke were regarded, by me, to be the 'most dodgy.'

Ronnie Green lived in Poplar fire-station. His father, imprisoned for arson in the early 50's had used all his experience for starting fires, in order, to gain a job with the London fire brigade. He was directly responsible for putting out most of the fires that his son and my brother had started. Ronnie considered himself to be something of a hard nut, he would practice his right hook on my torso whenever I was unfortunate enough to be anywhere near him. He would find our records and put them onto the dansette. I would tell him that he could

A Life Like No Other

not load more than six at a time, he took no notice of me until one day he broke the arm of the record player by stacking eleven 45's onto the spindle. I got my own back when I tied some black twine around the knocker of the door opposite and when he came racing down Venue Street on his bike, I pulled it tight, and he went flying. He was so thick that he did not have a clue as to what had happened to him. Ronnie had the physique of a bear; his plumpness prevented him from running. He was the first person that John and I named after a song, he was, of course, "Running Bear" we would sing this to him. His denseness meant that our tormenting of him went over his head.

Tony Brazil lived in a block of flats just around the corner from us. He was more rotund than Ronnie Green and would sit on me after the pyrotechnic had punched me to the floor. I quite liked him, but he would show off to the others. His father drove a large car transporter and one night Tony took the keys, but my brother drove it, as he had nicked the most cars and knew how to drive. They loaded three cars, all of which were stolen from outside the owner's door, onto the transporter and took them to a scrap yard in Canning Town. They received £30.00 from the dodgy scrap dealer. The owners got the insurance money. Everyone was a winner. Although Tony was nearly thirteen, he would cry whenever he was picked on, he would say, "I wanna go Home" we took no shame in singing this Lonnie Donegan song to him whenever he was in distress.

Bobby Bedfont was, by far, the largest of our brothers' friends. To us, he was a young Harry Secombe. He was unable to go upstairs on a bus. His mum reminded us of Hattie Jacques; however, his dad could have been used to check the oil of a car. Unable to participate in any sports at all, Bobby was at his happiest when taking part in Poplar's famous 'pie eating' contest, which took place on the first day of April, every year. I always considered him to be a something of a strange boy, as he did not seem to fit into our brother's gang. He had, large brown eyes, that would enlarge and blink, uncontrollably. He was quite happy to hear us sing, "What do you want to make those eyes at me for." On the 1st, April 1962, at the age of fourteen, Bobby Bedfont, whilst trying to consume his twelfth pie, had a heart attack and died on the debris that the older boys called 'the dirty park.' For thirteen years, a metal sign, bearing the picture of a 'Fray Bentos' steak and kidney pie, swung outside the front door of his house. When the house was demolished, in 1975, the sign disappeared.

Johnny Darke, two years older than the others, was the enforcer of the 'infamous five.' "Darkie" as we referred to him, was a fearsome fifteen-year-old. He had the mental capacity of our baby brother and would be easily led into trouble by the younger members of the gang. John and I were terrified of him, he lived just around the corner, however, whenever he strode into our street, we either ran off, or hid. Officially, he was not allowed into our house, but he never understood that. He would enter the 'forever open' front door of our house and although he knew that we lived upstairs, he would firstly open the door of the downstairs living room and frighten the life out of grandad Ted. We never minded this, as we always thought that this would provoke a heart attack for the old sod that never had a kind word for anyone. In 1965 our prayers were answered, more of that later. Darkie was the first person that I ever knew, that could extort money from others, simply by his physical presence. He did not get to see his sixteenth birthday and you will have to wait nearly two years to find out why.

Without doubt the most memorable theft perpetrated by the elder boys was that of the stealing of a double decker bus from a scrap yard in Coventry Cross. Somehow Johnny Darke had been able to get the bus started and between them they were able to drive it through the flimsy gates of the yard. They managed to drive it as far as the large debris at the end of Empson Street, whereupon it died a death and became the play-bus for hundreds of kids for several months before the scrapyard claimed it back.

14 – The Jukebox

On the last Friday of October 1960, John and I were pushing baby Graham, in his pram, for yet another visit to our mum at the record counter in Woolworths. As we turned the corner into Brownfield Street, we noticed, what looked like, a brand-new pram, with a brand-new baby, snuggled up under the pristine blankets that covered it. Without any discussion, John picked up our little brother and I did likewise to the very small bundle that appeared to be fast asleep in the other pram. Within seconds, we had switched the occupants of the prams and legged it towards Crisp Street and the sanctuary of Woolworths. We did the deal on the records and exited through the rear doors of the store and strode, quite normally along East India Dock Road, until we reached Brunswick Road. This route would mean that we were not going anywhere near to the scene of the crime. Strangely, our mum never enquired as to how we had managed to obtain an almost new perambulator.

Just fifty yards from the left turn, that would take us all the way home, we saw that the shop front of what was once a second-hand shop, (of which there were hundreds in Poplar) was now a gleaming new premises. We were looking at the very first 'milk bar' to appear on one of East London's major roads. Pressing our noses up against the newly installed plate glass window, we could see five or six teenagers. Two boys were playing on a pinball machine, two girls were sat, drinking milk shakes and a couple, holding hands, were studying the list of records that were inside the jukebox. We had never seen a real jukebox, we had seen them on the tele, but not in the flesh. John hoisted Graham from his new pram, placed him outside the door and the three of us entered. Courtesy of our mum we both had the £1.00 note that she had placed in the bag's containing our latest additions to the record collection. I went to the counter and ordered two chocolate milk shakes and a candy floss for Graham. Whilst we waited for our order to be delivered to the red formica topped table, we ambled over to the jukebox and noted the records that it contained. I went back to the counter, handed over a sixpenny piece and asked for two 'thruppenny bits.' The girl behind the bar opened her blouse and exposed two perfectly formed breasts. I dropped one of the coins into the slot and John selected, "It's now or never" which was one of the records that we had just lifted from Woolie's. Our little brother was mesmerised by the fact that music was coming from the large machine, that towered above his small frame. When Elvis had finished, we lifted our little 'shit-arse' up and let him drop the money into the jukebox and then asked him to randomly select a song. He chose "Shaking all Over" by Johnny Kidd and the Pirates and for the next two minutes and twenty seconds he shook his body so violently that the owner of the milk bar picked him up and snuggled him to his body. Two years later, the owner, known to all as the "Milky Bar Kid" was up in court on a charge of 'interfering with children.' We had no idea what that meant.

With our mum's help, we were able to increase our collection by 12. Our dad would give Rosie a £1.00 note and ask her to pick three records for him. In return for our silence, she would inform him that three of the songs that John and I had obtained, were in fact, for him. Mum of course, pocketed the money. These were our October 1960 purchases. All were copies of the originals.

Bob Luman – "Let's think about Living."
Elvis Presley – "It's now or Never."
Sam Cooke – "Chain Gang"
Johnny Burnette – "Dreaming"
Johnny & the Hurricanes – "Rocking Goose"
Johnny Mathis – "My love for You"
Piltdown Men – "MacDonald's Cave"
Billy Fury – "Wondrous Place"
Johnny Kidd & the Pirates– "Shaking all Over."
Frank Sinatra – "Nice N' Easy"
Johnny Kidd & the Pirates – "Restless"
John Barry Seven – "Walk don't Run."

We had bought "Walk don't Run" an instrumental, by the **John Barry Seven**, not because we liked it, but because it meant that we had the entire **top 20** at the end of October 1960. We had already purchased a version by a very old bunch of musicians by the name of the 'Ventures.'

The statistics were that we had **109** single records, of which **32** were in the UK top **40**.

Brother Graham - October 1960

15 - Bonfire Night 1960

The build-up to bonfire night had been fraught with problems. As John and I grew older, we were encouraged to help with the gathering of any combustible materials that we could lay our hands on. Our elder brother, was, as usual, at the forefront of ensuring that our tribute to Guy Fawkes was the biggest and the best, within the local area. Every street in Poplar had a house, or houses that had been taken out by the Luftwaffe and the debris that had been created between two, or more houses, was the ideal place to build a bonfire. On Venue Street, our home, three of the four corner houses had been flattened by Hitler's thugs. Corner debris were not ideal for the erection of a bonfire, as burning-embers could easily spill into the road, this tended to annoy some of our neighbours. We threw our hat in with the top half of Teviot Street where two houses had been raised to the ground in 1943, this created a larger space on which to build our bonfire. The bottom half of Teviot Street had its own very large site. They had a debris that had been created by the destruction of around twenty houses, meaning that their guy would burn at the top of a wigwam of wood, that was at least fifty foot in height.

During October, the Teviot boys began to create an impressive pile of wood. They were led by the thug that once controlled the flicker card craze, none other than Ronnie Watson. From mid-October, Watson's gang guarded their ever-expanding pile of firewood, 24/7. One boy, the future arsonist and murderer, Lennie 'pyro' Richardson was someone that, if you had any sense, you would never challenge. Although fully embedded into Watson's crew, 'Pyro' had his own little gang. Together, during the small hours of the night, they would steal whatever they could carry, from other bonfires and add their bounty to their own. Some mornings we would see that our, once proud, stack of timber, had almost all disappeared. The result of all of this was that a mass bundle would take place, normally after school had finished for the day. We would have to replenish what we had lost, and we did not care where the fuel for our fire was going to come from. We would dismantle wooden fences from both the front and rear of people's properties. Garage doors, which were almost always made from wood, were fair game, as were the large wooden market stalls that were simply parked in the street at night. We dug out the stones from under railway lines and took the sleepers, rendering the local train service inoperative. Ronnie Green, even at the age of thirteen, was an ace at dismantling things. He would unscrew street doors from their hinges and

A Life Like No Other

arrange them at the foot of the bonfire, he even built a small room inside and would spend many hours guarding his contribution.

Two nights before the big event, around thirty of Watson's gang, including 'Pyro' turned up at our debris. We were outnumbered two to one. They were armed, they carried large pieces of wood, bricks, and iron bars. Pyro held aloft a milk bottle that was half full of petrol. He lit the rag that hung limply from its opening and threw it into the middle of our pride and joy. Within minutes the whole stack was alight. Watson and his henchmen fled. Flames were shooting forty-foot into the air. The fire quickly spread to the piles of wood that were close to the sides of the houses. The wooden fences of both the Morris's and the Austen's back gardens were on fire. Ronnie Green fled the site and entered the fire station, just three hundred yards away. He alerted his father, the chief of the station. Two engines were dispatched and within ten minutes of it being a raging, out of control fire, it was extinguished.

The next morning, we re-grouped. We had to accept the fact that we would not be lighting any fire the following evening, as all our timber was either burnt through, or just too wet. Big brother convened a meeting of the elders. It was decided that retribution was to be the order of the day. At the older boy's school, it was agreed that a fight would take place between, Pyro and Johnny Darke. The winner would take control of the Teviot Street bonfire, which, was by far, the largest of its kind in Poplar.

At 4.30 in the afternoon of November 4th, 1960, Ronnie Green placed two fingers into his tooth decaying mouth and whistled. This sound was the signal for 'Pyro,' standing in the Teviot corner and 'Darkie' who was being held back by his Venue Street cornermen, to begin the fight that would determine whom it was that would control Poplar's largest bonfire night festivities. There were around one-hundred spectators, they were mostly children, of ages that varied from 3 up to 15. Just outside the circle of cheering supporters stood PC Crocket, better known to all of us as 'Davy.' Pyro danced out into the centre of the ring. Darkie was finally released by the overweight pairing of Tony Brazil and Bobby Bedfont. Darkie threw one punch and as they say in the world of boxing, it was 'goodnight, Vienna' or, more importantly, on this occasion, it was lights out for the fourteen-year-old that would go on to start over seventeen fires, accounting for four deaths. By the age of twenty, Lennie Richardson, alias 'Pyro' would be banged up in a mental institution on the Isle of Wight, which, two years after his confinement, would mysteriously burn down. Pyro set fire to himself in 1967. He was so badly burned that there was no need for a cremation.

And so, our gang had control of the following evenings events. November the 5th was a Saturday, the very best day on which to have a bonfire. Around twenty of us spent most of the day nicking wood from other, less spectacular memorials to Mr Guy Fawkes. John and I, in control of our young sibling for the whole day, used his pram, with Graham still on board, to convey large stacks of filthy dirty and often soaking wet timber from sites that we had raided, returning our spoils, back to our massive timber wigwam. The youngest and lightest of our gang would climb up the outside of the stack and place what we had stolen securely in place. This made the whole stack both higher and wider.

At 5.30pm on the 5th, November, brother Graham was hoisted onto the outside of the sturdy stack of wood. He was handed a piece of string with a loop at the end. The loop was placed over his hand and tightened around his wrist. The other end of the string contained the guy, which had been formed, out of 'Pyro's' clothes and had then been stuffed with newspaper. Three-year-old Graham Lucas, akin to a fleet footed monkey, climbed the fifty-foot-high structure, secured himself and then, bit by bit, dragged the guy up to where he was. He then undid the string from his wrist and tied the guy to the top of the telegraph pole, that had been uprooted from Spey Street two weeks previously. What came next still resonates with me until this very day.

In a 'preplanned' arrangement, that nobody had bothered to tell Graham about, eight of the older, and stronger boys, had unfolded one of our dad's thick, navy-blue army blankets. A blanket that served as an additional bed cover during the winter months. The eight lads opened the blanket and held it tightly underneath where Graham was perched, some fifty-foot above. Pyro, being an expert in starting fires, had already emptied the petrol from the jerry can that had been stolen from the back of Jimmy Ferry's open back truck. As he threw the burning, petrol- soaked rag onto the bottom of the pyre there was a loud boom, almost at the same time, Graham jumped from his position at the top and landed slap bang in the middle of the blanket. John picked him up and placed him gently into his pram. Pyro threw the blanket onto the fire. Graham and I were a lot colder during the winter of 1960.

At 7.15pm on 'bonfire night' 1960, the four engines of Poplar fire station arrived and began to put out the fire, that had spread uncontrollably to the houses on the far side of the debris. We were to have many more bonfire nights; however, none were as memorable as this one.

Whilst most of our time had been taken up with the building of our bonfire, we still found the time to make the weekly journey to Woolworth's, where our mum continued to deprive Woolies of some of its profits. When the month of November had begun, we were the owners of 26 of the top 40. Consequently, there would be just 14 'new entries' into the New Musical Express UK pop charts and now that we were able to listen to records before we bought them, we were finding it difficult to choose songs that we really wanted to have. We would leave our dad to buy the more, cheesy of the records that had made it into the charts.

Between us, John and I only added the following **4** songs to our collection – ours were fakes.

The Shadows – "Man of Mystery"
Duane Eddy– "Kommotion"
The Viscounts – "Shortnin Bread"
Bill Blacks Combo – "Don't be Cruel."
Slim bought these – his were by the real artists.
Connie Francis – "My heart has a mind of its Own."
Nat King Cole – "Just as much as Ever"
Gary Mills – "Top Teen Baby"
Mark Wynter – "Kicking up the Leaves"
Frank Sinatra – "Ol' MacDonald"

At the end of November 1960, the stack of 45's on our living room floor had reached **118 in** total.

We were missing just **5** of the top **40** and even our dad was not going to buy them.

16 – Christmas Presents – Part 1

December, in most children's lives, is a special month. The expectation of what one might receive on the 25th is hard to contain during the previous 24 days. From the very beginning of the month, John and I would systematically search the house for signs of what we might be getting in our pillowcases, on Christmas day. Nannie Lil would not give us any clues and the miserable old git that masqueraded as our paternal grandad, simply refused to acknowledge that Christmas even existed. At the end of the first week of December we had not been able to find anything resembling a Christmas present, even the large workshop in the backyard was void of clues. John and I decided to pool our resources in order to buy presents for our mum and dad, nan, and grandad, two other brothers and of course, for Mrs Eisel, the old lady that lived next door to us, and whom, for the best part of our lives we had managed to torment, to such an extent, that she had started to poison the Victoria sponge that she baked for us, every week.

Around the middle of the month, we found the first clue to the fact that we might possibly be getting some reward for the countless hours, days, and weeks that we had, safely guarded our little brother, thus allowing our mum to go out to work six days a week. The clue was that Rosie had started to keep the Daily Mirror. A stack of the nation's favourite daily newspaper had begun to emerge in the corner of her bedroom. We were able to breathe a sigh of relief as we now knew that presents were on the agenda, as mum always wrapped them in newspaper.

By Saturday the 17th, of December John and I had amassed a sum of £6.00, which was mainly by courtesy of the fact that mum was giving us our £1.00 back when purchasing records from Woolie's. £6.00 in 1960 was a princely sum for two East End kids to have ownership of. The average weekly pay was just £7.50. John and I sat down and worked out how much we would spend on each of our relatives. We added into our calculations the fact that there would be every opportunity to nick some presents, especially from Woolworth's, where the security consisted of just one person, namely Ivan Coppin. Ivan was a man of around twenty-years-old. He had arrived in London aged five, just after the end of World War 2. His parents, having fled the ravaged suburbs of Warsaw, found themselves living in squalor, in a rat-infested cellar of a house just off East India Dock Road. Ivan had never been educated, he spoke no English and was not entirely aware of the fact that his job was to guard the entire stock holding of his employers. Ivan, not entirely happy with his parent's choice of abode, decided to live in the stock room at the back of the store. It was warm in the winter and had several 'mod-cons' that were not available in his parent's cellar. The stock room had double doors that opened to the outside world. Deliveries were taken in through those doors. We had made it our aim to befriend Ivan, although we did not understand one word of the Polish that he spoke. We communicated through gestures. We would simulate eating and Ivan would fetch some cakes for us. He was oblivious to the fact that he was stealing them from his employers. John would mimic a monkey and Ivan would bring us some bananas. The best wheeze was when John and I hid our shoes in Graham's pram and pointed at our hole ridden socks. Ivan brought us two pairs of black plimsols each. Ivan would, quite innocently, assist us in making sure that we got all the presents that we needed for our relatives.

On the Monday prior to Christmas, having already broken up for the festive school holidays we marched confidently into the Crisp Street entrance of Woolworth's. Woolie's would have many items simply stacked up in front of their antiquated counters. Young Graham, with the actions of a latter-day 'Oliver' would lean out of his pram and swipe something within his reach and place it under his blankets. We never knew what he had nicked until we were well away from the shop. Once we had taken, yet another six records, without paying, we made our way home. On the way we rolled back Graham's blankets to reveal, a hairdryer, a set of plastic knives and forks, a Cadburys selection box and woman's bra. Once at home, we took the items from the pram and made our way to the backyard workshop, via the door that gave us access to the outside, without the need to go through our nan and grandad's living room. We were to repeat our pilfering until Friday 23rd, December. In addition to the goods that our little brother had managed to stow, undetected, under his well-worn blankets, we had also managed to procure several items from Ivan's closely guarded stockroom. These included a whole box of Christmas wrapping paper and over a hundred cards. After our parents had left for work on Christmas eve, John and I spent most of the day in the workshop, carefully wrapping the presents that we would hand to our family the next morning. Graham was tucked up, snuggly in his pram, outside. We were oblivious to the fact that the constant heavy rain had penetrated his blanket and that he was shivering like a jellyfish underneath. Old misery guts, Ted, kept sending nannie Lil out to see what we were up to. She brought us tea and biscuits and then reported back to the man that she would gladly, had suffocated in his sleep, telling him that we were making something for him, our favourite grandad.

One by one, we lifted each of the stolen items from under the large workbenches, having covered them over with the large planks of softwood that our dad had somehow amassed. Once they were assembled on top of the benches that were wrapped around three sides of the workshop, and which accounted for half of the area of the backyard, we then decided who would get what and duly laid out the first sheet of wrapping paper. We had agreed that we would wrap each present in the order of the seniority of our family members. All the presents were to be from all three of us. We included Graham as he had lifted, many of them from woolies shop floor.

Grandad Ted – We wrapped three bottles of Vick Vapor Rub.
Nannie Lil – She got a navy-blue bra and four packets of Atora Suet Mix.
Uncle Ted (Ticker) – We wrapped three of our dads Anthony Newley's records for him.
Aunt Lil (Teds wife) – The plastic knife and fork set.
Uncle Harry – A harmonica. This was taken from him by his wife Lil as soon as he took it from the paper.
Aunt Lil (The controller of the family) – Two baking trays. She was always baking.
Dad – 4 Screwdrivers, a spirit level, a pair of plyers and a small saw. Graham had excelled when lifting these, from the DIY counter.
Mum – The hairdryer, a large box of OMO, a pair of Wincey Ette Pyjamas, Six Plastic Beakers, and a Copper Bottom Pot and Lid.
Big Brother – A Swiss Army Knife. This gift would be used in several of his forthcoming misdemeanors.
Graham (From John and I) – The Selection Box that young Fagin had nicked from the display in Woolies.
Mrs. Eisel – For the frail old lady next door, we had stolen a padded footstall, thinking that she could rest her chin upon it, rather than allow the bottom of her head to drag along the floor.
For Ourselves – I got a small Dansette Transistor Radio and a new pair of shoes, which were still in their Bata cardboard box. John had chosen a lace-up football and a heavy-duty catapult. All four items were courtesy of Ivan, whom, unsurprisingly, did not return to his duties after the festive season.

17 – Christmas Presents – Part 2

Even though we knew what each of us was getting, we still wrapped them up and would place them under the tree that we had stolen from outside Jolly's the Greengrocers some ten days prior to Christmas day.

After we had finished our wrapping, we placed all the presents onto the bench behind us and then took four of the six-foot planks from under the bench by our feet. We cut four smaller pieces and nailed them all together. After placing the presents inside the six-foot wooden box, John painted "GRANDAD R I P" on the lid. We then carried the box into the backyard, noticing that our young brother's face was almost blue. We entered our grandparents' back door, carried the box into the living room and placed it at our grandad's feet. His reaction was predictable.

"You little gits," he yelled. He had a way with words.

"Wait until your father gets home."

Nannie Lil was bent over she was in hysterics as she let out a loud fart.

Just as we had placed the last present under the tree, our dad arrived home. As he walked past, en-route to putting the kettle on, he looked down at the coffin and enquired –

"Is that for your grandad?"

"Yes, it's just a joke dad."

Replied a slightly nervous John.

"Looks like you have done a good job. Might save us some money when the time comes."

We removed the wooden box and laid it at the foot of our grandparents' bed. Little did we know, at the time, that old misery features would be needing it sooner than expected.

Dad made tea for the three of us. He had come home early, to start cooking the Turkey, Beef and Pork for Christmas dinner. Our oven was tiny, therefore the meats had to be cooked and ready to eat long before our mum cremated the potatoes, parsnips, turnips, and Yorkshire pudding.

Suddenly, a shout, that was so shrill that it woke Mrs. Stephenson, our totally deaf neighbour, from a drunken slumber. The shout had come from under the stairs and had risen from the stomach of nannie Lil.

"Slim, Slim there is something wrong with 'Sputty' he is completely blue, wringing wet and ice cold."

A Life Like No Other

Our dad was out of the traps faster than 'Spark Vicar' a well-known Hackney Greyhound. John and I followed him down the stairs, but not into the back yard. We entered John's bedroom and laid underneath John's single bed. From our vantage point we saw two pairs of legs rush past us. One pair belonged to our dad, the other to our nan. Once they were out the door and into our dad's lorry, we found the courage to come out from our hiding place. There was a trail of water running along the entire hallway. At that very moment our mum arrived home.

"Where is your dad going?

I have just seen his lorry turning onto the main road."

"He is taking 'Sputty' to the hospital, nannie is with him."

"What have you done to him this time?" asked our mum.

"Nothing, but he may have got a bit wet in the backyard." I replied.

Rose went into the yard. We followed her. She pushed back the hood of the pram and lifted the heavy blanket from inside. She then wrang out several gallons of water. She did the same with the two pillows.

"How long has he been outside in the rain?"

"Not long mum, just ten minutes or so." Replied John.

As we passed grandad Ted on our way back upstairs, he asked –

"How about my dinner? I have not had anything to eat since lunchtime."

"Get your own dinner, you, miserable old sod. Or you will have to wait until Lil gets back."

One nil to our mum, we thought.

By way of explanation, brother Graham was born on the 1^{st,} September 1957. On October the 4th the Russians launched the first ever 'man-made' object to be propelled into space. Wally Smith, a close friend of our parents, seeing Graham for the first time on the day of the launch, nicknamed the newest member of the Lucas family as 'Sputnik' this would later be shortened to 'Sputty' and to some people Graham would be known as this for the rest of his days.

Mum, not being able to find out anything in respect of Sputties welfare, until Slim and Lil returned from the Hospital, carried on with the cooking of the Christmas day meat. There was to be a Christmas Eve party, starting at 7.00pm and soon people began to arrive. John and I helped put out the food. Most of it had been a donation from Woolworth's, although they were not aware of their contribution to our Christmas Eve celebrations.

Whilst Rose carried on with the preparations upstairs, John and I stood at the street door and welcomed our guests as they arrived. We handed them cups of ginger beer; we took their winter coats and threw them on the downstairs bedroom floor and then ushered them upstairs. Uncle Ticker, a Sid James lookalike and Aunt Lil were the first to arrive. Uncle Harry, a man whose facial skin was so tight that he looked like a living skeleton and Big Aunt Lil were next. Big Aunt Lil had a mountain of cakes with her. John and I knew for sure that she would love her Christmas present. Wally Smith, a man so short sighted that he nearly always knocked next door before realising that he was at the wrong house, had brought three large bags of booze with him. He was accompanied by his wife, Connie. Ted and Dorrie Winterflood, with daughter Janice in tow arrived. Ted, a well-known Council leader, was already three sheets to the wind. Dorrie and our mum had met in St Andrew's hospital in March 1951. I was born ten minutes before Janice and our mums had labelled us as 'the twins.' I spent 21 years trying to avoid my twins' amorous advances. Several other couples, not as well known to us, began to trickle in. There were up to thirty people in a living room that measured no more than 80 square feet.

It must have taken twenty minutes or so before anyone asked as to the whereabouts of Slim. Our mum simply informed them that Graham had a fever and that Slim, and his mum had taken him to the hospital. Anyhow, the absence of her husband and youngest child did nothing to prevent Rose from having a good time. John and I put her to bed, much the worse for wear, at around 12.45 on Christmas morning. Her departure was a sign that everyone else should leave. Ted Winterflood was the last person to leave, we had to physically prevent him from entering our mum's bedroom and then we had to drag him downstairs, step by step after he had passed out. He was not a small man, weighing in at around 19 stone. His head hit every single step on the way down. When our dad and nannie Lil arrived home at 7.30am, they had to step over Ted, who had fallen asleep inside our small front porch.

Slim, having made black coffee for Rose, climbed the five steps that led from our living room, he crossed the landing, and disappeared behind the bedroom door. The left ears of John and me were pressed firmly upon the white painted door. It took a few minutes for Slim to wake his wife from her unconscious state, we then heard the words that sent tremors through our respective bodies. The tremors were so violent that we heard a large thump as grandad Ted fell from his downstairs bed. Momentarily we prayed that we had killed the old misery guts, safe in the knowledge that we would never face trial for murder. The words that we heard our dad mutter, and which are still remembered to this day, were –

"They don't think that Sputty is going to make it. His body temperature was so low when we got him there that they had to put him in the large fridge to thaw out, that's how cold he was."

"Well, that's one less mouth to feed, Slim." Said Rose.

Our ears were still stuck on the door when our dad fled. Our ears remained on the door throughout Christmas.

A Life Like No Other

Unbeknown to us, at the time, Slim had run all the way to St Michael's Church, where he had prayed for one hour. He later revealed that he had not been praying for the recovery his youngest heir, he was simply asking God not to allow Rose to burn the Christmas dinner.

Sputty recovered and was back home on the 30th, December. By then, John and I had eaten his Cadbury Selection Box. We were told that we would never be allowed to take our little brother out in his pram ever again. We made a small replica of him and would wheel that around, as we needed the pram to both hide, and carry our ill-gotten gains.

We were not taken to see Mr. Cohen at his Victorian record shop, in Brick Lane on boxing day, 1960. Whilst this was somewhat disappointing, it was not the end of the world, as, with our mum's help, we had managed to add 14 records to the collection. Our visitors on Christmas Eve were not impressed with the music offered by woolies fake singers, however they still managed to dance to –

Cliff Richard & The Shadows – "I Love You"
Nina & Frederick – "Little Donkey"
Johnny Tillotson – "Poetry in Motion"
Max Harris – "Gurney Slade"
The Ventures – "Perfidia"
Emile Ford & The Checkmates – "Counting Teardrops"
Matt Monroe – "Portrait of my Love"
Ray Charles – "Georgia on my Mind"
Everly Brothers – "Like Strangers"
Lonnie Donegan – "Virgin Mary"
Bobby Rydell – "Sway"
Acker Bilk – "Buona Sera"
Russ Conway – "Even more party Pops"
Marty Wilde – "Little Girl"

We had nearly made it. There were just **4** records missing from the top **40** of December 1960. We would have bought them had we made it to the 'flour graders' shop on boxing day.

Our total for 1960 stood at **132** singles. We were running out of floor space.

A quick check of the top 100 chart for 1960 revealed that we had **83** of those songs. In **2021** I would find myself downloading them all. Many contained video footage that I had not seen for more than **60** years.

18 - Radio Luxembourg

The small dansette transistor radio that I had given myself for Christmas, 1960, would prove to be one of the most treasured of presents. It did not get much use during the day as radio Luxembourg only broadcast to the UK in the evenings. There was no radio Caroline or London at the time, therefore the only real place to go to listen to 'pop music' was on the '208' waveband. There was no need to search for the station on the radio as it clearly showed 'Luxembourg' on its dial. The radio came with a single earpiece that plugged into the back. At night I could listen whilst laid in bed, without disturbing my precious little three-year-old brother, that laid peacefully by my side. I can recall the names of a few of the DJs from that era, there was Barry Aldis, who hosted both 'Smash Hits' and 'The Top Twenty Show.' Muriel Young and Shaw Taylor jointly fronted 'Friday Spectacular' and as the 60's progressed Don Wardell, Paul Burnett and Tony Prince joined in the fun. A good number of Luxembourg's DJs would later join Caroline or London before moving on to the BBC.

Whilst the ownership of a radio would not register at all in today's world, for me it was like magic had happened. John and I would no longer have to go to Woolie's, stand in the listening booth and ask our mum to play new releases for us. We were able to hear them all from this tiny music box. I still remember the first record I ever heard on the dansette radio. It was 'Are you lonesome Tonight' by 'Elvis Presley', which would become the new year's second number 1.

I was still nine years old and brother John just eight, we were like two kids that had been locked in a sweetshop. Even at our tender ages we were hooked on music. We were now able to march into Woolworth's and collect our records from our mum without the need to listen first. On the second Saturday of 1961 our mum handed over two brown bags. In each bag were three records and the £1 note that she was meant to have put in the till, obviously an oversight on her part. Between us we inherited the following six songs –

'Are you lonesome Tonight' – **Elvis Presley**
'Save the last dance for Me' – **The Drifters**
'Goodness gracious Me' – **Peter Sellers & Sophia Loren**
'You're Sixteen' – **Johnny Burnette**
'Blue Angel' – **Roy Orbison**

A Life Like No Other

'Rubber Ball' – **Bobby Vee**

These six (fake) records were to be the last that John and I received courtesy of Woolie's as mum was taken off the record counter and transferred to the sweet counter, which in its own way became just as beneficial for my brother and myself.

When our mum came home from work that evening, she had brought with her another three records –

'My heart has a mind of its Own' – **Connie Francis**
'My love for You' – **Johnny Mathis**
'As long as he needs Me' – **Shirley Bassey**

We were much too young and naive to understand the message, however at 8pm mum put those three records on, picked up the portable extension speaker and guided our dad to the bedroom. John and I listened at the door as they grunted their way through those three 'love' songs.

Our collection of 45's now stood at 141, which we deemed to be quite good for just one year.

As I have mentioned previously, John had lifted, with the help of Ivan at woolie's, a heavy-duty catapult, and he was putting it to very good use. From the safety of Manorfield School playing ground he was easily able to pick off most of the windows of both the Spratt's dog food factory, and those of the Far-Famed Cake Company building. From our windowsill in Venue Street, he could hit the calf of most of the people passing by in nearby Teviot Street. Our cousin Michael Roberts, a seventeen-year-old from Bromley-by-Bow had become a glazier at fourteen. John would shatter the windows of houses and later Michael would pop round and offer his services to the injured party. We were normally given enough money by Michael to enable us to buy a couple of singles, every other Saturday.

One Sunday evening John and I were enjoying some jelly and ice cream in our nans downstairs living room when there was a loud thump on the street door. Our dad came down to investigate, he opened the door to reveal the largest of police sergeants, he asked my dad as to the whereabouts of two boys aged around ten. When dad asked as to why he wanted to see them, he replied,

'There have been a number of windows broken in the area and that his two boys have been named as the culprits.'

John and I were now under nannie Lil's table, a table that completely hid us as the tablecloth touched the ground on all sides. Our nan flew out of the room, pushed my dad to one side and told the officer, in no uncertain way,

'Those boys have been with me all day, they have not left the house, there are many brothers around here, perhaps you should call at the Whalley's house.'

Nan returned to us and said,

'You can come out now, boys.'.

Our dad watched as the Sergeant crossed the road and knocked on the Whalley's door. I can still hear the torrent of abuse that Mrs Whalley levelled at the upholder of the law. He never knocked at our door again.

19 - The Swinging 60's

Early In 1961, fed up and often frustrated by his son's naughtiness, and continual running in and out of the house, Uncle 'Ticker' came up with the idea of pegging his two male offspring onto the washing line in the backyard of his house in Hackney Wick. What started out as a punishment for his two lads soon became a great sense of fun, not only for Brian and Stephen but also for all their friends, who would wait patiently for their turn to be 'hung out to dry.' Queues, of both girls and boys used to form, outside his terraced house until it all ended abruptly one Sunday morning. That is when 5-year-old Stanley Smith slipped from his moorings and spent the next three months in Homerton Hospital recovering from both the trauma and several broken bones. After this 'mishap' Aunt Lil, not known for her sense of humour, forbid her husband to continue with this form of amusement. Stanley went on to join the circus. He was not, as you might think, a trapeze artist or a high wire devil. He simply gave out the goldfish on the shoot a duck stall.

Just two of the many young boys that enjoyed being hung out to dry.

20 - The Music Box

On the 25th, March 1961 I struck my first ever bet. My mum had picked out about ten horses by the time that 'Smiley' the local bookies runner knocked on our door. I had been studying the runners and had read that no grey horse had won the world's most famous steeplechase for 90 years. Nicolaus Silver was not only a distinctive silvery grey in colour, but he was also to be ridden by a little-known jockey by the name of Bobby Beasley. I always had a liking for grey horses, ever since I had first met my Yorkshire grandad's grey shire horse, whose name was snowy. In addition to this, a boy of nine, named Bobby Beasley, lived in Lochnagar Street, which was not far from our house. Bobby would sometimes play on the debris that was an equal distance from our respective abodes. He also tended to wear light-grey clothes, an omen, if ever there was one. I had exactly a pound left from my birthday money, I decided to bet the lot. When Smiley knocked on our door at around 2pm my mum had already added my bet, of 10 bob (50p) each-way. Smiley, a former jockey, was as small as any man could be. At ten years old I towered above him. He seemed to have the largest ears of anyone I had seen and given his diminutive size the wingspan of his hearing devices was almost as wide as he was tall. Mum handed him her bet, she had also staked a pound, albeit she had bet a shilling (5p) each way on no less than ten nags. The 1961 Grand National welcomed two Russian horses, and their jockeys and the Russian flag flew over the Aintree grandstand. Mum and I listened intently to the radio; we had no TV as it had been reclaimed by rediffusion for not paying the monthly rental. With two fences to go, Nicolaus Silver drew level with the long-time leader, Merryman and the grey led over the last and eventually won by five lengths. The winner was returned at 28/1, I had the princely sum of £18 and ten shillings to collect from Smiley. From the ten horses that my mum had backed, not even one of them managed to finish in the first four, which was quite a feat. Normally the bookies runner would return the following day to pay out any winnings. As the following day was a Sunday, I was not expecting to collect my bounty until Monday. After arriving home from school, I had to wait, firstly for mum to come back from work and then for Smiley to knock on our door. There was no knock. Mum crossed the road and knocked on the door of the Skeel's house, as Charlie Skeels was also a regular punter with Smiley. Charlie gave her the bad news; the pint-sized, big eared ex jockey had been attacked when leaving his local pub on Saturday night and had died in St. Andrew's hospital on Sunday afternoon. He

A Life Like No Other

had no money at all upon his person when found by the police. I was never to receive my winnings. Betting shops became legal in the UK on the 1 st, May 1961. Had the grand national been run five weeks later then I would not have required the services of Smiley the runner.

With our mum no longer working on the record counter at Woolworth's, our record collection had become stagnant. We were listening to many new releases via the Dansette transistor but were unable to get our hands on any of the 7 inch 45's that we wanted. Mums transfer to the sweet counter was to be more beneficial to us than we could have imagined. We were able to fill our duffle bags with an unlimited amount of 'pic n' mix' which we sold to most of our school friends. On the first Saturday in April, we were sent to Crisp Street market by our nan to get some live eels for our dinner. As we passed the 'Music Box,' one of the many small businesses that operated from the exterior of the arcade, we saw that Tony Brazil, one of our elder brothers' friends, he was working behind the counter. We had a brief chat with him, he seemed to be extremely busy, with many customers waiting to be served. At a little after 6pm, John and I returned to the market and waited for Tony to be released by his boss. Walking back home, we gave the extremely overweight thirteen-year-old 'an offer he could not refuse.' We promised not to grass him up for the stealing of the bus last year or the fact that he had nicked half a dozen books from Poplar library, if he agreed to hand over three records and return ten shillings of the £1 that we would pay to him. We had to further explain that he could keep the other ten shillings for himself. Tony, a few sandwiches short of a picnic, got there in the end. The following Saturday we collected three 45's from Tony, who for some reason, returned the whole of the £1 that we gave to him. We continued to obtain our records in this way until February 1962, when Tony Brazil became so obese that he could no longer get through the opening under the counter.

The first three records that we obtained from the Music Box were –

"Are you Sure" – **The Allisons.**
"Will you still love me Tomorrow" – **The Shirelles.**
"You're driving me Crazy" – **The Temperance Seven.**

21 - The twin Tub

Part of my 10th birthday reward was that I received a pair of my eldest brothers worn out shoes, albeit with brand new cardboard inside to cover the holes in the soles. I also received a 'red rover' all day bus ticket, brother John was also given one and we had a whole day of complete mischief to look forward to on the Saturday. My nan had cooked stewed eels and mash for my tea and the miserable old git that sat in the corner of the downstairs living room gave me a chisel and a small saw from his vast collection of pre-WW1 carpentry items. I would continue to get tools from him until he checked out of life when I was fourteen. I did not receive any records for my 10th birthday, this was maybe because our mum was no longer in charge of the music in Woolie's. Our collection had come to a standstill, but we had now found an alternative supplier.

"Walk right Back / Ebony Eye's" was the number 1 record and "Wooden Heart" by Elvis had been at number 2 on the day of my 10th birthday.

Shortly after my tenth birthday my mum announced that I was now both old and strong enough to take the dirty washing to the 'bag wash' and hand it over to a lady that we knew only as 'Laundry Lil.' When East Enders first hit our screens, both John and I always referred to Dot Cotton as 'Laundry Lil,' as Lil was never without a fag hanging from her lips. There were always two bags of washing to take, the 'lights' and the 'darks.' We were supposed to hand them over and leave the rest to Lil. However, as my brother and I were budding entrepreneurs, we decided that we would put all the clothes into the same washing machine and pocket half of the money. When we opened the machine at the end of the wash all the whites and light-coloured items were now pink. We took only the darks back home, telling our mum that Lil had managed to give *her* 'lights' to someone else. Our mum was not the slightest bit fazed by this news, she simply muttered –

'Oh well, less ironing to do.'

Our visits to the 'bag wash' lasted for just a month, as our dad, sick and tired of listening to his wife moaning about the state of the clothes when they came back from being washed, had a big surprise for her on her 33rd birthday. Her birthday was on Sunday 16th April. On Saturday the 15th, mum and dad went to work as normal. At 10am dad returned and parked his TK Bedford lorry outside the Puxley's house, leaving enough room for Sid Whalley, our most notorious of neighbours to park his large van directly outside ours. By

A Life Like No Other

10.20 Sid and dad had carried mum's birthday present from the van and placed it inside the downstairs front room, which was nan and grandad's boudoir. As Sid and our dad shut the back doors of the van my dad asked,

'How much do I owe you Sid?'

'Let's call it a tenner, Slim.'

Dad handed over ten one-pound notes, which was equivalent to a week and a half's wages at the time.

On Sunday morning, John, little brother Graham and I were all on our mum's bed, handing over the presents that we had lovingly wrapped in last week's East London Advertiser. I presented her with 'Blue Moon' by the Marcels and John gave her 'Theme for a Dream' by Cliff, she loved Cliff Richard. Graham gave her a box of Maltesers, which he later consumed. During all of this, our dad and eldest brother were busy carrying the heavy present up the stairs and into the back kitchen, and whilst dad set it up, big brother arrived in the bedroom, with coffee and toast for the birthday girl.

Half an hour later our mum entered the kitchen and squealed with delight when she saw her brand-new Rolls Rapide, Twin Tub, washing machine, with a bunch of red roses nestling on top. Ten minutes later she loaded a pile of 'darks' into the washer and poured in some of the OMO that dad had lovingly bought for her. When the washing machine had come to a halt and its contents had been 'spun dry' John and I were despatched to the back yard, in order, to hang the newly washed clothes onto the line. The machine came with a formica cover that mum was able to use as an extra kitchen worktop.

Two weeks after receiving the 'roller' from Sid Whalley, he was arrested. He was charged with stealing goods from outside shops. Our machine had been stolen from the pavement outside a 'white goods' shop on Stratford Broadway. In court Sid asked for 76 other offences to be considered. He received six years. He was 35 years old and had spent 14 of them at her majesty's pleasure.

One year later that washing machine was to play an integral part in our young brother's formative years.

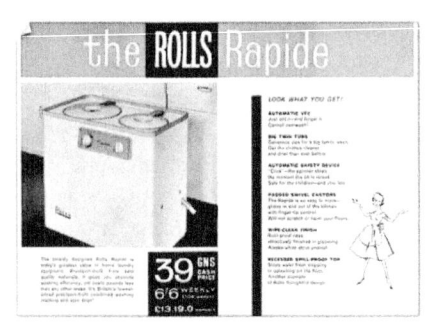

The 'Rolls Rapide' was to become the most popular washing machine of the 1960's.

22 - Up the O'S

On Saturday 28th October 1961, my dad left for work, taking my eldest brother Peter, and my younger brother John with him. I faked a bad stomach in order that I did not have to go with them. My Mum headed off to Woolworth's to take up her position on the sweet counter, she would take our youngest brother, Graham, with her, and he would sit behind the counter all day eating whatever our Mum could get into his mouth. At the tender age of 10 and a half I was home alone and able to hatch my plan, to watch Liverpool, play my beloved Leyton Orient. At 9.30 am I informed my grandparents that I was going to purchase a "red rover" (all day bus ticket) and that I would be with three friends. My grandparents had no concerns with this and just presumed that my Mum and Dad were aware of it. My Nan gave me two shillings (10 p) my Grandad gave me sod-all, as he was as "tight as a duck's arse". It took 15 minutes for me to walk to Bromley-by-Bow underground station, from there I proceeded to Euston and took the big train to Liverpool, Lime Street. I had been saving up some of the £1.12sh 6p (£1.62p in today's money) that I earned every week for delivering newspapers, every morning, and every evening, except Sunday evenings, I had amassed the princely sum of £5.00, which was basically what my dad earned each week. The Big train was packed, I sat on a large brown suitcase that belonged to a man dressed as Sherlock Holmes, he even had a monocle. I arrived at Lime Street at around 2.15 pm and quickly found the bus terminus. I had no idea how I would be getting from there to the football stadium and as I stared one way and then the other way a man with a red and white scarf asked me, in a broad scouse accent, 'are you going to Anfield, whack?' I nodded, he pointed at the blue double decker bus that displayed, "football special". I wondered how he had guessed that I was going to the match, then it dawned on me, must be the blue and white scarf and wooden rattle. I was the only person in blue amongst a great sea of red. The bus stopped almost right outside the stadium, it cost me 2 old pence. I joined a queue with other kids and OAP's. The board above the turn style showed 1 shilling and 3 pence (6p today). Ten minutes later I was in the now, world famous Anfield Stadium and nobody in the World knew I was there. For those football buffs amongst you, this was a division two game, the first division later became the premier division. Leyton Orient had never been in the top-flight of English football and Liverpool were top of division two. Helen Shapiro with, "Walking Back to Happiness", was at number 1 on the day I visited Anfield. I

A Life Like No Other

was at the end of the ground known the world over as, "the kop", and I think I was the only Leyton Orient supporter there. I got passed down, from, the back of the stand, to the front, over the heads of the scoucers'. I ended up pressed firmly against the wall that held us all in. It is a little-known fact that Anfield was originally the home of arch-rivals Everton, who were evicted from the stadium after seven years, for non-payment of rent. The game itself was magnificent, end to end stuff. Orient lead three times, Liverpool equalised three times, it ended 3-3 in front of 36,000 Liverpool fans, and me. Liverpool had the likes of Gerry Byrne, Gordon Milne, Ron Yeats, Roger Hunt, Ian Saint John & Jimmy Melia, all famous Internationals. Orient had Dave Dunmore, once of West Ham fame, he scored twice. I had become something of a celebrity, a 10-year-old cockney kid, amongst thousands of scoucers'. I was escorted out of the ground by my new guardians and was told that I was going to be taken, by taxi, back to Lime Street Station, I thought nothing of it. Imagine that happening today! The driver of the black cab and his mate escorted me from the taxi, bought me some tea and a pie from within the station and took me to the waiting train. The train pulled out of Lime Street at 6.10 pm and I was on my way back home. When I eventually arrived back in Venue Street it was 10.15, my dad, looking over the brim of his tea-cup, seemed a bit upset and asked where I had been. I told him that we had ended up at Heathrow to watch the planes taking off and did not realise it was so late and that it had taken nearly three hours to get back from there, which it did, by bus. That day lives on with me, as vividly now as when it took place. Liverpool and Leyton Orient were both promoted to Division One. Liverpool went on to achieve many league titles, plus FA and European Cups. Leyton Orient went straight back down, never to return to the top-flight of English football in my lifetime. In 2017, for the first time in their 138-year history they were relegated out of the Football League altogether.

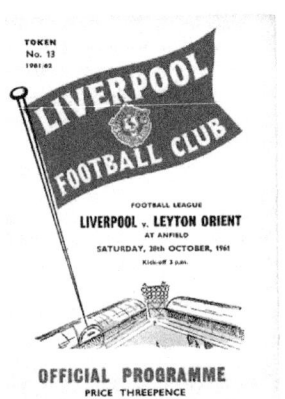

The official matchday programme from my first ever away game.

23 - Neighbours – Part 1

At an early age we were able to observe, from the safety of our windowsill, the daily routines of our neighbours. We lived in Venue Street, Poplar E14. Venue Street was half-way between Bromley-by-Bow station and Blackwall Tunnel. My ever-curious mind helped me to learn, that all the adjoining streets had been named after places in Scotland. All 26 letters of the alphabet had been used, there was Aberfeldy Street right through to Zetland Street. A Scottish Laird, Andrew McIntosh, had bought many acres of Poplar in 1823 and had then employed John Abbott to build a few thousand houses upon the land. One of the longest streets in the neighbourhood was called Abbotts Road. Every house was Victorian in appearance and consisted of the same layout, with each house having an outside toilet, and a small backyard.

The families, ours included, that occupied those terraced houses, were unique and individual, whilst also being almost identical, if that makes sense? Venue Street was rare, as half of it was from the 1820's era whilst the other half had been rebuilt after the war, due to it having succumbed to the extensive bombing of Poplar by our good friends, the Luftwaffe. Originally there would have been three blocks of eight houses on each side of the road. The first block of eight houses, those nearest to Brunswick Road, had all been demolished after the war and all that was left was a debris or bombsite. Debris were, full of bricks, earth, weeds, planks of wood and glass. They were very much, our playgrounds when we were kids. Our block of sixteen houses, originally eight on either side of the road, were all intact, except for three of the corner houses, they had become small debris. The third block were all new builds from the late 1940's. They had indoor loos and bathrooms. We therefore had six neighbours on our side of the road and six on the other side and as I write this chapter, at the age of seventy, I can still vividly remember all of them.

On our side of the street, lived the Newman's, a family of thirteen. Freddie and Enid Newman were the parents. There were six sons and five daughters. They had nothing, and I mean nothing. Our Mum gave them money, clothes, and food, as we had less nothing than they did. Freddie was a lazy sod, he never did a day's work, he just rode around on a bike, a woman's bike. He wore the same dark grey duffle coat every day, summer, or winter. Whatever the elements offered, it made no difference to Freddie Newman. The children really did have the "arse" hanging out of their short trousers, both boys and girls. Their abject poverty meant nothing to us because it was very much the

A Life Like No Other

norm in the East End in the 50's and early 60's. We did, however feel much better off than they were.

Next to the Newman's were the Brown's, a family of eleven which included the grandparents. They were all extremely overweight. Mrs. Brown was not able to weigh herself on one of those machines that they had in Woolworth's, as it could only manage weights of up to twenty stone. When she reached twenty-nine stone, Mrs. Brown was fitted with a gastric band, the first of its kind in London. The operation was carried out in Tyler's Garage, which was situated at the end of our street. Only a car hoist was able to lift her onto the makeshift bed. We had little to do with the Brown's as our Mum had told us to stay away from them, branding them as, "being up to no good," as, according to her, they always seemed like they were doing OK, when they should not be.

The Robertson's, just the two of them, lived next door to the "fatties." Mr. Robertson was the Gentleman of the street, he looked 60 when I was eleven but was probably much younger. He always dressed smart, mostly in a suit and tie. Unfortunately, he went off the rails, today they would say he had dementia, back then he was simply a "looney." One Sunday evening, having finished our bathing ritual, we all sat down, as a family, with our, bread and dripping on our laps, to watch Sunday Night at the London Palladium. As we did, into our small living room walks Mr. Robertson. We had two armchairs and a two-seater sofa, therefore two of us would always have to sit on the floor. My dad was in the kitchen, making yet another cup of tea. Mr. Robertson sat in my dad's armchair, stared at Bruce Forsyth, looked around and then proclaimed,

'Oh dear, wrong house.'

My dad took him home, much to the relief of Mrs. Robertson who had sent him out to get some sugar earlier in the day. Mr. Robertson went out one Monday morning for a newspaper and was never seen again. From that day on Mr Robertson would be eternally known as 'wrong house' Robertson.

The Puxley's were our immediate neighbours to the left of us. There was Bert and Vi and children Joyce and Raymond. To us, as kids, the Puxley's were the rich, family of the street. They had a telephone. This telephone became the lifeline of the whole street. My Mum would receive calls from her family in Yorkshire on the Puxley's, "dog and bone". Bert Puxley had an Austin van, and for some time was the only vehicle parked on our street. Joyce seemed to always be away, seeking a career in dancing. Initially, at just 17, she worked at Butlin's, along with Ringo Starr and Dave Allen. She moved on to London theatre and then to Europe. She met and married the son of the President of A C Milan. All the Milan team were at her wedding. Joy, as she likes to be known, has lived in Italy for over 50 years and is now a regular poster on the East End FB page. Raymond (Ray) was one of our playmate's and remains so to this day. Joy sadly passed away in October 2022 (R I P).

To the right of us lived Mrs. Eiesel and Mrs. Stevenson, both were war widows. Mrs. Eiesel, whose Christian name we never knew, lived downstairs in this shared house. She was a gentle and small framed lady, her diminutive size accentuated by the fact that she was constantly bent over, almost hunch back in appearance. Being mischievous young boys, we would constantly knock on her door and run, she would open the door, her chin almost touching her front step, nod her head and go back in. Occasionally she would hand out bread pudding to us, we would politely take this from her and then go off and brother John, an ace at throwing, would break some of the Far-Famed factory windows with it. It was, after all, much too hard to eat. Mrs. Stevenson was somewhat strange, we never saw her go out and never saw her go in. She was found one Sunday afternoon, rocking peacefully in her chair, having died some weeks earlier. When we moved to a luxurious flat in Blair Street, Mrs Eisel moved in next door, she refused to go anywhere else.

24 - Neighbours – Part 2

On the opposite side of the street, to the right of our front door, yet another debris occupied the corner where a house had once stood. Next to this were the Sugar family. Harry Sugar was a black cab driver and was only occasionally seen. His wife, a sweet lady, seeing us all perched on our windowsill, would sometimes cross the road and hand us a small slice of cake that she had brought back from the Lyon's corner house, her place of work.

Next to the Sugar's lived the Rowe family, they were weird. All of them looked like Groucho Marx, yes, all of them, Mum, Dad and their two Sons. They were taunted so much by the local inhabitants that the youngest Son took his own life, choosing to suspend himself, with the help of a bedsheet, from his bedroom window at the back of the house. I still remember his funeral, just one car and a bloke that looked like Charlie Chaplin following behind on a pushbike.

Exactly opposite our house, lived the Skeels family. Nan, Grandad, their son Charlie, his wife Pam and their three Children, Johnny, David, and Ian. In addition, there was Millie Skeels, Husband John and later their two Sons, yes big families, in one small house, was the norm for the East End in those days. Charlie, Pam and the three boys moved to Granada House, Limehouse, which was still in Poplar, when I was eleven. Johnny Skeels, four years my senior, would become my best friend, until he sadly passed-away in 2007, aged 60. When I wrote this chapter Pam was still around after all those years but then she was only sixteen when giving birth to Johnny. Sadly, Pam passed away in 2020 (RIP). Covid prevented us from attending her funeral.

Immediate neighbours to the Skeels clan were the Saint's. Frank and Emily Saint. They were neck and neck with the Puxley's in the race to be crowned Venue Streets most prosperous family. Frank and Emily ran a small abattoir from a side street off Silver Town Way, E16. The Saints were the second family in our street to have their own car. I remember the car being an Austin A40 and in time honoured tradition Frank would spend countless hours on Sunday's, lovingly polishing the chrome that adorned the front, back and sides of this popular black painted 1950's motor vehicle. Once he had finished his cleaning, and gone back indoors, brother John and I would let both of his offside tyres down.

A Life Like No Other

A frail old lady, known to us only as Mrs. White lived next door to the Saints. Ghost like in appearance and rarely seen during daylight, she boarded the 108-bus early one morning and never returned.

There was no forgetting the inhabitants of the next house, it belonged to the Whalley family. Mrs. Amanda Whalley was a mammoth of a woman, weighing in at between 25 to 30 stone. Her only rival for Venue Street's heaviest woman award, was Mrs. Brown. Amanda's Husband, Bob Whalley, was about nine stone soaking wet, how they ever managed to produce thirteen offspring was beyond my wildest of dreams. I used to imagine Bob, rocking gently in and out of his, "whale-like" wife. It is impossible to remember the names of all the kids. Those that have not been erased from my memory were Twinkie, Cola, Poppet and Sid, as these were the ones that were arrested at least twice a week, every week. Bob Whalley was a frightening man to look at, my Mum used to say that Bob Whalley was, without doubt the World's ugliest man. Mrs. Whalley ran the house, if not the whole Street. On the debris, next to their house, they kept a goat and a donkey. They had a three-legged dog named Jackie and a parrot named, "you dirty bastard" this name derived from what Mrs. Whalley would shout out every time it, "shat" on her head. There was no barrier between their back fence and the debris. They had no back door to the house. The donkey and the goat would enter the hole where the back door should have been, walk through the house and come out of the front door and into the street. The front door had no lock, it was open every day, hot or cold. At night, two of the kid's slept in the hallway, laid up against the door as security. God knows why they needed security as they had absolutely nothing to nick. When Mrs. White failed to return from her 108-bus journey, the Whalley's knocked a hole through their wall, this gave them access to another house. They occupied Mrs. White's house 'free of charge' until the day they left Venue Street. Mrs. Whalley never had a good day, she would stand, massive arms folded in front of her gigantic breasts at her front door, just waiting for the next old bill van to arrive. At least one member of her clan would be in prison at any given time. When she really had the hump, poor Jackie, the three-legged canine would bear the brunt. One summers day, we were sat on our windowsill when Jackie came hurtling from the house, thrown by Mrs Whalley, only to come to a halt under the wheels of a passing motor bike. The rider of the motor bike was thrown, head-first into the only lamp post in our street. Poor sod, what were the chances of that happening? Our nan tended the poor bike rider until the ambulance arrived. On another occasion, ugly Bob had been upstairs, looking out at the street, through the only pane of glass still left intact at the front of their house, when Mrs. Whalley took hold of both of his ears and crashed his head straight through the window. They now had a full set of broken windows but more importantly Bob was badly hurt. When he returned home from hospital three weeks later, he was accompanied by the police. As she was being loaded into the black Mariah, Mrs. Whalley shouted out obscenities to the mass of onlookers. Mrs. Whalley died in Holloway in 1965. She was just 28 stone.

25 - The lost Opportunity.

In June 1962, my dad announced to the family that he had been offered a job by the company directly next door to his present employer's, Laurier's Sack and Bag Company and that this job offer would give us the opportunity to leave the East End behind. The company in question was relocating to Bletchley, Bucks. Dad would be elevated to the position of vehicle maintenance manager, he would have four assistants and oversee the maintenance and repair of the 50 lorries that belonged directly to his prospective new employer's. His salary would nearly double, and he had been offered, "an executive four bedroomed detached house" as part of the deal. The next step would be for all of us to visit Bletchley to view this, too good to be true opportunity. The following Saturday all six of us clambered into a rented Vauxhall Zodiac and made the much-awaited journey to what we believed would be our new abode. After meeting his potential new boss, we followed him to a rather large housing estate. We pulled up outside a row of smart modern terraced houses and my dad was given the keys by the boss. Dad immediately queried the fact that he thought he was being given a detached four bed property. The boss, looking very shady, explained to my dad that the four bed properties were for management only. My Dad threw the keys he had been given, we all climbed back into the Zodiac, and I was never to visit Bletchley again. Elvis Presley's, "Good Luck Charm" was at number 1.

Dads about turn in respect of the job offer, for which I never blamed him, had left several repercussions for the family. Firstly, having already given his notice to quit to Laurier's Sack and Bag Company, effectively meant that dad was out of work at the end of the month. Fortunately, dads' brother, uncle Ted 'Ticker' Lucas found him a job as a lorry driver for a small timber company and mum was able to return to her job with Mr Lloyd at one of his four shops just 100 yards from our house. For myself, I had been offered a place at Bletchley High, Grammar School, a prestigious place of learning, situated within the grounds of Bletchley Park and recognised as one of the finest Grammar Schools in the Country back in 1962. I had passed my eleven plus a few months earlier. My first choice School had been Coopers Grammar, regarded as the best School in East London. I had now lost this place. After a lot of help from my then Primary School Headmistress, Ms. Anderson, I was offered, and accepted, a place at George Green Grammar, an old and equally prestigious School in East India Dock Road, Poplar.

Looking back, this change of heart by my father could be regarded as the first significant, "corner" of my life. Had my father taken the job and had we all relocated to Bletchley then everything that followed in my life would have been totally different. I would not, for instance, have written this book. I think we all have these, "Turn a different corner" episodes in our lives, I just seem to have had more than most.

26 - Summer in East Yorkshire - 1962

Whilst my dad and his four Sons were born and bred in the East End of London, our Mum was from Beverley in East Yorkshire. Her father, our paternal Grandad, was a coal merchant. He was a strict disciplinarian, kids from the East End of London were alien to him. He always wore a black waistcoat; his trousers were held up by a thick brown belt. Whenever he touched the buckle of the belt John, and I would scarper. We were quick to note that 'grannie Lil' did almost everything for him, he was, without doubt 'the man of the house.' My Mum had been brought up, together with her three sisters and two brothers in a large house that stood beside Beverley Beck, a short canal built in 1296 to bring goods from Hull to Beverley. My Dad had been stationed at Catterick Camp during the war and would visit Beverley during his time off. Originally my dad had courted my mum's elder sister Elsie, but he later decided on the younger version, (God knows why) Rose, to be his wife. They married, in Beverley in 1947. Throughout our school years my brothers and I would spend most summers in the big house in Beverley. This change of scenery was a world apart from the East End of London. There were trees and fields and every day we got to eat our grandma's freshly cooked food. Now deemed to be old enough, we would go out with our grandad or one of his employees to deliver coal in and around Beverley. The large shire horses that my grandad owned would travel as far as the seaside town of Hornsea, some eight miles away. We would return home to, "beck-side" as black as the ace of spades, having had to nestle between the sacks of coal on the back of the cart. We were not allowed back into the house until we had washed ourselves under the outside showers at the side of the house. Some days we would be allowed to travel on the barges that my grandad owned. Pulled by a small tug, we would cruise the one mile from the house until we arrived at the river Hull, from there it was about a seven-mile journey, in much choppier waters, until we entered Hull Docks, where we would stop alongside massive piles of coal that had been discharged onto the quay by one of the many bulk carriers that arrived in this busy port each day. We would have to hop onto the tug whilst the barges were filled with hundreds of tons of black, filthy coal. Once full, we would make the return journey to beck-side, stopping right outside my grandad's house. Twenty to thirty men would be waiting outside the house, one of those men was, of course, the small, hunchbacked man by the name of Clary Daggart. Clary had been introduced to us a year earlier. John and I could not resist the constant

A Life Like No Other

murmuring of 'the bells, the bells.' During the unloading of the barges our grandma would arrive with tea and cakes, and nobody seemed to care that we would eat and drink without washing the filth from our mucky paws. The discharge of coal from the barges to the coal store was completely undertaken by hand. The men in the barges, including my brothers and myself would fill large wire baskets with coal, the baskets would then be hoisted from the barges onto the quayside and other men would carry them some 50 yards to the coal store, where they would be tipped and returned empty to the barges, after which the whole process would then begin again. It normally took three days to unload the three barges that my grandad owned. Ernie Otter would say to my Mum,

'Look at them boy's Rosie, like pigs in shit.'

It is true to say that we loved every minute of our time in Beverley, even though we had to sit on the steps of the pub every night whilst our grown-up relatives got merry. We did, however miss the sound of music from our Dansette. Grandad's house was very much a 'noise free' zone. I still visit Beverley today, as my Mums youngest Sister is still alive and well. There was one major disaster during our stay. We managed to lose baby Graham's pram. Well, we did not exactly lose it but somehow it ended up in the river, fortunately our little brother, now nearly five years old, was not in the pram at the time. We told our parents that we had left it outside a sweet shop in the market square and that it had been stolen. My mum said that it was a good thing that it had gone as it was about time that her youngest offspring started to walk. Three years later, whilst the river was being dredged, the pram was found. We continued to deny any wrongdoing. The big house and the coal business are long gone, the quayside now being home to many "yuppie" type apartments. There is a street named jointly after my grandad Otter and another local tradesman, whom I knew as Mr Birch, the street is called 'Otter Birch Way'.

27 - Our poor little Brother

We had returned from Yorkshire on the last day of August 1962. Saturday September 1 st was our little brother's 5th birthday. It was also just 2 days before I would begin my Grammar School education.

Young Graham woke at 9.15, having stayed awake during the whole ten-hour journey back from Beverley the previous day. My parents, nan, brother John and myself eagerly awaited his arrival into our tiny living room. Our eldest brother had gone out early, he and four of his delinquent friends, all aged 14, were helping Mr Yeoman, a local builder, to lift the tiles from the roof of Burtons the tailors in Crisp Street.

As Graham entered the living room, nanny Lil hugged him and kissed him with her toothless mouth. On the floor were five parcels, all wrapped in newspaper. He had been given 2 record's, one each from John and me. They were, 'Sheila' by Tommy Roe and 'Telstar' by the Tornados. Once he had listened to them, they were added to 'our' collection. Mum and dad had bought him a 'Jungle Set.' This consisted of a camouflage jacket, a belt with bullets, a gun, a knife (plastic) a hand grenade and an army type water bottle. He was most impressed. From nannie Lucas there was a Mars Bar and a Milky Way. The last present to be opened was from the grumpy old git from downstairs that was glued into his armchair. From grandad Ted, Graham had got a bag of four-inch nails. At Christmas he would receive a claw hammer.

Mum and dad, having not seen their friends for a while, announced that they were going out at 5pm and would not be back until late. Graham was, unfortunately, left in the care of John and me.

Brother John, now in his 10th year, had perfected the art of 'throwing.' He normally threw stones, his main target was windows, however he would sometimes take aim at cars, bikes, buses (he loved hitting buses) if there was a stone laying around, you could be sure that John was going to throw it at something. He was well known in the neighbourhood for his ability to hit almost anything if it was within his range.

He also liked to throw potatoes. Not long after our parents had departed that evening, John dragged the large bag of potatoes out from under the butler sink, pulled down the kitchen window and took aim. He hit the window of a house some 50 yards away. The house belonged to a Mrs Barclay, her son, at just sixteen years of age, stood 6 foot 2 inches. He was, for some reason know as 'Nancy Peprow.' When the window smashed there was no reaction from the house. At this point young birthday boy wanted to be involved. John and I lifted him up onto the top of the twin tub and gave him a few small potatoes. He was only able to throw a short distance, his potatoes landing in our backyard. John then threw three more King Edward's, each with such ferocity that they all went straight through Mrs Barclay's window. John and I hid, either side of the window, but Graham was still stood on the washing machine and in full view. As Mrs Barclay sounded off a barrage of obscenities towards us, John pulled our little cherub's arm and Graham fell, with a sickening thud onto floorboards below. I can still hear the shriek that our young sibling let out. A man riding his bike in Upton Park, fell off. Graham was now 'break dancing' on the kitchen floor. We took knives, forks, spoons, and the potato masher from a drawer and proceeded to operate on his right arm. Our nan arrived and enquired as to why her little grandson was rolling around in agony. She then saw the blood and the bone that was protruding from his elbow, the bone that John had been trying to put back with the masher. There was a shout from downstairs,

'Lil, where's my tea?'

For the very first time we heard our nan swear. Grandad Ted was firmly put in his place. In 1962, we had no phone, we could not call for an ambulance. There was not a single car in the street, so no one could take us to the hospital. I was in the street, running up and down, like a headless chicken. Nan came out, with Graham. She had somehow made a sling, from what looked like a pair of the old gits long John's. Brown streaks ran down one side of the makeshift support. We walked to the bus stop, some 100 yards away, Graham was almost delirious. We had a choice, we could go either to St Andrews or Poplar hospital, it purely depended on which side of Brunswick Road the bus arrived from. The bus came from the direction of Bromley-by-Bow; therefore, it was going to be Poplar Hospital, just a few bus-stops away. Nan boarded the bus with our screaming young brother. John and I began to plan exactly how we could get to Germany before our parents arrived home. To cut this story short, Graham was in hospital for five weeks and had several operations, however his arm was never fully straightened and for that reason he has never been able to play golf, cricket, or ten-pin bowling, amongst other things.

Once out of hospital and back into the safety of our care, Graham was keen to join in the outdoor activities of the elder boys. It was a day when we had no football, so we played cricket, using the three painted stumps, that were drawn onto the wall of Kate Jones house as the wicket. This part of Poplar, known as the 'Teviot Estate' had drains with lids that lifted from the pavement, this created a gap between the pavement and the road that was big enough for a cricket ball to disappear into and within five minutes Graham failed to prevent the ball from dropping into one of those drains. John and I held Graham's feet as we dangled him headfirst into the drain and for some reason that we still do not know, he slipped from our grasp and plunged, headfirst, into the sewer. At that precise moment the 6-foot 2-inch frame of Nancy Peprow was cycling by. He ditched the bike and reached into the drain and began to pull Graham back to safety. A lady passer-by laid him on his side and hit his back hard, water was ejected from his nose and mouth, his lungs, kidneys, and liver laid dormant on the pavement. He was taken to hospital in our dads' lorry. His stomach was pumped out, at last, we had found the VW Beetle dinky toy that had gone missing a few weeks since. Poor Graham later developed a fever but after two weeks or so, he was allowed back home.

A week after his release from hospital Graham threw an apple core at me. I chased him across the road, he was hit by an oncoming motorbike and spent another six days in the care of the NHS.

At Christmas 1962 Graham was taken to Yorkshire by our dad, he stayed with our aunt, our mum's youngest sister for the duration of the school holidays. He was to do this on every subsequent school holiday occasion until he joined the police force as a 17-year-old. Even then I managed to involve him in a frightening episode of violence in a notorious East End pub. For some reason unbeknown to us, Graham now has nothing to do with John or myself.

28 - George Green Grammar School -- Part 1

Back in 1962, almost all Schools insisted on the wearing of uniforms and George Green Grammar was no exception. From my first ever day at secondary school I would have to wear neatly pressed shorts, black shoes, grey socks, white shirt, the George Green tie, a black blazer with the George Green badge sewn on the breast pocket and to round it off, a cap. The cap would have either a yellow or red band around it, depending on which schoolhouse one was in. Yellow was for East India House, and red for Black Wall. Amongst the fifth year "prefects" was a boy, feared by all younger students, he was Robert Liddiard, he would delight in removing the caps of his more junior schoolmates, throwing them up onto the roofs of houses. The "cap less" student would receive an hour's detention for not wearing the topmost part of the uniform. Fifty-Four years after I had last set eyes upon Mr Liddiard, we were reunited, courtesy of Facebook. Rob now resides in Perth, Australia. A letter, from, George Green School, to my Mum, had informed her that I would be in East India House and that she should prepare me accordingly. My attendance at Grammar school would prove to be a financial burden for my parents, as, apart from the cost of the uniform, there were many other items that they would need to provide for me. The uniform could only be purchased from Harry Neave and Son, a shop in Crisp Street, Poplar that normally my Mum would never have entered, as the cost of everything in there was just too prohibitive for her. My entire school uniform was purchased by using, "provident cheques". Provident Cheques worked as follows, a man in a grey suit would knock on our door every Monday evening. He would ask my mum and my nan if they wanted any cheques that week. Should my mum ask for a cheque then the suited man would issue it and then record it into her Provident Book. They would charge interest on the cheque plus any outstanding monies. It was the yesteryear version of credit cards, with no cards. At least 60% of retail shops in the East End, would display a sign in their window stating that they, "accepted provident cheques". I would go to Harry Neave and Son, armed with a provident cheque whenever I needed to renew any of my school uniform.

There were very few other young boys and girls in the immediate vicinity of Venue Street that had been given scholarships to George Green, the majority, including my eldest and youngest brothers were to go to Hay Currie, regarded as the lowest form of learning at that time. My younger brother John would go

A Life Like No Other

to St. Pauls Way School, which, to all intents was somewhere in the middle of George Green and Hay Currie.

George Green Grammar School had been built around 1856 and the main hall of the school resembled the inside galley of a ship. This design was very much the work of its founder, George Green, a famous shipbuilder of his time. He had also built Black Wall Tunnel. The headmaster, and teachers all wore long black robes, and mortar boards adorned their heads. For a boy of eleven, with such a poor and lowly background, George Green School was almost Cathedral like in appearance, it was both frightening and awe inspiring at the same time.

It was a long walk to school, just over a mile and a half. I undertook this walk four times per day, as I also walked home to enjoy lunch with my nan and grandad, as my mum was almost always working. Wintertime was horrendous, as shorts were not the most suitable attire for long, icy cold periods. I had no topcoat to go over my blazer. I, along with numerous other children were to suffer the horrendous winter of 1963. The first two years at George Green were spent learning Latin, French, History, Geography, Maths, English, Religious Study, Woodwork, Chemistry, Biology, Physical Education and stealing. I would later excel in the latter subject. The curriculum was set to fill each student with as much knowledge as possible in those subjects within the first two years and then to spend the following two years revising what we had been taught. The fifth year was set aside for exams. George Green excelled in GCE pass grades. If you did not leave at sixteen with six, seven or more GCE's then you were deemed to have failed.

George Green was a small select school, each year consisting of just twenty-eight boys and twenty-eight girls, split equally into two classes. Some years there were no form teachers, the school was very much, "pupil lead", at the beginning of each term every class would elect a "form captain", and it was he / she that would sit at the desk at the front of the classroom and take the register of attendance prior to the whole school congregating in the galley for morning assembly. After assembly, all pupils would file out and proceed to whatever classroom was holding their designated lesson. At the end of each lesson, normally forty minutes, the whole school would change classrooms, this would create mayhem in the small narrow corridor's but there was no other way to do this as no lesson ever consisted of, exactly, the same pupils. There were no sporting facilities at the school, the boys had no playground, just an outside space where the toilets were located. The girls enjoyed the wide-open space of the roof of the school, boys were not allowed to go there. Football, cricket, rugby, and athletics were the main physical activities for the boys, whilst the girl's enjoyed netball, rounders, cooking, ironing, and knitting. On, "games" day, all pupils of the entire year would have to get a double decker bus from East India Dock Road to the school's own private sports ground on the Isle of Dogs, just a stone's throw from what is now Canary Wharf. We were all given two thrupenny bits to cover the cost of the bus journey to and from the Isle of Dogs. Some of us would walk home after games and pocket the three, old pennies. I was good enough to play both football and cricket for the school, which often got me out of lessons for a day each week.

School work during the first two years was not easy, homework was required every night and not wanting to miss out on playing out after school, most of my homework was done from 9 pm until 2 am or later. My parents never asked about or made me do homework, neither did they scald me for not appearing to sleep until the early hours of each morning.

I was still doing my paper round, and this normally started at 6 am, however this lack of sleep never seemed to have any adverse effect upon me. A few months into my third year at George Green, at the age of 13, one of my friends from the next street, who attended Hay Currie School, suggested that we try playing truant. For some strange reason, I had been voted in as form captain and therefore occupied the front desk. I was responsible for ticking off everyone's name in the class attendance register, this gave me the perfect opportunity to avoid going to lessons. I would tick off my own name in the book, the book was then taken to the headmaster's secretary, she would make a note of whoever was not ticked off, and if that pupil were missing for three days, she would then send a letter to the parents of that child, asking why he or she had not attended school.

George Green School – East India Dock Road – Circa 1900

29 - New Years Eve - 1962

There had been no snow in East London on Christmas day, however after clearing the ice from our bedroom window on boxing day morning we could see that it was snowing heavily, it continued to snow for the next three days and almost every kid in Poplar was outside. We were dressed in just our underpants and stringed vest, the plimsolls that covered our sockless feet were wet through, but no one cared, that was except for Eden Aylett, a classmate and neighbour that was cocooned inside an electric blanket that wrapped around him several times.

At 10.00am on New Year's Eve 1962 ten-year-old Eden was finally let out by his mum Ethel. Mrs Aylett was a woman aged just twenty-four, she had conceived her only son when she was only thirteen after a brief encounter with Derek, the vicar of St. Michaels Church of which the young Ethel was a member of the choir. Derek had been re-assigned to a church on the Isle of Bute shortly after the bump in Ethel's mid-drift had begun to show.

As Eden opened his front door he was bombarded with scores of snowballs, we had laid in wait for him. To his credit the boy, whose only visible parts were his eyes, stood firm and choose to walk towards us. He was normally the skinniest of specimens, on this morning he had ballooned to twice of his normal size, courtesy of the sheer amount of clothing that his over-protective mum had dressed him in.

To gain his confidence, we ceased hostilities, we lured him to the playground, got him to stand dead still on the roundabout and then built a snowman around him. We had no idea if he was happy or sad as six of us started to move the roundabout until it reached a frightening speed. When we left the playground Eden was still spinning around at a rate of knots, frozen to the steel platform of the roundabout. He did not return to school the following week.

By lunchtime we were all so cold that we returned to our respective homes, hoping to thaw out. Brother John aged ten and I, now eleven managed to edge our way onto the four-foot by four-foot rug that covered the bare floorboards in front of the open coal fire. Baby Graham, now just over five years old was as red as a pillar box, having been laid naked on the stone hearth by our mum, who had returned to her bed having completely forgotten to dress her youngest son. John ran downstairs and returned with a very large snowball. He placed

A Life Like No Other

the large piece of ice on Graham's belly button, and we watched as it melted, it was gone within seconds.

With no sign of anything to eat in our kitchen, and with our dad outside in the street trying to start the long-nosed Bedford that had laid dormant for four days, John and I made our way downstairs and entered the living quarters of nannie Lil and the grandad that had never once smiled at us since our respective births. We had arrived at just the right time as grandad was drinking his tea from a saucer, something he always did, and Lil was in the scullery stirring the very large black pot that sat constantly upon the gas stove.

'Do you want some nice hot soup boy's' asked our totally toothless grannie.

'What's in it.' I replied.

'Well, there is the chicken bones from Christmas day, some potatoes, turnips, carrots, swedes, cabbage and me teeth, which fell in when I sneezed into the pot whilst adding the pepper.'

'I think I will pass on that, but thanks nan.'

John, not being as fussy as me ran upstairs, turned Graham over and returned with the bowl that our mum normally made her cakes in.

I went outside to find that my dad was frozen to the door of his lorry. Bert Puxley from next door and a man from Tyler's, the garage, were trying to prise him off. Even the blow torch that had singed his hair and burnt his Christmas jumper could not manage to get him free.

Once John had finished his soup and accidentally fell over grandad Ted's legs on his way out, making the most miserly man in Poplar grimace in pain, we both went up to the front bedroom to see how our mum was, we were shocked to see that she was almost blue in colour, I legged it downstairs and out into the street, I was just in time to see my dad slide slowly down the side of his lorry, he ended up on his arse in ten inches of snow.

'Dad, come quickly, I think mum has died, she is completely blue.'

Slim composed himself and followed me back into the house, he went straight up to the bedroom, seconds later he came into the living room, lifted Graham from the hearth rushed back to the bedroom and put our smouldering little brother in the bed next to mum. The iced over front windows steamed up and were then quite clear.

'What time is it Slim.' Asked our mum.

'It's just after three, I can't get the lorry started so we are going to have to walk to Lil's.'

'I won't be able to go, why don't you just take the boys and your mum, and I will stay here in case Peter is released later.'

Slim removed baby Graham from the bed and dressed him in his new Christmas clothes, which were in fact John's hand me downs from five years ago. This was known, even then, as 'recycling.' John was sent down to tell nannie Lil to get ready.

And so, Slim, John, Graham, nannie Lil and I made ourselves look presentable for the new year's gathering at aunt Lil and Uncle Harry's house just the other side of Bromley-by-Bow station. Nannie Lil propped grumpy Ted up in his chair, put a blanket over him, placed his sputum and 'piss' pot within reach, turned up the oxygen that kept him alive and put a bowl of jellied eels upon his lap. Her last act was to put his mittens, with the cut off fingers on his hands. She accidentally kicked him in her haste to leave, he was still screaming as we all exited through the front door.

Ten minutes into our expedition we noticed that the canal that ran alongside the flour mills had frozen over, before Slim could say 'oh no you don't' John, Graham and I were skating on the ice.

As you may have guessed, it was only baby Graham, by far the lightest of us, that managed to find the small hole in the ice, he fell headfirst into the river. Our dad and the solitary fisherman managed to get him out, we spent New Years Eve and most of the following day in St. Andrews hospital.

30 - The Beatles

It has been said by millions of people that were born in the 1950's and subsequently became teenagers in the 60's that this was, without doubt, the most musically influenced period in the history of mankind. I personally endorse those feelings as my brother John, and I discovered 'pop' music when our dad brought home that Dansette stereo record player in December 1959.

The Beatles had their first UK chart entry in 1962. 'Love me Do' only reached number 4, although it topped the charts in Australia, New Zealand, and the USA. It was in 1963 that the four friends from Liverpool became known throughout the UK. In that year 'From me to You' 'She Loves You' and 'I want to hold your Hand' all topped the UK charts.

In March 63 the Beatles hit the road, for the first time outside of their native home, Liverpool. I exclude their stints in Hamburg. Their very first UK 'live' concert away from 'Penny Lane' was held at none other than the Granada Cinema, East Ham, London E6. Surprisingly, John and I were not aware of this major event. That was not to be the case when the Beatles returned to East Ham on Saturday 9th November 1963.

John, George Downey, (we were only missing Ringo) and I had tickets that cost 7 shillings and six pence (37.5p). We obtained them by lining up with thousands of other kids a week before the gig. The doors were due to open at 18.50 and the show was to begin at 21.00. After having not moved along Barking Road for over half an hour we ditched our limo (a number 15 bus) and started to walk. Half a mile from the cinema the crowd was immense, blocking the whole of what was, one of London's major arteries. Being savvy, we crossed the road and took to the side streets. We finally managed to get ourselves into a queue where a man with a megaphone was shouting 'ticket holders only.' At 19.45, nearly one hour after the doors had opened, we were in. We got to our designated seats only to find that three girls were occupying them. The girls did not have tickets. Hundreds of ticketless people had managed to get in. There were around a dozen or so commissionaires, fully striped up, that were seemingly controlling the crowd. They were of little use. We sat on our seats and let the girls sit on our knees, after all, there was no way out at that stage. I believe we saw Tommy Row; I think he sang 'The Folk Singer' and 'Sheila' however he was not audible over the continuous screaming of girls, some as young as five. When the lads hit the stage, the din was deafening. John said something, Paul followed him, exactly what they said, we would never know.

A Life Like No Other

The opening song was 'I saw her standing There.' I think the closing tune was 'Twist and Shout' the screaming never relented. Girls were passing out all over the place. St. John's ambulance service had one of its busiest nights for ages. Back in 63 each guitar was plugged into a single Marshall Amplifier, a microphone was placed beside the drums, the sound quality was as poor as it gets, however that did not really matter as young girls will out scream any music system.

The Beatles released 63 singles in the UK between 1962 and 1970. The first was 'Love me Do' in 62, the last was 'Let it Be' in 1970, strangely neither of them reached number 1. Believe it or not, 'Wandering Star' by Lee Marvin and Clint Eastwood kept 'Let it Be' off the top spot. John and I owned every single Beatles 45, plus 18 of their Ep's and all their studio albums, of which there were just 12. All of those reached number 1 except for 'Yellow Submarine.' In May 1963, Gerry and the Pacemakers, another Liverpool group, made it to number 1 with 'How do you do It?' From then on there was a steady stream of British groups making it big, but one group stands head and shoulders above them all, 'The Beatles.'

In 1973, my father-in-law to be, Bill Harrison, a former Army Sergeant Major and then a commissionaire at Tate & Lyle, informed me that he had been one of the security team on duty back in 1963. He was not keen on the Beatles, preferring the sound of military marching bands.

31 - Christmas Day - 1963

At 4.52am on the morning of my 12th Christmas I heard a loud banging which seemed to be emanating from downstairs, the living quarters of my paternal grandparents, Ted, and Lil Lucas.

I withdrew the single earpiece that had come with my dansette transistor radio, which had been lifted from Woolworth's three years previously, this was most annoying as I was listening to the Christmas number one, which was "I want to hold your hand" by that little known group, the Beatles. I was still awake as I had been left to supervise baby Graham as he was clearing up from our parents annual Christmas eve party, which had ended at 3.00am. Graham was now six and he was more than capable of cleaning up the mess left behind by the thirty or so visitors that had been present just a few hours before.

I returned the earpiece to my lughole, Gerry and his wonderful Pacemakers were singing the previous number one, which was of course "You'll never walk alone" the banging was becoming louder, I again withdrew the earpiece, I was amazed that brother's Peter and John, lying next to me in the same bed had not stirred. I managed to peel back the nine army blankets that pinned all three of us to the two inch thick mattress, I then slipped out of the bed, put on my dad's trench coat and stepped out onto the top floor landing, falling over Graham, who had passed out on the bare floorboards after consuming almost all of the alcoholic dregs that had not been consumed by our guests, the last of whom had left just a couple of hours since.

I tiptoed down the three sets of stairs that led to my grandparents living room, passing nannie Lil, who looked resplendent in a pink candlewick dressing gown that swept up as she walked. The Ena Sharples hairnet that covered her hair did nothing to disguise the fact that she was ugly, there was no doubt in my mind that she would once again win the Poplar gurning contest for the fifth year running on New Year's Eve.

'Your grandad has gone mad.' Said Lil through a toothless mouth.

I walked down the hall to the living room, I could no longer see through the half-glazed door, the old sod had nailed planks of wood across the door frame, the door opened inwards, it was not possible to open it.

'Grandad, what are you doing.' I asked.

'I don't want to see anyone, your nan has spent all of our money on Christmas presents, I can't go to the pub, I can't buy any baccy and she has bought a second-hand turkey.'

To the right of where I stood was a door that led into the backyard, I went out, it was pouring, I walked to the other back door, the one that led into my grandparent's scullery, it was locked, there were seven bolts on the inside, old Ted was certainly security conscious. I went to the back of the house, next to the outside loo there was a window, it was also locked. As I looked through this curtainless window I saw that some towels had been laid across the bottom of the door, I could smell gas, I had a choice to make.

I returned to the hall, the banging had stopped, should I wake my dad up and tell him of what was going on downstairs or should I return to the comfort of my overpopulated bed and put the sounds of radio Luxembourg back into my ear. As I passed my nan, she told me that her false teeth were bathing in a cup of bicarbonate of soda in the scullery and that she must have them if she was going to be eating a big dinner later. I informed her that there was a strong smell of gas coming from the scullery.

'I hope he lights up and blows himself to pieces, I've had more than enough of him, I really have.'

With that she turned and went back into her boudoir, soon after I heard her peeing in the gazunder.'

I returned to the boarded-up door. I called out to the grandad that absolutely hated children –

'Come on grandad, please open the door, nannie is very upset, and she needs her teeth.'

There was no response from the man that had been on this earth for some sixty-six years but had never once smiled or offered any kind of compassion whatsoever to any of his grandchildren, of which there were ten in total.

At 7.15 I could take no more, I walked into my parents' bedroom, my dad (Slim) came out of the wardrobe, fully naked, my mum (Rose) slinked under the covers. I filled Slim in on the events that had occurred downstairs. He put a sock on his sizeable manhood, slipped into Rosies nightie, wandered downstairs to our kitchen, and put the kettle on. I told him that the kettle just did not go with the nightie, he took it off, replacing it with the toaster. Much better I thought.

All this mayhem meant that none of us kids had been presented with the off-white pillowcases containing our presents, that would normally have been placed at the foot of our bed before 6.00am.

Immediately after he had consumed his second cuppa, Slim slowly descended the stairs, he took the now full chamber pot from his mum, opened the front door, and threw the contents out into the street. The unfortunate boy that was our next-door neighbour, fourteen-year-old Ray Puxley, received a full frontal covering of my nan's urine as he rode past on his brand-new push bike.

Slim was now stood outside the boarded-up door, his dad, that charmless old git known as Ted Lucas would not respond to his sons' pleas to end his self-imposed incarceration. Within minutes Slim had climbed into his lorry and was off. Half an hour later he returned. With him was his sister, Lilly Roberts, we all called her big Lil as our dad's brother, 'Ticker' had also married a Lil, she was little Lil, she was just 4 foot nine, weighed 5 stone 13 lbs and had the most enormous mole protruding from the middle of her forehead. When no one was within earshot John, and I always referred to her as the unicorn.

Big Lil had married the infamous 'Harry Roberts' and because of this she was feared throughout the land. If *she* could not get her father to surrender peacefully then no one could. For the next fifteen minutes she pleaded with him to stop being silly, her words were interlaced with expletives that only Bernard Manning could match. She would never make it as a negotiator. Halfway through her attempt to lure old Ted out of his hideaway there was a knock at the door. Mrs Eisel from next door had come to give nannie Lil her spare pair of teeth. As she opened the street door, she saw that old Ted was sat on the windowsill, she called out, everyone gathered around the man that had an almost grim reaper look about him, at that very moment there was an almighty explosion from within the downstairs scullery.

And that was how we finally managed to get rehoused.

32 - George Green Grammar School – Part 2

And so, in November 1964, with my name ticked in the attendance book every day, meaning that my mum was never going to receive a letter from the headmaster in respect of my absence from school, my lengthy period of truancy began. After handing in the register, I then had to make my escape from the school, this was not easy. To the side of the main doors that led into East India Dock Road was the "sergeants" office. The sergeant was in-fact an ex-sergeant in the armed forces, his assistant was Ron, nicknamed 'Corporal' by yours truly. Corporal was a kind and gentle man. Sergeant was a six- foot, fifteen stone, brick, "shithouse." You were never impolite to him, even though he wore a light brown dress and matching high heels. Corporal dressed entirely the same. Sergeant's actual name was Donovan, although most called him "bastard." Their job was to guard the front door, open it to visitors, Jehovah's witnesses, delivery men and whomever else might want to come into the school. I had got to know that immediately after assembly both Sergeant and his sidekick were busy re-stacking the chairs that had been put into position for everyone to sit on prior to assembly taking place. This activity allowed me the opportunity to make my escape, uninterrupted. Once out into the street I had a difficult choice to make, turn right, and I would risk sergeant, or corporal seeing me through the hall windows. Turn left and I had to walk past the windows of two classrooms. After a few days of this I decided it was just too risky to leave by the front door. It dawned on me that the side door, which the boys used to enter the school each morning was still open until 10 am. It stayed open to allow for latecomers. This escape route was ideal for me as there were no classroom windows to pass and it put me out into a side street and not in the full glare of the front of the school.

After my escape, I would meet my fellow truant, George Downey, at the foot of the steps that led up and over the local railway line. At the beginning of our days out of school we would simply walk around or visit the large graveyard in Bow. Sometimes we would walk along the towpath of the various canals that crisscrossed Poplar and Bow. After a few weeks, we got to know other boys that were playing truant, there were soon enough of us to be able to play eleven a side football matches either side of lunchtime. I still went home to my nans for lunch, with George Downey, so as not to arouse any suspicion.

Not long after we had started missing school, my brother John joined us. We found a café on Bow Road owned by Millie and Jack, an elderly couple

A Life Like No Other

with no children of their own. Whilst Millie adopted us, Jack continually told us to, 'fuck off' back to school.

We would do odd jobs for them. Millie would give us tea and sometimes even a cake. We found out how to corrupt the pin ball machine that they had at the front of the café, each replay was worth 3p and although you could not get cash back for this, the replays could be exchanged for food and drink. We became so successful at duping them every day that Jack would turn the machine off and say to us,

'You're knackered now, ain't yer, you little sods".

It was strange that Jack called us, 'little" as we were all much taller than him. He stood at no more than 5 feet 2 inches in his platform shoes. We turned up one morning and the café was shut. Jack had cooked his last sausage at his Bow Road eatery. Oh well, everything comes to an end one day.

Although I was not attending school, I still played football and cricket for George Green, our sports teacher had no idea of what I was up to as we only ever met once a week. I even managed to represent the school, at the age of 13, in the final of the U-15's National Grammar Schools Cricket Competition at Lords. I was sat in the England dressing room when my right ear was twisted back, thinking it was one of my team-mates, I half turned and nearly uttered some obscenity only to find that it was Mr. Wilks, the Headmaster, that was doing the ear tweaking.

'Nice of you to turn up, Lucas, I would like to see you in my study tomorrow morning.'

The following morning, fearing the worst, I had pulled on three pair of underpants, one pair of which was my brothers and as we only had two pairs of underpants each, I remember thinking,

'What will John do if he had, "shit" himself that day?

I fully expected to be severely caned for the disgrace that I had brought to the school. Instead of receiving the corporal punishment (from Ron) that I most certainly deserved, Mr. Wilks simply asked me what I was going to do when I left George Green school, for good, in two years-time. I informed the headmaster that I was going to work in a Bookmakers, I could see the rage in his face,

'So, you intend to follow that other no hoper, Puxley?'

His veins were attempting to burst through his neck, when he said,

'Over my dead body.'

I had no choice, I shot him. I left his study, crossed the galley, descended the 110-year-old staircase, passed Sergeant's office, managing to pass wind, loudly, as I did, and walked out onto East India Dock Road.

I did not attend school for even one single day after this event, however in June 1966 my mum received a letter from the headmaster requesting my attendance at the school. To ensure that I went, my mum accompanied me to the front doors of the school and handed me over to the sergeant. I was then frogmarched to the heads study.

'I have arranged an interview for you at the Daily Mirror, as an apprentice Journalist, make sure you attend.'

The headmaster asked if I had changed my mind in respect of my future career, I said that I had not. Mr. Wilks handed me an envelope. I turned and left. Corporal Ron shook my hand as he let me out into East India Dock Road.

I was just 15 years and 3 months; I should have been leaving school at 16.

I have never returned to George Green School. it still stands today, looking no different to when it was built, over one hundred and sixty years ago. I achieved no academic reward for my two years at Grammar School. I have no GCE Certificates to wave around. If only I had listened.

George Downey got expelled from his school, which is exactly what he wanted. My brother John returned to his, once I had officially left George Green. Well, he no longer had anyone to keep him company. At the end of July 1966, The Kinks, "Sunny Afternoon" did the honours at number 1.

Officially, I left George Green Grammar School on Friday 22nd July 1966. I was 15 years and four months old. Unofficially, I had left George Green in November 1964.

England were to play West Germany in the World Cup Final on Saturday 30th July. That day would turn out to be one of the most traumatic days of my life. Out of respect for Mr. Wilks, the Headmaster, I did attend the interview at the Daily Mirror in Fleet Street, and whilst I was tempted by what they had to offer, my mind was made up, I was going to become a Bookmaker. Looking back, this decision, made entirely by myself, would become my second, "corner" as, had I been tempted to join the world of the tabloid press then my life would have likely taken a different course, almost certainly for the best. But then I will never know.

George Green U15 Cricket Team at Lords in the summer of 1964. I am 3rd from the right.

33 - The Red Rover (The naughty one)

On the 10th, July 1965 brother John was thirteen years old, I had celebrated my fourteenth year on this earth back in March. In his birthday card from our mum and dad were two red rover passes, one for each of us. The tickets had been purchased from the bus garage at Leven Road, Poplar. We would be able to use them on Saturday the 24th, July. Later that day we informed our mates, George Downey, a long-time truant friend of ours and John Duggan, a classmate that often let me out of the locked door at our school, enabling me to play truant totally undetected. Duggan shared the same birthday as me, both of our friends were able to get their own parents to buy them red rovers for the same day.

And so, at 8.00am on the 24th, July all four of us boarded the 108 bus that would take us to East India Dock Road, where we would change and then take the number 15 that would be on its way to Ladbroke Grove, Kensington. John Duggan had brought with him a whole duffle bag of sweets, courtesy of his parent's sweet shop in Crisp Street, although they were not aware of their contribution to our day out.

The first part of our journey would take us along the entire length of Commercial Road until we reached Aldgate bus garage. From there we continued along Leadenhall Street on the edge of the City of London. We crossed into Cornhill and as we stopped at the second bus stop, George Downey initiated the first bit of mischief.

A man, dressed as though he was attending Buckingham Palace was quietly reading his newspaper, which was a broadsheet, possibly the Guardian. He was seated in the back seat of the bus, a spot where we would have liked to have been sitting. The spread of the newspaper in front of him meant that we could only see the fingers of his hands. We were each having our second cigarette of the day, I had nicked my mums nearly full box of Consulate, you know, the one with the menthol taste. George got up from his seat, struck a match and set fire to the bottom of the newspaper, the man's reaction was to throw the paper into the air, it landed under the seat in front of him. As the man was busy ringing the bell, the conductor, a large West Indian bloke came up the stairs, he momentarily froze and then repeatedly shouted, "my God de bus on fire, de bus on fire." The four of us were down the stairs and off the bus before anyone challenged us, we legged it down a side alley off Cornhill and came out into

A Life Like No Other

Threadneedle Street, the Bank underground station was ahead of us. John and I still say the words "de bus on fire" today.

Against the railings at the top of the station stairs there was a very large newspaper, and tobacco stand. I asked the proprietor if he could show me the way to Gresham Street as my mum worked as a caterer in one of the banks and I needed to ask her to come home as grandad Ted had tried to commit suicide by laying in front of the steam roller that was pressing the newly laid asphalt in the road outside our house.

'Where is your grandad now?' Asked the concerned news vendor.

'He is in St. Andrew's hospital, wards nine, ten and eleven.' It was lost on him.

Distracting him away from his stall gave John Duggan the opportunity to stash about fifty cartons of various cigarettes into his duffle bag.

By now there was a small queue waiting to be served. We were never to learn if he realised that he had been hoodwinked by four young entrepreneurs. To be honest we really did not care, we would earn a nice few quid from selling the fags later.

To avoid going back to the scene of the crime we decided to walk along Gresham Street, and then turn left, knowing that we would end up at the bus stop outside St. Pauls underground, we would then be on the A40, a road that would take us, by bus, all the way to our ultimate destination, London Airport. We simply had to change buses at Hatton Cross. London Airport was renamed as 'Heathrow' at the end of September 1966.

Two hours and fifteen minutes after leaving St. Pauls we arrived at the airport that now bears no resemblance whatsoever to what stands there today.

Our first port of call after arriving was to head to the 'viewing gallery' which, back in the day was open to everyone and no one got frisked. There simply was no security at all. All kinds of people, from every walk of life would be waving friends, family and loved one's goodbye. John and I had been to the airport on a few occasions and had set eyes upon the likes of the Rolling Stones, the Hollies, Wilfred Bramble (Steptoe), Harry Worth and Rolf Harris, who always seemed to be surrounded by young children whilst playing with his diggery-doo.

Duggan managed to sell about thirty packs of cigarettes within twenty minutes of arriving, telling the buyers that they were surplus to duty free requirements. We then staged, what we called our 'Shaking' all over, routine.

This involved brother John falling to the floor, after which he would shake violently, I would call for help, a crowd would gather, I would inform them that my little brother suffered from seizures and whilst they were stooped over him, George Downey, a pickpocket of some renown, would relieve three or four gentlemen of the contents of their jacket pockets. I would slap John's face and he would become normal almost immediately.

With the bounty nestling in the bottom of Duggan's duffle bag we would calmly file down the stairs and board the first available bus, irrespective of where it was heading.

On the top deck of the bus, we counted the proceeds of our visit to London Airport, we had amassed the princely sum of £38.00 and still had nineteen packs of cigarettes in hand. As the bus passed through the west end we decided to alight, we were hungry. We blew all the money in the Aberdeen Angus Steak House near to Piccadilly.

There were to be several more 'Red Rover' days before we all started work, none however, were as memorable as that of the 24th, July 1965.

34 - The <u>World Cup Final</u> – July 30th, 1966

My path into the shady world of bookmaking was laid by two people, my mum, Rose, and next-door neighbour, Ray Puxley. My mum was an avid punter and prior to the legalization of betting shops, on 1 st May 1961, the "bookies runner" would be a regular visitor to our front door. My father never struck a bet in his life. The bookies runner would take bets from punters wherever they liked, at home, at work, at the pub, even hospitals had, "runners" and it was all totally illegal, but half of the population of the East End were, "at it". Once betting shops were legalized, the runners disappeared, some of them in strange circumstances. Most Saturdays from 1961 onwards, our small upstairs living room would resemble the inside of a betting shop. I would help my mum fix the racing pages of the Daily Mirror and the Sporting Life to the wallpapered walls of the room, and we would stand, as if in a betting shop and pick our fancies for the day. At the age of 10, I would have to take my Mums handwritten bets to the top of Spey Street, and turn the corner to Joe Jones, "your trustworthy bookmaker", a more contradiction of words you would not find. At the betting shop, I would hand the bet to any man that might be going in through the door and a few minutes later the man would return and give me a ticket that I would take back to my mum. I soon found that I too was becoming a gambler, as I would bet some of my hard-earned paper round money, sometimes losing it all, sometimes winning a bit. Bets would be written out on any kind of paper and bookmakers would accept it. My mum used Izal Toilet paper when nothing else could be found. She used to tell me when she used Izal that, "her horse was likely to be shit hot," that was my mum.

Ray Puxley, from the house next door, had been introduced into the Bookmaking world by one of his sister's boyfriends, Billy Newman. Billy was the son of a Licensed Course Bookmaker, Billy Newman Senior, or shovel nose, as he later became known to me. Newman Snr had the License, and I presumed that Newman junior had some dosh, as he was to open several betting shops in the first year of them becoming legal. By 1966 the firm, William Massey, the name derived from Father and Son's Christian name and the Doberman dog, named "Massey" owned by Billy Snr. By 1966, 46 shops in East London, Essex and Kent had been opened. Young Billy had offered Ray Puxley a job in the Head Office of the firm, situated in Alie Street, Aldgate East, London E1. Ray had also attended George Green School and much to the disdain of the headmaster, Mr. Wilks, he had, prior to me, turned down a

A Life Like No Other

job at the Daily Mirror, to venture into the unglamourous world of Bookmaking. Later in life, Ray became a writer and has published several books. One day, in his thirties, Ray bumped into our former headmaster who was quick to inform him that, "Lucas and Puxley" were his biggest disappointments. Ray was then two years older than me, and surprisingly, he still is. He was already sitting in the number two chair in the racing room at the Head Office when I was invited to join William Massey.

My first day at my first ever full-time job was to be on Monday 8 th August 1966, however before this landmark in my life, I was to go on holiday with my parents, for what would be the last time as a youngster. On the 30th, July 1966, twenty-four of us, made up of myself, my brother John, youngest brother Graham, former truant companion George Downey, mum and dad, Uncle Ticker, Aunt Lil, cousins Stephen and Carol, Uncle Harry, Aunt Lil and their son, Tom, friends Wally and Connie Smith, their daughter Jill, her boyfriend Chris, Ted and Dorrie Winterflood and daughter Janice. 86-year-old Mrs Eisel from next door and the three youngest Newman kids, whom had never had a holiday, joined us. We would board a coach at a depot in Bow, destination, New Beach Holiday Camp, Chichester. My dad had never really been an avid football follower and therefore had not seemed to have been aware that on this day at 3.00 pm, the World Cup Final would be taking place. England were playing the most important match in their long footballing history. Yes, it was the World Cup final, forty million people in England were aware of this, my dad was oblivious to the fact!

The coach, cream and green, just like the ones that you would see in an old carry-on film, was due to leave Parnell Road in Bow at 11.00 am, giving us plenty of time to get to Chichester in Sussex, before kick-off time. We figured that we would easily reach our destination by 2.00 pm. We would get sorted out and then watch Bobby Moore, Gordon Banks and the rest raise the Jules Rimet (World Cup) Trophy. Well, it just did not work out like that, as my uncle Ticker had decided that his holiday would start at 8.00 am. Ticker had downed a whole bottle of whiskey before he tried, in vain, to drive the 2 miles from his house in Hackney Wick to the coach station. We later found out that he had lost control of his motor bike and sidecar, which contained his wife and two of his children, somewhere along Carpenters Road. He had ploughed into a bus stop, fortunately no one had been killed or seriously injured. In a drunken stupor Ticker flagged down a passing lorry, loaded the family and luggage onto the back and finally arrived at the bus depot at 12.15pm. The effect that this had upon us, waiting by a coach, on a hot sunny day in July was, without doubt, extremely traumatic and Uncle Ticker was never forgiven. With a worse for wear, intoxicated, leather clad uncle now on board, together with his upset wife, little Lil, and equally despondent children, Carol, and Stephen, we finally upped anchor at 12.30 pm. We had just 2 hours 30 minutes to make it to Chichester, but it was still doable. Well, it had been possible when we set off, however, what with two unplanned stops, one to allow Ticker to be sick, and the other for an extended stop at some halfway house in Kent, together with the fact that the driver had no idea as to the whereabouts of Chichester, it was never going to happen. We arrived at New Beach at around 5.15pm, we raced to the club house, a rickety wooden hut that had once appeared in Colditz and built to hold about 60 people, but currently occupied by around 200. We were stood outside the opened doors when we heard those immortal words, "they think it's all over, it is now." It was a full five minutes before we found out that England had won the World Cup and we had managed to miss every minute of it. Some part of me still thinks that Ticker, having been born in Scotland when nannie Lil was on the run for poisoning grandad Ted, had deliberately sabotaged our departure time. I spent the following week trying to prevent the ugliest 14-year-old in the camp from putting her tongue down my throat. I was to see the World Cup final about two years later when it was made into a film and shown, in full technicolour, at cinemas across the Country. It was not the same as seeing it live, as I already knew the score. When, dads brother Ticker prematurely passed-away, due to yet another accident, I planted a small flag of St. George into the grass above his coffin. The greatest day in England's football history had been missed.

The coach that would take us to Chichester on the day of the World Cup Final

35 - My first day at work – Part 1

My big day had arrived, Monday 8th August 1966. "Yellow Submarine" by the Beatles was Top of the Pops. Together with Ray Puxley, I walked from 18 Venue Street to Bromley-by-Bow station and took the district line train to Aldgate East. It was just a few minutes' walk from Aldgate East to William Massey's four-story building situated in Alie Street, on the edge of the City of London. There was only one entry and exit door for the whole of this building, this was at street level and behind this door was one of Massey's betting shops. I followed Ray through the shop, behind the counter and up two flights of stairs. At the top of the first flight there was a toilet. At the top of the second flight and to the right was a door with a Brass Plaque, inscribed as, "General Manager", directly in line with the stairs was a steel door, this door gave no indication as to its use but was, in fact, the "racing room." This room was to be where I would spend a lot of my working life for the next seven years. Ray introduced me to the 'racing manager.' Alan Rose was probably 30 years old but looked and dressed like someone twice that age. I was to quickly find out that Alan Rose had absolutely no sense of humour, not even when I started a small fire under his chair one Saturday afternoon. There were four chairs lined up under a worktop that stretched the whole length of the room, these chairs looked out onto Alie Street. The first chair belonged to Alan Rose, the second to Ray Puxley, whom by now had the title of assistant racing manager. Next to Ray was Alan McCauley, an ugly, evil looking prat who looked like, and was, a complete "arsehole". The fourth chair was mine, although I only got to sit on it very briefly during the first few weeks in the job.

    The introductions having finished, Ray was asked by Alan Rose to show me around the rest of the building. We climbed the stairs to the top floor, there was a board room and another quite empty room, the same size as the racing room, at my suggestion, this would later become the "security" room. Going back down the stairs to the second floor I was taken into and introduced to the Company Secretary, a large rosy faced man by the name of Jim Rainbird. An unlit fag dangled from his lips his whole body was akin to an ashtray. Sat on a chair next to Jim was Grace. She was stunning, with long blonde hair draped over her shoulders, she wore the tightest mini skirt I had ever seen, and her knickers were very visible. Her breasts were enormous, and I must have been drooling as Jim looked at me and said,

    'Easy Son,'

A Life Like No Other

His dog end falling from his mouth as he spoke. I always knew when Grace had a day off, as when she was in, the noise from her well-heeled shoes would sound like a horse in a courtyard. When Grace climbed the stairs, every man in the building watched her curvaceous "arse" wriggle from side to side, until it disappeared out of view.

Ray informed me that below the betting shop there was a basement where the General Manager, Terry Bishop (TB) and Billy Newman Snr (shovel nose) spent most of their time. Back in the racing room I was asked, by Alan Rose, to perform my first working task, this was to put the kettle on and make tea for us and the occupants of the basement. In the far corner of the room there was a worktop containing a kettle, several mugs, containers of tea, coffee, and sugar. The mugs were filthy. Under the worktop was a small fridge. I asked Ray as to where I might fill the kettle and wash the mugs,

'In the karzi' was his reply.

I loaded a tray with the kettle and several mugs, Ray had buzzed the basement, and two teas were required down there. As I descended the stairs, mugs rattling on the tray, possibly because of my nervousness, I was startled by the karzi door being flung open from the inside, I saw a pair of legs, trousers around the ankles and then a very gruff voice bellowed,

'Where's the fucking toilet paper, get me some, bloody paper.'

I knew not what to do. I placed the tray and its contents onto the landing floor and as I was stooped, in order, to perform this task, my head being just outside the open door, a very red faced, ugly old git, poked his head around the frame of the door, and made eye contact with me.

At that very moment, the sliding door at the bottom of the stairs slid back and a bloke, whom I had not yet met, shouted up,

'Hold on Bill, I am just getting it for you.'

The bloke that was to get old shovel nose his "arse" wipes, was Johnny Rugg (or Ruggie) as he was called by almost everyone. Ruggie would play a big part in my life for many years to come. Ruggie was the Alie Street betting shop manager. Shovel nose wiped his arse and pulled up his trousers, he did not bother to shut the door, neither did he wash his hands. Dirty old sod, I remember thinking. Billy Newman Snr disappeared back down the stairs. I entered the karzi, to fill the kettle and wash the mugs, no sooner had I entered when I had to leave. The stench was unbearable. Back in the racing room I had now managed to prepare and make six mugs of tea. I then had to take two of those mugs down to the basement, where I would meet the General Manager, Terry Bishop, and of course renew my acquaintance with old shovel nose, whom I already disliked. At the half landing, below shop level there was a steel, reinforced door, I tapped on this, but no one heard. I stood for a while, no one came. From up above, Johnny Rugg told me that he had phoned the basement and asked them to open the door. The door in front of me opened, I was beckoned in by a man in his early thirties, I noted that he had a Bobby Charlton, comb over hairstyle. He closed and locked the door behind me. I then entered another room, through yet another reinforced door, shovel nose was sat at a desk that contained massive piles of cash. I had never seen so much money before. I took the two mugs of tea from the tray and placed them on the desk, my hand shaking uncontrollably. Shovel nose picked up his mug, sipped and snorted,

'This is stone bloody cold, get me another one, for fucks sake, Son.'

After no more than one hour I wanted to leave this employment!

Back in the sanctuary of the racing room, I noticed for the first time, that on the left-hand side of the room there were fifteen telephones. They sat on top of the purpose-built, full-length desk. Above the desk was a shelf, again along the whole length of the wall, on the shelf sat another fifteen telephones. Each phone had a label with a name on it, each phone had a light above. It was around 1.00 pm when the first of these phones burst into life, a loud ring and a flashing light emanated from the phone labelled, "Mile End." Alan McCauley, being the anus that he was, told me to answer the phone. Hello, I said quietly into the mouthpiece,

'I want a £5 acca.'

Said the cockney geezer on the other end.

I knew not what to do. My three brand new workmates fell about. Even Alan Rose smiled. Puxley shuffled over and rescued me. He listened whilst writing onto one of the betting slips that were piled at the front of each phone, he then told the caller to do one, and hung up. My next-door neighbour showed me what he had written. There were the names of five horses and underneath them were the words £5 acca.

'It's that easy.'

'You have done this for your mum hundreds of times,' said Ray.

In fact, it was that easy.

I had written accumulators out for my Mum many times before, but I guess being the "new boy" with all eyes on me had put me off the task. Puxley explained that thirty of the shops had direct lines to the racing room, whilst the other sixteen would ring on one of the eight outside lines that were fixed to the wall directly in front of where the four of us were sitting. Private punters would also ring on these phones and would place their bets accordingly. As time went by, I learnt that these, private account punters would settle their losses on a weekly basis. Failure to settle would mean a visit from one of Massey's heavies. Were they still not able to pay their bill a visit from Reggie and Ronnie would be arranged, they always paid up then. These account punters had special carbonated betting slips, copies of which were posted to them each Monday

A Life Like No Other

morning and they were expected to, "settle up, in cash", by the following Friday. Some of their names are still with me some fifty plus years later. There was, "polo", he got his name from the hole that he had in his neck, which he breathed through. There was, "Mrs Gee" she was from Mile End, she refused to frequent the shop as she had polio and the punters in the shop would take the piss out of her. Another account punter was the Old Etonian, Mr. Doughty. If you were unfortunate enough to answer the phone to him you would hear him, say,

'Doughty here.'

He would then spend twenty minutes, or more, giving you about one hundred different bets, none of them were his. He worked at Lloyds of London and would place the bets for his work colleagues. Doughty did not bet, he simply collected seven and a half per cent in commission from Massey's for every bet that he placed. At around 12.45 pm every day three of us tried to distance ourselves from the outside telephone lines so that Rosie would take Mr. Doughty's call.

A gathering of some of the William Massey managers at Christmas 1966
Ray Puxley is 2nd from the left – Alan 'Rosie' Rose is 6th from the left and 'Old Shovel Nose' is 2nd from the right. I am not in the photo as I took it.

36 - My First Day at Work – Part 2:

At 1.30 pm the "guvnor" arrived in the racing room. This was Billy Newman Jnr. He was very polite, introducing himself to me and making me feel more relaxed than I had been up to that point. He was aware that I lived next door to Ray Puxley and asked me if I was one of those little sods that had thrown ice cream into his Mercedes convertible when he had parked it up in Venue Street before he picked up Joyce, Ray's sister. Of course, I denied his enquiry, but I was in fact 'guilty as charged.' Billy, said I could call him Billy, a nice touch, I thought. He was dressed like a golfer, Lemon trousers, Pink Fred Perry, white shoes, and bright red socks. To me he looked like a Neapolitan ice cream, but then he was paying my wages, so I allowed him to dress in any way that he wanted to.

'Right Son,' Billy said to me.

'Go and get the coffees before racing kicks off.'

Turning to Puxley, Billy asked if he would show me where to go. My first ever boss took a bloody great wad of cash from his pocket and said,

'Here's a sky diver, Son.'

He was probably testing me, but I knew full well that a sky diver was a fiver in cockney land.

'Ask everyone if they want a drink,'

Puxley and I left the room and made our way down two flights of stairs. As we opened the sliding door that led into the betting shop, a massively over-dressed tall bloke came over to me. He put his hand by the side of my head and appeared to pull a ten-bob note (50p) from my ear. This, I was to learn, was Stan Romaine, the best dressed employee that ever worked behind the counter of a betting shop. I later found out that Stan's father was a Director of Dunn and Co, Gentlemen's outfitters. Why Stan worked as a mere settler (he who works out the bets) only became apparent some years later. Ray then introduced Johnny Rugg to me, I instantly liked this man. "Ruggie", was the Manager of the shop and had known Billy for many years. He had hardly any hair but was only in his early thirties. The other person working in the shop that day was Susan, and to me she was unreal. Susan had blonde hair, piled up on top of her head, her face contained more make-up than Max Factor could ever have produced in a month. They must have returned a sizeable profit each year, based entirely upon Susan's purchases. Her eyelashes looked like they were going to attack me, her breasts were so large they frightened me. I hoped

A Life Like No Other

that I would never have to fondle them. Susan was a replica of Marina from the TV program Stingray, look her up on google, she is her twin sister. By now, Ray had used the shops internal herring bone to call downstairs and take the order from Terry Bishop and old shovel nose. Ray and I went out of the shop door, turned left, walked 20 yards, turned left, and entered Micks Café. In a most distinctive Greek voice, a man, the size of Demis Roussos, and dressed completely in white said,

'Hello Raymond, what the hell can I get for you?'

'Mick, this is Paul, Paul this is Mick,' introductions over.'

'Get me seven cappuccinos, two bacon sandwiches, two sausage sandwiches, four slices of toast and a plate of chips.'

Having written all this down, Mick walked the length of the café, his food splattered kaftan rising above his hole ridden tights, due entirely to the amount of displaced air that the enormity of his garment created. He handed the note to the kitchen staff. Upon his return, Mick asked for £3 and 18 shillings (£3.90). I handed over the sky diver and Mick gave me £1, two shilling's change. The oversized "bubble and squeak" then started to make seven frothy coffees. I had never seen a cappuccino machine before. After making the first two coffees, Mick handed them to Ray and myself and asked that we sit at a table whilst we waited for the order. Two minutes later, a plate of chips was put onto the table,

'For you, enjoy,'

Said a man from the kitchen, whose once white apron was covered from top to bottom with all kinds of food staining. I looked at Ray, he explained,

'Every time you come in here, they will give you something while you wait. I am so pleased that I do not have to do this anymore as it was making me feel sick.'

The day that I started at William Masseys I weighed just under eleven stone. Two years later, aged seventeen I weighed in at a massive seventeen and a half stone. I had a thirty-inch waist when I started work, it was forty-four inches when I weighed more than Cassius Clay. Mick had done a fine job into turning me from a light middleweight into a super heavyweight. Ray and I carried a tray each and one of Micks staff trailed behind us with a third one as we made our way back to the betting shop. After handing Billy his cappuccino, I remembered his change. I offered the £1, two shillings to him, he just waved it away.

'Keep it he said.'

For those of you that may be much younger than I am, £1 and two shillings (£1 & 10p) could buy nine pints of beer back in 1966.

It was now nearly 1.55 pm, the first race of the day was just 5 minutes away. Billy locked the reinforced racing room door. No one would be allowed in once racing was under way. If you wanted to take a "piss", only Billy could unlock and relock the door. Billy, as I was to learn, was an extremely superstitious man. There was a "dumb waiter" in the corner of the room, I knew it was dumb as it never once answered any of my questions. The 'thick' waiter was used to send the empty cups and plates down to the shop below, for them to dispose of. In return, Marina would send Troy Tempest up with more tea and coffee. From 2.00 pm until the last race of the day, which could be 5.00 pm or a little later, the telephones never stopped ringing. On this, my first day of working within the hub of the company, I was not allowed to answer any of the outside lines. Rosie had instructed me to answer only the internal lines, I obeyed his instruction. For the first hour or so I raced over to a phone that was ringing and lighting up, only for Billy Newman to physically nudge me out of the way.

'Leave it, this one is mine.' Billy would say.

I finally got to, "take a bet", from the phone labelled as Grundy Street. Massey's shop in Grundy Street, Poplar, was well known to me, as I had passed it every day for two years, on my way to School. After taking the bet, which I was more than capable of doing, the slip of paper then had to be handed to Rosie. He would record the bet onto a large sheet of paper, which covered most of the desk in front of him. This sheet of paper was known as, "the book", and this procedure had to be followed for each, and every race, every day of the week. Just before a race was to begin, "Rosie", as he was commonly known as, would inform Billy as to which horse or horses in the race would lose the company money. Billy would then tell Rosie either to "hold" or to "lay-off". Hold would mean, do nothing, and take a chance that the mentioned horse(s) did not win. Lay off would mean that Rosie would have to call William Hill via the direct line that was on his desk and lay off an amount of money to cover any potential losses. Now that may all sound quite a simple thing to do, however back in the day when there was not even a calculator to help with maths, everything had to be assessed and acted upon by using one's brain.

On busy days, there could be up to 36 horse races plus 12 greyhound events sandwiched in between. They all had to be weighed up and acted upon in the split seconds just before the "off". It frightened the life out of me, God forbid I ever had to sit in Rosie's chair! After each race Rosie would go through the stack of betting slips piled up in front of him and either strike a line through them, if they were losers, or work out the amount there was to come back, if they had won. Each slip would then be passed to Puxley, he would check Rosie's calculations and if correct, he would initial the slip. Puxley would then pass them to, the snide, McCauley, who would take them over to where the tea was made. On the wall above the worktop was a purpose-built set of Pidgeon holes, 48 holes in total, each belonging to a betting shop, all in alphabetical order. The "snide", as I had named him, would then file the slips. It seemed to

A Life Like No Other

me that I was surplus to requirements, however I was soon to find out that I was not. During the afternoon, I would hear Billy shout various expletives every time Rosie informed him that the last race had lost him money. On the plus side, 90% of the day's results were winning races for Masseys. After the final race of the day, the, ugly faced snide went over to the Pidgeon holes and took out all the slips, carefully arranging them in order, so that Rosie and Puxley could quickly go through each individual shop, adding and subtracting, without the use of pen or paper. Each wad would then be stapled, and a figure would be written on the back. As an example, the Mile End shop may have placed 22 bets during the afternoon, six may have been winning bets whilst 16 were losers. After some lightening mental arithmetic, the figure of C £252 would be written on the back. Now I knew a lot about the betting world, but I did not know until that day that the letter "C" meant "cop" and cop meant win. Had the figure on the back been B 52, then we could expect a raid from the US Airforce. In fact, B 52 would have meant a loss of £52 as "B" meant "blew" or lost. Even today, I still do not understand why some idiot had turned win or lose into cop or blew. At almost ten minutes after the end of the last race of the day, Billy would unlock the door, in would walk TB and shovel nose. I learnt in time to be at least two feet away from TB otherwise his Bobby Charlton, "comb over" would brush into my eyes, blinding me. TB and shovel nose would pick up each internal telephone in turn, TB starting at one end of the room and shovel nose at the other. They would ask the same question to whomever had answered their call,

'How much are you sending?'

They would then write down whatever figure they had been told. If the Leyton shop had told them £300 then this would be the amount that had to brought to them before 6.30 pm. After contacting all 46 shops, TB would add all the figures together and tell Billy 'Cop' £6,200.

If the last race of the day had been at 5.00 pm then Billy would be gone by 5.30. TB and shovel nose would retreat to the basement, awaiting the arrival of potentially forty-six brown envelopes full of cash. Until 6.30, apart from taking an occasional bet on the nights greyhound racing, there would be nothing for the occupants of the racing room to do. Rosie had it in his power to let one or two of us go home early, but because he was a tight git that had once worked in a synagogue, he never once did.

Johnny Rugg would walk into the racing room most evenings after racing had ceased and he would set up the "shove halfpenny" board. On that first day of work, I watched as Ruggie, Rosie, Puxley, and the snide played a game that I had never seen before. They played for money, all putting 2 shillings (10p) into the kitty. There were two semi-finals and then a final. It was all over in ten minutes. Winner of the final won six shillings (30p). Several games took place before it was time to go home. Puxley won four finals and was eighteen shillings (90p) to the good by the time they called it a day. Puxley was my best friend and next-door neighbour, but he never bought me a drink with his winnings. During the time that the shove halfpenny competition was happening I watched out of the window and saw car after car arrive outside. The driver would disappear into the shop below, envelope in hand. The envelope would normally be given to Stan Romaine, without the person who had brought the envelope ever being allowed behind the counter of the shop. Romaine, envelope in hand, would bend down, open a letter box that had been built into the floor, under the counter of the shop, and simply drop the envelope into it. The envelope would fall onto the floor of the basement and either TB or the shovelnose would open it, count the dosh, and then add the amount to the ever-increasing pile of cash that adorned their desks. Later I would find out that there was a third desk, which was there simply to pile money upon.

Puxley and I left the office at just after 6.30 pm and headed for Aldgate East Underground Station. I was eager to ask him the many unanswered questions that had built up in my head during the day. My first enquiry was to ask if TB and shovelnose would have to wait for all the envelopes to arrive from 46 outlets. He told me that only the shops that were close enough to the Head Office would be bringing their money each evening as some shops were too far away to make it there by 6.30. Puxley already knew which shops had to deposit their money, each day. He explained that all shops had to settle-up the previous weeks balance on a Tuesday morning, adding that I would see this for myself the next day. I carried on with my questions.

'So, Billy owns the whole show, how about his old man, shovel nose?'

'With clear annoyance beginning to show in his voice he replied:

'Billy has a partner, Peter White, you will see him tomorrow as he only comes in three days a week. The Old Man owns nothing, he just happened to have a bookmaker's license and Billy Junior and Peter White used it to get their first shop. They then changed the license into their name's and therefore do not need the old "fart" anymore, now stop asking me stupid questions!'

'So why is the old fart there?

'He just is, now stop asking me bloody question's'.

'Just one last thing then,' I said, half expecting a thump from my agitated next-door neighbour.

'What on earth do they do with all that money?'

'You will see when you are next in the basement, just look at the large chimney breast, that is all I am saying'.

My mate, of fifteen years, who had won one sixth of his weekly wage less than an hour earlier then buried his head into the Evening Standard that he had purchased outside Aldgate East Underground and never looked up.

37 - My second day at work

I could not wait for Tuesday the 9th, August 1966 to arrive. I was so eager to get to work to learn more about this world of "cash and characters". When Puxley and I arrived, there were at least twenty-five people standing in the street, outside the shop door. Some I recognised from the previous day, others I had never seen before. Shovel nose was the first to air his disdain at having to stand outside a closed door in the rain.

'Where is Ruggie? He must be, shagging that young bit of skirt again,' snorted old shovel nose. His face redder than the post box that stood on the corner of the street. Before the words had left his mouth, Ruggie appeared, completely unfazed by the fact that so many people, including his General Manager, Terry Bishop, had been waiting in the rain for several minutes. TB's hair had been flattened down by the rain and the comb over was now plastered to the left-hand side of his face. Marina could not have been impressed.

'Where are *your*keys, Rosie?', asked Ruggie.

'Left them at home.'

Shovel nose could not contain himself,

'Left them at home, you, fucking moron.'

Rosie ignored the former boxer that had so obviously never won a fight.

Ruggie opened the shop door, turned off the alarm, and the rain-soaked crowd shuffled in. No sooner had I got upstairs when the internal phone rang, Rosie answered it and then passed it to me.

'Hello', I said, nervously.

'Have you made the tea yet, son?' bellowed old shovel nose.

Had I had a gun at that moment in time I would have gone down to the basement and shot that old bastard. As I was not armed, I went and put the kettle on. As I left the racing room to descend the stairs to the basement, I could hardly not notice that there was a queue of blokes, starting right outside the racing room and continuing all the way down to the basement door. This is what Puxley had mentioned the day before, these were the managers of the shops, lining up to present their previous weeks paperwork and outstanding cash to TB and shovel nose. I was just fifteen-years old. These were full grown men, fat ones, skinny ones, tall, short, old, and young and they all had one thing in mind, to relieve me of the two cups of tea that were shaking violently in my hands. By the time I entered through the second steel door there was, nothing

A Life Like No Other

at all left in the once full mugs. I knew what was coming as I placed the mugs on the desks of TB and shovel nose.

'Where is the tea, Son? I could read your future from the tea leaves in this mug, in fact, I have read your future, and you do not, bloody well, have one. Now go and get me a mug with something in it'.

I could hear the loud laughter from the blokes occupying every step outside, and now I had to walk past them all on my way back upstairs to make more tea. As I passed the open door to the shop, Ruggie said,

'Don't worry Son, you'll get used to it.'

As time went by, I did of course, get used to it. I soon learnt to give it back. I also realised that I had been given a new name, I was no longer named Paul, I had become "Son".

Upon my return to the basement, with nearly full mugs of tea, I was spoken to by a man who introduced himself to me.

'Hello, I am Colin, you must be the new boy?'

'Yes, I am,' I said, trembling in front of about twenty-five shop managers.

Colin Scales was about five-foot one inch tall, he weighed in at under eight stone. His jet-black hair was stuck down with brill-cream, he wore a dark grey pinstripe suit with matching waistcoat, a white shirt, and a black tie. He offered his hand it was sweaty and limp. I thought he must be an undertaker. From above, the managers were heckling,

'Watch him, he's a shirt lifter.'

'He's a brown hatter.'

'Don't let him get behind you.'

'He's a fudge packer.'

These were just some of the jibes coming from the mouths of the blokes on the stairs. As I made my way back up, I was subjected to various comments, all made with very effeminate pronunciation.

'I think he likes you Colin likes them young.'

'Did he touch your knob?'

'He is as bent as a nine-bob note.'

I thought I was street wise up to this point in my life, but this was a whole new experience to me. I had never met a "queer boy" before. I was determined to stay well out of Colin's way, even though I could have laid him out, no problem.

At 12.30 pm the internal phone rang in the racing room. Rosie answered it, turned to me, and said,

'They want you in the basement.'

'Oh Christ, I thought to myself, what am I going to have to endure this time?

Upon entering the basement, I saw that Ruggie was there, I felt at ease. I liked Ruggie. The old man told me that I was to go with Ruggie to the Bank. On the floor were four carrier bags, each bag had a towel neatly folded on top, making it difficult to see the contents. Ruggie stuffed something into his inside jacket pocket, picked up two of the bags and beckoned me to pick up the other two, we left the room. As we entered the shop, Stan Romaine came over to me, he gave me a big bear hug and said,

'Be careful out there, there are some nasty people around the East End.'

Stan Romaine, I had been informed by Ruggie, lived in Great Portland Street in the West End of London, what the heck did he know about the East End? Ruggie and I walked at a brisk pace until we reached the Nat West Bank in Whitechapel High Street. As we entered the bank, a bloke in a whistle opened a door and in we went. Two other bank employees joined us and then the counting started. One bag contained £2,600, Ruggie handed over a paying in book, it was stamped by the suited man and handed back. The next bag also contained £2,600, another paying in book was duly stamped. The third bag had £3,900 in it and the fourth contained just £2,100. We had just deposited £11,200 in paper money. No one asked any questions, there were no forms to fill in, no statements to make in respect of where the money had come from, and the bank were certainly not going to report us to the 'money laundering squad.' How simple having money was back in the day. We left the bank and Ruggie asked if I wanted a sandwich, my reply was affirmative. We had only walked a few yards when my new best mate opened the door to Blooms Restaurant. He let me walk past him. I had heard of Bloom's it was recognised as being the most famous "kosher" restaurant in the UK. It was renowned for its, salt beef sandwiches. Ruggie ordered the food, I bit into the bread and instantly spat it out. Looking inside the bread, I found it to be covered in mustard.

'I don't like mustard.' I muttered.

'Never mind, I will get you another.'

Ruggie was not at all put out by having to do this for me. He then told me some fascinating stories about Blooms. Charlie Chaplin used to eat there. Frank Sinatra too. They had a unique scheme of charging. Each waiter had to buy every dish they served from the kitchen, they would then sell the dish on to the customers. There were menus, but these showed no individual prices. The waiters made their salary on whatever they could add on top, plus any tips they received. At the end of their shift, the waiters would 'settle-up' with the kitchen staff. It was a very Jewish way of doing business. Blooms closed in 1996 due to the downturn of Jewish East Enders. They had moved out to Golders Green and Ilford. I enjoyed many salt beef sandwiches' during my years at William Massey, a lot with Ruggie, but even more, courtesy of Billy Newman, who would send me over there once a week to get salt beef for everyone in the

A Life Like No Other

office. I normally made about £3.00 from this errand and as my take home pay, each week, was just £7 and 2 shillings you would understand why I liked going. It cost me a lot of money when I got promoted and no longer had to do the fetching and carrying.

As I sat in Blooms with the man that was to teach me so much, I could not help quizzing him about our little deposit at the Nat West. I asked,

'So, we just paid in £11,200.'

I never had a bank account, so this was all new to me, in fact I do not think I had ever been in a bank before that day.

'Yes, a lot of 'spondoolies' (money).

I quickly worked out that at my present rate of £7.2 shillings a week, it would take me 28 years to earn that amount of cash.

'Why four different lots then?'

I now felt that Ruggie was becoming uncomfortable.

'A lot of questions, from a kid of fifteen.'

There was now a different tone to Ruggies voice.

He went on, pointing to his mouth.

'If I tell you, then you have to keep this zipped.'

'Of course.'

'Well, Billy gets £2,600, as does Peter White. The £3,900 goes into Massey's account and Jim Rainbird received £2,100.'

'Every week?'

'No, not every week, sometimes it is more, sometimes it is less.'

Based on this information, I did not give a hoot if Billy Newman let me keep the change every time that I did an errand for him. After all, I did most of his donkey work. For the record, Peter White never gave me a farthing. Terry Bishop was always generous if I did something for him, like keeping quiet about the fact that he was regularly shafting Marina in the basement. By the time I left Masseys employ I think old shovel nose owed me money, as he never paid me when getting his newspaper or the fisherman's friends that he liked to suck. Tight old Bastard. I always wanted him to die on his front so that I could park my bike right between the cheeks of his hairy "arse". Arriving back at the shop, Ruggie gave me the four paying in books and asked me to take them down to the basement and give them to TB. Both doors to the basement were locked, but I had already learned that I had to knock quite loud before they would hear. TB answered the door and waved me in. What I saw, I still remember some 50 plus years later. In the fireplace was a pair of shoes, looking up, a pair of legs and then a waist, it looked as though a body had been cut in half, it had not of course, it was old shovel nose. He was removing piles of cash from the third desk in the room, bundles of £1 and £5 notes and then stuffing them up the chimney. Ducking under the fireplace opening, his eyes saw me, he turned to TB and let out a torrent of abuse.

'What the hell have you let him in for? Do we want everyone in the world to know what goes on down here? You bald headed faggot.'

TB, remaining as cool as a cucumber simply replied,

'If only they had taken you to the gas chamber with the rest of your family.'

A furious shovel nose, responded,

'Well, you would not have a job if they had, and you wouldn't be shagging that doll either, would you?'

TB, turning to me, said,

'Thanks son, you can go.' I left.

As I climbed the stairs to the racing room, Billy and another bloke were coming down. Billy stopped, turned, and went back to the half landing. The other bloke said to me,

'He will never pass anyone on the stairs, its bad luck.'

As I arrived on the half landing, the very place that I had first come face to face with old shovel nose, Billy informed me that the other bloke, (who did not care about passing me on the stairs) was Peter White. Peter wore a suit and tie, he always did. He was polite, he had thick lenses in his black rimmed glasses, he did not fit the image of being a bookmaker, but then he was not a bookmaker. Whenever Billy was away or unable to come to the office, Peter would be somewhere in the building, but he had no real interest in being in the Racing Room. On those days, it would be left to TB to assume Billy's role. Within a couple of weeks, I had got to know everyone working at the head office. Bob White, Peter's brother, oversaw security. He was around in the morning's but had pissed-off somewhere by 1.00 pm. On most day's he would be accompanied by Harry Rose, uncle of Alan (Rosie) Rose. Harry was the firm's enforcer. The first time I met Harry he looked at me and asked me to hit him.

'Come on son, you are a strapping lad (I was six feet but only eleven stone) hit me as hard as you can, anywhere you want.'

Of course, I did not take Harry up on his invitation, he seemed annoyed. At that moment one of the direct telephones rang and as I brushed past him to answer it, he gave me an almighty punch, right onto the top of my arm, the force sent me hurtling across the room.

'That's what you will get if you ever do anything naughty.'

Sod this, I thought. This was the second time that I had wanted to quit, and within just two days of starting! Yes, Harry was a hard man and he kept company with some of the most notorious villains in the East End, but he never hit me again.

Just before 6.30pm on only my second day at work I entered the basement unannounced, my mission was to collect the empty teacups. At the tender age

A Life Like No Other

of 15 I was to witness TB fondling the well-endowed Marina. I left, leaving the cups behind. For weeks afterwards I was unable to make eye contact with the man with the blond comb-over. We never spoke about this until some years later, when Marina left to join the cast of Star Trek.

38 - My very first 'pay-day'

On Friday 12th August 1966, Jim Rainbird, all twenty-three stone of him, ambled into the racing room, ash falling from his unlit fag, he was carrying a rectangle wire tray, he took out four dark blue envelopes and gave them to Rosie. Rosie then handed one to Puxley, one to the snide and one to me, keeping one for himself. Dog-end Jim left, he still had more of the dark blue envelopes in his tray, which he would distribute to the rest of the staff. It was weird, I had in my hand my first ever, legally earned wage packet, the three other members of the racing room had theirs, also. None of us opened the envelopes. I waited until I went out to get the coffee and grub to open mine. There it was, a wage slip, with my name and national insurance number on it. There was a total of £7. 2 shillings inside, made up of 6 x £1 notes, 2 x 10-shilling notes and a 2-shilling piece. I had made £4 and 5 shillings from errands on top. I was rich. I had no credit cards to pay off, no overdraft, no mortgage and no loan sharks chasing me. My Mum only wanted £2 a week from me, and I still had Saturday to go, where, given a slice of luck I could earn a little bit more.

At lunch time, I strolled over to Levy's record shop and purchased six 45 rpm singles for £2.00. These were to be added to our joint record collection. Together with my brother John, we bought over 4,000 singles and 800 LPs from 1960 until 1974. By the time we started our DJ business we had every record anyone ever asked us to play. After a few weeks, Billy got to know of my record purchases and asked me to buy him some LP's. He left the choice to me, as he knew less about music than he did about bookmaking, and he knew 'sod-all' about bookmaking. I would buy him the kind of music that I liked however he was in his mid-thirties and had not grown up with the music the sixties had to offer. Billy would give me a fiver and I would buy him 2 LPs for £3. 15 shillings. I would always get to keep the £1. 5 shillings change. He would take-home whatever LP's I had purchased for him. A few days later he would bring one, or both, back to the office and hand them to me and say,

'Sorry son, Vera (his wife) is not keen.'

I soon learnt never to buy Billy something I already had, as invariably I would get a copy back from him, free of charge.

Three weeks after starting my job at Massey's, with Jim Reeves, "Distant Drums" in prime position, at the top of the charts, Puxley was asked to give up his position as number two to Rosie and become a shop manager. He could

A Life Like No Other

not wait to go. I was quite gutted that I would no longer have my mate to work alongside me and back me up when others were on my case. Puxley took on the job of relief manager, which meant working at a different shop every day, to cover for managers that were either sick, on holiday or just skiving. His departure meant that the 'snide,' Alan McCauley, moved into the seat next to Rosie. I moved onto the snides chair, and my chair became vacant. How I, really hated' snide features, and with Puxley's departure, life, for me, was going to become decidedly worse. Fortunately, for me, Billy did not like the snide either, however the fact that I was being recognised as Billy's blue-eyed boy was beginning to get up the ugly gits nose, he became even nastier to me.

What progress I had made, within just three weeks of starting my first ever job, I had moved up from being number four in the racing room, which meant making tea, going to the café, the bank, Blooms, the record shop, the newsagents, plus undertaking every other menial task they could throw at me, including the unblocking of the bog after shovel nose had discharged "turds" that resembled oxygen bottles into it. Now I was number three in the hub of the empire. I was still responsible for all the afore mentioned, but with the unwanted bonus of having to sit next to a bloke that was so facially ugly. The addition of about six thousand black heads on his boat race did nothing but enhance his vile looks. Still, if that was the price, I had to pay for rapid promotion, then I just had to accept it.

About three weeks after Puxley had left the head office, I began to realise that snide features, having become the number two in the room, was leaving his chair less and less when the phones rang. It was left to me to race across the room to answer the direct lines. Sometimes I would answer two phones at the same time and write down two bets simultaneously.

'What a clever little sod you are,' Billy would say.

This would wind-up old spot features, so I did it even more. Eventually, having heard Billy sing my praise's just once too often, the snide jumped up from his chair, to beat me to the draw. I stuck out a leg and he went flying. He got up and squared up to me, I had no option, I smacked him right between the eyes, it was the punch that I wanted to land upon Harry Rose but never had the bottle to do so. Billy got between us Rosie just carried on reading the Beano. The rest of the afternoon was quite weird, everyone seemed to have lost their voices. At 5.45, after TB and the old man had finished their, "ring around", I was called into TB's office.

'Billy has told me what happened earlier.' TB, with a stern voice informed me.

'I must say that McCauley is a horrible little specimen, and I for one will be glad to see the back of him. Please send him in.'

138

It dawned on me, as I left the room, that I had not been sacrificed, even though it was me that had thrown the only punch of our brief physical encounter. I told the snide that he was wanted in TB's room, he smirked as he brushed past me, he must have thought that I was out. He returned just a few minutes later and picked up his cigarettes, lighter, tube of blackhead cream and loose change from the desk where he had been sitting and left. There was a rumour that he was to become the understudy to the elephant man. I was now number two in the racing-room, I was still only fifteen years old. Not only did I have to undertake most of the tasks mentioned previously, I now, had to work out bets, file them, add up the totals of forty-six shops and worst of all, I had to sit next to Rosie. On Friday, when the grossly overweight Jim Rainbird gave me my dark blue envelope, I found that I had been given a £2.10 shilling's rise, an increase of 33%. I was now on a tenner a week. I could buy one hundred pints. Rich beyond my wildest dreams.

The following Monday morning, a young kid (he was in fact the same age as me but looked about twelve years old) arrived with Rosie. He had one over-riding feature, his nose. It was enormous, side on he looked like a Macaw Parrot. Ronnie and Reggie had hidden behind this nose, from the police, for over six-weeks. The kid was Ray Rose, younger brother of Alan, nephew of Harry, and he was thick. It now fell upon me to show him the ropes. I had to go through all the things with him that Ray Puxley had gone through with me, just six weeks previously. Soon after the "nose" took his first mugs of tea down to the basement, the internal phone rang, Rosie answered it and then handed it to me.

'Have you seen the nose on legs?' enquired TB.

I presumed that the nose had already left the basement. I was put on the spot by this quizzing from the bishop. I seemed to be the one that everyone looked to bounce things off. Rosie was dull and not really "in" with anyone, he had his wife, Iris, whom everyone called flower, due to her being named, "Iris Rose" together they had his twin boys, TB had nicknamed them, "Laurel and Hardy", I saw them only once, at a Massey football match, my god, one of them was fat and ugly and the other sported a moustache, aged just ten months! So now I was, in effect the assistant racing manager, how I got ribbed by the shop managers every Tuesday morning.

'Wiped Billy's arse today?'

'Cleaned Billy's car recently?'

'Bought Billy any nice records lately?'

These were just a few of the nicer remarks that would befall me as they queued outside the open racing room door. Suddenly, I had noticed that these men, that had previously poked fun at me, were now a little wary of me. Rumour had it that I was Billy's spy. I think this filtered its way back up the chain, as Billy told me not to worry about what people were saying. Shovel nose even smiled at me now and again. I both liked this and resented it at the same time. I noted that Ray "the nose" Rose never got to keep Billy's change.

During one of our walks to the bank, Ruggie had told me that Billy and his wife, Vera, had a son but unfortunately, he was not normal. He was, in Ruggies words 'a bit backward.' Ruggie went on to say that Billy seemed to be treating me as a substitute for his son and that is why I am the apple of his eye. I remember telling Ruggie that this situation is often embarrassing for me as everyone thinks that I am licking Billy's arse, when, in fact, I am not. Ruggie just told me to put up with it as no one else on the firm gets treated the way that I do. I guess I was lucky.

39 - Foinavon

On Saturday 8th April 1967, amazingly over half a century ago now, there remains one race that is etched into millions of minds, well at least the minds of those of us that are still alive. Eurovision song contest winner "Puppet on a String" by Sandie Shaw was at number one. It was Grand National Day. The Grand National is the single most gambled on sporting event in the World. This would be my first "National" at Massey's. We started at 9.00 am that day, the only day of the year when we had to get out of bed early. The phones started ringing at 9.15 and never stopped all day. There were so many betting slips by the time the race started that I fully believed that we would all still be there until Sunday morning. TB, who normally went to one of the shops on Saturday afternoons, was seconded to the racing room. Even Peter White was there, God knows why, as he did nothing to help. In the morning Honey End, the mount of Josh Gifford, and trained by one of the most crooked of trainers, Captain Ryan Price, was priced at 12-1. Throughout the entire country, punters were putting their money on this horse. Masseys and every other bookmaker would have lost a fortune had this won the race. At the off, Honey End was down to 15-2 and most bookmakers in the UK were on a hiding should Josh Gifford manage to ride him to victory. The race itself remains the most remarkable in Grand National History. There were forty-four runners, at the 23rd fence, which is now named after the winner of the 1967 Grand National and is the smallest fence on the racecourse, a loose horse, Popham Down, who had lost its jockey some way back, veered in front of the pack, bringing down every horse still racing, every horse except the 100-1 outsider Foinavon. Foinavon, was so far back that his jockey was able to steer him around the mountain of horses piled up on both sides of the fence and successfully jump over it. By the time some of the jockeys reclaimed their horse's and remounted, Foinavon was already a whole fence in front of the ensuing pack. With two fences to jump, Foinavon was still over 200 yards ahead of Honey End. Honey End was, however, gaining with every stride. Billy left the room, Peter White poured himself another Brandy, TB was shouting,

'Fall you bastard, fall.

His shout being directed at Honey End.

Foinavon jumped the last fence, Honey End was still gaining, I had backed Honey end at 16-1 a week earlier, I had mixed reservations about what should happen. The finishing line came too soon for Honey End, and Foinavon had

A Life Like No Other

just won his owner £17,000 in prize money. Remarkably neither the owner nor trainer of Foinavon were present at Aintree, both feeling that Foinavon, who normally fell over in every race, had little chance of getting around the course, let alone win. You can re-live the race by visiting - www.grand-national.me.uk

For those horse racing buffs amongst you, Anne, the Duchess of Westminster owned one of the greatest and most well-known of all racehorses, Arkle. She also owned Foinavon but sold it on, as her trainer had told her that it would never win a race. Prior to winning the greatest steeple chase in the World, Foinavon was out hunting foxes.

On the "ring around" that evening, one shop, in Roman Road, Bow, had reported that one punter had bet a pound each way on Foinavon, winning £125.00 for the lucky sod. In total Massey's had cleaned up to the tune of twenty-three-grand, This, would equate to well over half a million pounds in today's dosh. I know full well that only £5,000 of this money ever found its way into the bank. That evening, Billy took us all to the Blind Beggar, he paid for all the drinks for all the people in the pub, including many well-known figures from the underworld. Billy took me to the Beggar's in his two-seater Mercedes Sports, cementing what everyone was saying, that I was the son that he never had. In the car, he gave me a rolled-up bundle of cash and told me to buy something nice for my mum and dad. Before he left the pub, Billy handed over a wad of money to the barman in order that we could all continue to drink, at his expense. I had counted the money that Billy had given me whilst taking a leak in the pub toilet, I had been given £50.00, four weeks wages. The following Friday I bought Billy Disraeli Gears, an album by Cream, the next day Billy gave me it back, well it was not Perry Como, was it.

40 - The Bandit

It was during 67 that I was first introduced to the dodgy world of gangsters. I had begun to go to the Grave Maurice Pub with Ruggie at Saturday lunchtimes. Billy had found out that this pub produced the best Ham sandwiches in the East End, which they did. The Grave Maurice was just along from the infamous Blind Beggar, in fact, there were six pubs all within 100 yards of each other along Whitechapel Road, all were frequented by the Kray's and their entourage, although the "twins" were in custody for murder at the time. We would enter the "Grave" and people would fall over themselves to buy Ruggie a drink. Me, being his companion, would also enjoy a light ale courtesy of Jack the Hat, Freddy Foreman, or Tony Lambrianou. Ruggie would tell me,

'Son, don't ever get involved with any of these gentlemen.'

One Saturday in the Grave, Ruggie was approached by a man known locally as the "bandit", he pulled Ruggie to one side and had a brief chat with him. After the chat Ruggie told me to drink up as we had to get back to the head office before racing started. I picked up the bag containing several Ham sandwiches and we headed for Ruggies Ford Corsair. As he drove us back to Alie Street, he told me that if we were to go back to the Grave Maurice in a years' time then most of the undesirables that we had seen today, would be gone. How right you were Ruggie! They were all banged up or murdered. I did ask him about his chat with the bandit, but on this occasion, Ruggie remained tight lipped.

Two weeks later, a black telephone was put onto the desk in front of me and duly connected by the GPO. Every other telephone in the racing room was grey in colour. This telephone had no dial; therefore, no calls could be made to the outside world. Even Rosie had been kept in the dark about this. When Billy arrived in that day, I was called into TB's office and informed that I was the only one allowed to answer the new phone, when it rang. TB explained that this was a direct line between a room above one of the shops, in Commercial Road, Stepney, and "us". The phone would be for the sole use of the bandit and his gang of cronies. Apparently, as I was told by Billy, the bandit and his mates did not wish to gamble in hard cash within public view and had therefore, made an approach, via Ruggie, to have their own exclusive account. This would be settled, every day, between the bandit, the Commercial Road shop manager and myself. Well, that was what had been agreed, but it never quite worked out that way. Billy told me that I could take bets up to £100 without

A Life Like No Other

having to ask (equivalent to around £3,000 in today's money). I would be responsible for managing this account, this meant I had to decide if I kept the wagers or laid them off with William Hill or Corals. I was just sixteen years old, and I not only had the responsibility of losing Billy's money, but I also had to deal with a bunch of crooks that would skin me alive just for the fun of it! I was also informed that there would be an addition to the racing room in order that I could manage this account unhindered. At one minute before 2.00 pm the black telephone in front of me sprang into life. A very gruff voice said,

'It's the bandit here, I want £30 on this horse, £20 on another horse and a tenner each way on yet another.'

I could hardly hear anything that the illiterate gangster was saying, as the din from the other occupants of the room made it nigh impossible to do so. Anyhow, first race over, the bandit had blown it, £70.00 in the kitty. The next race just fifteen minutes later was even more of a farce. The bandit was trying to give me the name of a horse, but he obviously could not read, as what he was saying was incomprehensible. In the background, the cronies were all shouting out what they thought was the name of the horse, I had not written anything down because I could not understand what anyone was saying. The bandit hung up. Things were made worse for me as Billy insisted on almost sitting on my lap whilst I was on the phone. I was getting extremely nervous. Immediately after this race the bandit called and asked if I had got the bet and to confirm that they had just won over £300. After just twenty minutes we already had our first confrontation. I explained to Billy that this was not going to work, Billy told me that he would take over the phone for the next race, thankfully he did. When he took his first call, Billy was shouting down the phone,

'What the fuck are you saying? I can't understand you and I can't bloody well hear you. either'

Billy put down the phone and called the manager of the shop that was below the room where the gangsters were operating from. Unfortunately, the manager of the shop that day was none other than the petite effeminate Colin Scales, the limp wristed undertaker. Billy was not happy. He needed to send someone upstairs to meet with the bandit, but he did not want it to be the girlish gay-boy. Against his better judgement Billy decided that he had go with it. He explained to the gay shop manager, dressed that day in a long flowing silk number, that he should go upstairs, take the bandit somewhere nice and quiet and tell him that he needs to find someone that can speak very clearly on the telephone and that this nominated person would be the one that would be dealing directly with myself. Although we were not privy to the exact details of what happened, the story told was that Colin climbed the stairs, ambled over to the bandit, held out his limp, sweaty hand and asked him to go with him to another room. The bandit, being the "leader of the gang" did not like being asked to go somewhere private with this little poof and duly rendered him unconscious with one almighty blow. When Colin did not return to the shop below, one of the girls went up to find out why, she was subjected to all kinds of sexual connotations, she fled, never to return. Having heard nothing from the shop or the bandit for a good half an hour, Harry Rose and Bob White were dispatched to Commercial Road, just five minutes away. One hour later the black telephone rang, I picked it up. Harry Rose reported that all was now sorted and that in future I was only to accept bets from "patch". Patch, I later learnt, had a black, pirate like blob over his right eye, he had once upon a time been a bare-knuckle fighter and had the eye gorged out by an opponent's thumb. The opponent had mysteriously impaled himself onto patch's brother's knife whilst sat, minding his own business in the public bar of a notorious East End pub. Upon his return to the racing room, Harry Rose reported that there were at least forty undesirables upstairs from the shop. They were all drinking heavily and most of them would not have known what day of the week it was, let alone be able to read a horse's name from a newspaper. A speaker system was installed, and the racing pages of the sporting life were put up on the walls to make the upstairs room feel exactly like a betting shop. This situation lasted for about three months until the bandit was smashed up with baseball bats in Massey's West End gaming club. By my reckoning the "mob" collectively owed Billy around £17,000, but then, not even Harry Rose was going to enforce collection of that debt.

With Kenny (Winston) Churchill having been hived-out to one of the shops, as Billy deemed him to be responsible for the recent heavy losses, the new boy, Winston's replacement, had started as number four, meaning that the nose on legs had become number three in the pecking order, probably the highest position he would ever attain. Unfortunately for him, the new-recruit, Robin, was wearing a green shirt on his first day at work. Billy walked into the racing room, saw a green shirt, and backed out of the door.

'What the hell are you doing with that shirt on?' He bellowed from outside the racing room door.

Billy beckoned me over, gave me a sky diver and told me to give it to the new lad and ask him to go and buy another shirt, which must not be green. Robin, completely unfazed, gladly accepted the fiver and left, returning an hour later with a bright pink shirt. Pink was OK, but it made us all a bit suspicious of Robin's gender. In Billy's world, you could not, wear green, pass on the stairs, put a brush on a table, open a brolly indoors, use a red pen or let old shovel nose into the racing room. If you did any of these your days would be numbered. Robin survived just eight days and he was gone. He later moved in with Colin.

A Life Like No Other

For me, sixteen turned into seventeen and just after my seventeenth birthday, Billy asked me if I fancied working in the shop at Leysdown, on the Isle of Sheppey, Kent. This shop was widely recognised as being the busiest betting shop in the UK, but only during the months of May – August. At seventeen I was not legally able to work on licensed premises, but the term legally did not seem to be within anyone's remit at Masseys. I was already working evenings at the Young Prince Public House in Crisp Street, Poplar. Anyhow. I agreed to Billy's proposal but was a little wary when asked if, 'I could keep an eye on things' for him whilst at Leysdown.

41 - Bad Toe

A few weeks before I was due to leave for Leysdown for the summer season, I had to visit St. Andrews Hospital as I had a bad infection in the big toe of my right foot, the pain was unbearable. The verdict was that I had an ingrowing toenail, the nail would need to come off. I was asked to come back the following day. I was told that once they had treated the infection they would operate and remove the toenail. It was May 1968, "Young Girl" by the Union Gap topped the charts. I was just seventeen years old. The following day I walked the two miles from Venue Street to my place of birth, St. Andrews Hospital, every step was so painful. Upon arriving at the reception, I was taken to a ward, allocated a bed and asked to sit on it until the Doctor arrived. I was not stuck in A and E for hours on end and neither did I spend any time on a trolley in the corridor, things were so much more civilized "back in the day." When the Doctor, a man of Chinese origin, whom I named 'Who Flung Dat' arrived, I was asked to remove my shoes. Upon doing so I could see that my shoe was full of blood. A nurse left my bedside and then came back with a polythene bag, into which my right foot was placed. Doctor Dat spoke to the ward sister, and I was led, one foot bare and the other one clad in a plastic bag, to a cupboard at the end of the ward. I was asked to sit on a stall, a nurse came in with a small footbath, poured some boiling water and iodine into it and asked me to plunge my infected toe inside. The pain was the worst I had ever encountered in my short life, surpassing the time when my eldest brother had repeatedly beaten me on the head with a cricket bat, after I had bowled him first ball, at the age of ten. I was unprepared for the severity of the pain, which would get much, much worse. My scream alerted the sister to the fact that her nurse had just made me insert my right extremity into water that was far too hot for a human foot to endure. The sister called an ambulance, and I was taken to a soundproof room next to the morgue. By now, my foot looked like a lobster's claw, my infected toe was leaking puss. I now had five nurses in the cupboard with me, this was probably most men's fantasy, but for me it was a nightmare.

After wrapping about twelve feet of bandage around my foot, I was taken, by wheelchair, back to my bed. I was asked to undress; the curtains were closed around me. At that moment, a voice shouted,

'Show her your potato.'

I thought that I recognised the voice but could not put a face to it. Once in my pyjamas, which my Mum had bought for me as I never wore pyjamas and still do not, even at 70+ years of age. The pyjamas caused a bit of a stir as they were pink and white stripes and made from old army blankets. They had numbers and yellow stars on them. My mum later revealed that she had bought them, as part of a "job lot" from Mr Rosenblatt, a man of Jewish extraction, who had survived five years in Auschwitz. She had, as part of the deal, also inherited some gold teeth and a few pairs of broken spectacles! The curtains were drawn back and there he was, the perpetrator of the earlier obscene shout. It was none other than Vince McShane, a regular drinker at the Young Prince. Vince was what was known back then as "a half caste", being half black, half white. Fortunately for Vince, the black half was at the bottom. I do not think that we can say such things these days, but back then, you could say whatever you wanted without fear of being either murdered or sued. Most evenings, I worked behind the bar of the Young Prince, one of the most popular pubs in Poplar. This was quite illegal, as I was only seventeen, however there were no social services, and my parents did not object as I kept them supplied with vast quantities of nuts, crisps, and pork scratchings. Vince McShane, now laid in the bed opposite me, would arrive in the Public Bar of the Young Prince at 7.00 pm every evening, Monday through to Friday. He would order a pint of Guinness and a Barley Wine. He would do this several times during the evening, each time inviting me or whomever else might serve him to "have one yourself", which invariably we did. Vince would leave, stumbling, every weekday night. On Saturday evenings he would enter the 'posh' side of the pub, the Saloon Bar, or the Lounge as it was called, with his wife, Molly. He would be "suited and booted" and his nearest and dearest would always wear an evening dress. I never once heard Vince blaspheme when he was with his wife. He swore every other word whilst in the Public Bar.

Having Vince in the bed opposite me was both a blessing and a problem. A blessing because he was someone that I knew, a problem because he was known to be a groper of women. I had caught him in the "ladies" of the Young Prince one evening, he had his manhood out and was asking a lady, that was well past her sell-by date, to kiss his potato! After I explained to Vince why I was in the hospital he told me that he was having his willy shortened because it kept touching his girlfriend's tonsils and she was getting fed up with it, he added that his wife did not care as she had become a lesbian. Of course, he was kidding, (I think) he never stopped. Every time a nurse came to his bedside, he would ask her to touch his potato, it was a little embarrassing for me, a shy seventeen-year-old. My parents came to visit me on that first night in hospital, my nan came but not my grandad as he had decided to check out of life the previous year. All three of my brothers came, as did my entire Yorkshire family, seventeen of my friends, the milkman, the provident bloke, four dustmen, almost all my near neighbours, including the donkey and the three-legged dog, but, most importantly, the fiancé of my eldest brother was there. Vince called her over and asked her to touch his potato, she never visited me again, result!

The following day my treatment began in earnest. A short stroll to the broom cupboard, boiling water into a footbath, foot plunged in, a scream, and then a wheelchair back to bed. It was such fun to be hospitalised.

At around 2.00 am on my second night in captivity, I was disturbed by a bloke in a wheelchair, he was parked at the foot of my bed, he picked up the metal board that contained my notes and started to bash my feet with it, I screamed in agony, two nurses arrived and told the man in the wheelchair to get back to his own ward. I learnt later that day, that the wheelchair had contained Eddie, the schizophrenic. Eddie apparently only woke up at nights, as they kept him sedated during the day, after he had tried to mount the matron when she had bent down to pick up some old guy's teeth. God knows why they did not inject him at nights. He would wheel himself around the hospital, shouting obscenities and physically assaulting people, I had become his latest victim. Back in the 60's there was no real segregation of patients in NHS hospitals, the sane and insane shared the same wards and facilities. My treatment continued in much the same way for several days, until I was told by the Doctor that it appeared that the infection had cleared up and that the surgeon, a Dr Cutter, would be round to have a look at me. I remember thinking "bloody hell" I only have an ingrowing toenail, why do I need a surgeon? On the second Tuesday of my stay in St. Andrew's, which I think was the 14th, May 1968, "Young Girl" was still at the top of the hit parade, both of my legs were shaven. Vince had told me that "Eddie the wheelchair" always did the shaving, I was shitting myself. In fact, a very lovely looking Chinese nurse did the job, I gave her the name 'blood loss' as she took a chunk of skin from my knee. Fortunately, she did not go all the way up to my privates! Opposite, Vince was in a frenzy, shouting out, repeatedly, for her to, "touch his potato". At 8.00 am, I was wheeled out of the ward and into a lift. My feet overhung the bed, and the porter, not really giving a dam, slammed my bad foot straight into the wall at the back of the lift. I wanted to cry but being seventeen stone and six feet tall, I held it back.

I remember waking up at around 4.00 pm that afternoon, I also remember thinking "for God's sake, put me back to sleep", both of my feet were on fire. I was in the intensive care ward, widely recognised in the 60's as the place you were most likely to die in. I conjured up enough bravery to look down the bed, I could see that I had a frame over my feet, preventing the bed covers from touching them. I was wheeled back to the ward, I made sure that my feet were not overhanging when we entered the lift. At around six pm, the surgeon, Dr Cutter, arrived at my bedside, he informed me that the operation had gone well but had taken rather longer than expected, five hours in total. I asked him why

A Life Like No Other

both of my feet were so painful, he told me that he had removed both nails from my big toes, as in his opinion, the left one would have become a problem in time. He lifted the cover from the frame to reveal a bottom sheet absolutely covered with blood.

'This is quite normal,' he said, adding that he had to remove the nail bed and that my nails would never grow back again. Cutter left and I never saw him again.

During the night, Eddie the mad man returned, this time he was mumbling and making gurgling noises, froth ran down his chin, again he stopped at the foot of my bed, he lifted the cover from the frame and began beating my feet with his fists. I nearly passed out. Vince jumped from his bed, shouting 'nurse, nurse', it was too late, the damage was done. The blood was dripping through the one-foot-thick bandages that covered my feet. The sister came, then a doctor, then a porter, then the gas man, the plumber and finally the undertaker! I was taken away and my stitches were "re-stitched." I was in hospital for six long weeks, for an ingrowing toenail! For over 50 years I have had bits of nail growing out of my left big toe and I use plyers to keep it cut down to size.

Sadly, Vince McShane died during the night of my re-stitching, it was in fact his liver that had given up, alcohol had reduced it to one fifth of its normal size. At least that cleared up the myth surrounding his claim that they were shortening his potato. Despite his obscene bad manners, Vince was a good guy.

Every week whilst I was in hospital Alan 'Rosie' Rose would pop in and give me my wages. Billy had insisted that I be paid, as it was not my fault that I was off work.

I left St. Andrews hospital on the Thursday before my eldest brother's wedding, I was to be his best man. Whilst hospitalised, I had asked my Mum to take my best suit to be dry cleaned at the dry cleaners in Coventry Cross. I had to pass the dry cleaners in the taxi that was taking me home. Parking right outside the cleaners was impossible, I was on crutches, the tops of my shoes had been cut away as I could not have any pressure on my toes. It was pissing down. I managed to walk the 100 yards or so from the taxi to the cleaners, each step was extremely painful. I had no ticket, but I was a regular. Before I could utter a word, Mrs Sketchley, the owner, informed me that they had been robbed, just last week and that my suit was one of the items that had been stolen. I kicked the counter, a big mistake, I then cried. The taxi took me home, my Nan greeted me at the door, no one else was in the house. The next day I went to Phil Seagal's tailor shop in East India Dock Road and got measured for a 24-hour suit. The final fitting for the suit took place at Midday on Saturday, the wedding took place at 2.00 pm. The suit looked fine, the cut away shoes and the blood on my socks did not! 24-hour suits were a strange phenomenon, as exactly 24 hours later, whilst stood in the pub, the suit totally disappeared, leaving me stood at the bar in just my boxers, socks, and shoes. Two weeks later, Sid Whalley, one of Mrs Whalley's Sons, knocked on our door and asked if anyone was looking to buy a suit. He held up a hanger, it was empty. Anyhow, I took my suit back from him, telling him that I would keep quiet if he did not charge me for my own suit. This was the only deal I ever did with Sid Whalley.

42 - He's a bit short

Having been hospitalized for six weeks, I returned to work on Monday 24th June 1968, "Jumping Jack Flash" by the Stones had replaced "Young Girl" at the top. The nose on legs was still there, although he had been arrested and bailed for harbouring two of the great train, robbers inside his nostrils. Ray Puxley had been brought back into the racing room to cover for me whilst I was away. I began to get bored with the daily routine of the racing room, in fact it had been a whole lot more interesting when I was doing the errands, at least I was getting out and meeting people. I began to drop hints to TB that I rather fancied becoming a relief manager, or at least a settler in one of the busier shops. TB discussed this with Billy, and I was asked if I would become assistant to Bob White, the security manager. At first, I readily agreed, as this would get me out of a now familiar daily routine. The room at the top of the head office had been turned into the security room. Billy and Peter White had long since realised that fraud was being committed on a massive scale by a lot of the managers, several of whom were relatives of Billy. Part of my new position would be to check the bets that had been paid out. Every week the managers would bring the betting slips to the head office, they would then be taken upstairs to me. I was now becoming the enemy of the very people that I wished to have a good relationship with. One or two of the managers, both related to Billy, offered me money to turn a blind eye to what I might find. I was not happy in this job. Previously there had been no security at all, therefore any manager or settler could have worked out a bet incorrectly and paid themselves out, I found a lot of such bets and was torn between telling Billy and become known as a "nark" or not telling Billy and risk being accused of being in on it.

 I decided to talk to TB and explained my situation, adding that, in my opinion security would be best handled by people with no association with existing staff, TB readily agreed. Billy thought the idea was great and I received a £5.00 per week rise. I had to wait for someone to replace me before I could move on. I did not have to wait too long, as within three days a young man by the name of Peter Crutchley came for an interview. Peter unfortunately had contracted Polio as a baby and consequently his movement was very restrictive. His right leg dangled at a 45-degree angle, and he used a crutch to support himself, I considered at the time that he was very aptly named. He was as far removed from being a security guy as he could be. He got the job and started the following Monday. Not since big boobs Grace, had anyone clunked up and down the stairs like Peter Crutchley did. I had recommended to TB and Billy (hark at me, at seventeen recommending things to the guvnor) that they really needed to add a third person to the team, as often Bob White and myself had to go out together, leaving no one there to carry on the checking. Crutchley would now have to do the rounds with Bob White, leaving the security room unattended. The phone in the security room rang, I answered it. It was Ruggie, he said,

'There is a bloke down here saying he has come for an interview for the security job.'

Bob White was supposed to conduct this interview, but he was not around. I called TB, but I think he was busy examining Marina's personal parts. TB asked me to do the interview, my god I thought, I will be running this bloody business soon. I descended to the ground floor, slid the door to the shop back and was looking straight into Ruggies face when he said,

'I think this guy is a bit short, so he could do with a job.'

'Where is he then? I asked.

'He's there.'

'Where.?'

'On the other side of the counter'

Ruggie, was now sporting a wide grin upon his boat race. I peered over the half glass counter and there he was, all two feet nine of him. I could not help laughing, I did not want too, but it was Ruggies earlier comment,

'I think he's a bit short' which did it.

I asked the small man his name,

'Nobby, the cannon ball.' he replied.

I asked as to his last job.

'I was working for Bertram Mills Circus, I got fired just before it went bust last year.'

I thought, God, this is going to create some laughs. I knew that Nobby was going to get the job even before he climbed the four flights of stairs to the room at the top. There would be pandemonium in the office, Crutchley on sticks and Nobby dragging his leg onto each step. Billy would never be able to go up or down the stairs again. Together the misfits became known as, "Batman and Robin" and Bob White was the Joker.

'Fucking worst security in the whole of the East End.' old shovel nose said, sarcastically.

Peter Crutchley would sometimes pick me up from the bus stop in the morning, he had a specially converted automatic car, the only pedal was the brake, which was on the left-hand side since his right foot was nearly hanging out of the door. He controlled the speed of the car with a lever fitted to the dashboard. There was a knob on the steering wheel, which he used when turning corners as he had hardly any strength in his right hand. I must admit that I dreaded it when he stopped for me, as I never felt safe as his passenger. Nobby, the midget was found sleeping under a table in the room at the top, the sporting life covering his minute body, he was sacked and soon after we learned that he had died whilst being fired from a cannon at Billy Smarts circus.

43 - Mile End

One Friday night in July 1968, during a pub crawl around the Isle of Dogs, my brother John, Stephen Richardson (the newest member of our gang) and myself wandered into the Kingsbridge Arms, and there, behind the bar was one of my old George Green School mates, John Duggan. All of us were under-aged. I had not seen Duggan since he got caned for letting me out of George Green back in 1964. Like myself, he had been born on the same day as Janice Winterflood. Duggan and I never knew each other before attending George Green, aged eleven. My old school chum told us that we were in his parents pub. I had known his parents Bill and Cathy, as, during my schooldays they had a tobacconist come sweetshop in Crisp Street market and Duggan would take me there some lunchtimes and fill my duffle bag with sweets. We were to rekindle our friendship, he worked in the shipping business in the city and soon introduced us to his workmates, Brian Ellery (Herbie), Pat Ellis (Joe 90), and Vincent Steel (Vinnie). These three will feature later in my story, all for very, different reasons, but one of them would become notorious in the terrorism business, another for his affair with a nationally known gay figure and the third one for his utter abuse of our friendship. Once I knew these lads, my own social scene changed. Instead of pints in the local in the East End, I was introduced to the swanky cellar bars of the West End, the most impressive being Shelley's Bar at Green Park, where I was to meet many hooray-Henry's and posh Chelsea Ladies. I was earning well, and money never seemed to be a problem. It was not unusual to go on to Swiss Cottage, Notting Hill or Kilburn after a Friday or Saturday night out. Swiss Cottage and Notting Hill visits were always at the behest of some of the upmarket ladies that we met in Shelley's. The posh girls just loved a cockney accent, amongst other things. The Kilburn connection was totally down to Vinnie Steel, we mingled with people of a certain ilk but without the knowledge of whom they were or what they did. This was 1968, the summer of love had passed but the London scene was as buoyant as ever.

Upon entering the Kingsbridge Arms for the very first time, 'Arnold Lane' by Pink Floyd was playing in the background. This song reminded me of my nights at the Roundhouse at Chalk Farm. I had been there on the opening night in October 66, when the then little-known band "Pink Floyd" led by Syd Barrett were the headliners. During 68 and 69 I would see Hendrix, The Who, Led Zeppelin, The Doors (yes Jim Morrison no less, how great was he?) T-Rex and Fleetwood Mac, to name but a few. Admission, £ 1.25 to £ 1.50. I never took drugs, but you could get high from just being in there, it was colossal. We know its old hat, and everyone born in the 50's will tell you that the 60's music scene was, and still is, unrivalled, I could fill a book with the groups that I saw live. The sound was mainly "crap", compared with today's digital era, but the atmosphere was always electric, if anyone ever tells you differently, they are probably dead. You could sometimes just walk into a pub and some of the best-known groups would be playing, for free. How lucky was that?

In October 1968, our association with Venue Street would be at an end. The whole street was on the move. Our Nan had already moved, six months earlier, to Roman Road, Bow. She was in a warden-controlled environment. Brother John and I would visit her in, order to use her 'indoor' bath. Most times she would be asleep in her chair. We would both bath (separately) leaving a large cream cake on her table and scarper before she woke up. She was a lovely old lady. My two younger brothers, parents and I moved to Blair Street, just half a mile from where I had spent my first seventeen and a half years. Blair Street, as you might have noticed, carried on the Scottish street name connection. We had a ground floor flat. it was massive. We had a bathroom, yes no more fetching and carrying of the tin bath. We had a separate indoor loo, central heating, hot water, and a lounge bigger than the whole of the top floor of Venue Street. For us, this was utopia. On the minus side, Julie Fitzpatrick lived just 100 yards away and she was rampant, she had been chasing me since primary school. She was pleasant enough, I just did not fancy her, due mainly to the fact that she had only one ear, the largest 'arse,' of any teenager in the country and her breasts were inverted. I knew that I must avoid her at all costs. We had moved everything from the old Victorian house in Venue Street on the back of my dad's open back lorry, it was raining heavily, and my brother John and I were soaked through as we had to stand on the back of the flat bed, open truck just to make sure that nothing fell off. We also moved our next-door neighbour, Mrs. Eisele, as she too was moving, right next door to us in Blair Street. She had asked to be near to us as we were the only people she ever saw. When she died, we arranged her funeral, she had no-one. We did save a bit on the undertaker's bill, as at the time of her death she was bent over so badly that they were able to use a child sized coffin. The day we moved to our new house, Mary Hopkin singing "Those were the days" was at number one, they certainly "were the days" of 'our' young lives.

Boxing Day, 1968 "Lily the Pink" by the Scaffold was the Christmas number 1. In the bookmaking business, there were only two days off per year, Good Friday, and Christmas day. On this Boxing Day, the settler at the Mile End branch had failed to show up for work. TB asked me to go and cover for him, legally I was too young, but nobody really cared, so off I went. In fact,

Ruggie took me there in his car and warned me to be careful. This day was the launch of my career outside the gaze of the Head office. I arrived at around 11.30 am and there was not a single punter (customer) to be seen. Pat Brown, the manager was a little nervous that someone from Head Office had been sent to work there. My reputation as Billy's favourite was known company wide, combine this with the fact that I was working in security, and I suppose they had every reason to be on their guard. Pat suggested that I go next door and grab a sandwich and a drink. Next door was a gambling club, it consisted of several snooker and pool tables, dart boards, card schools, dominoes and even a roulette wheel. All totally illegal, but then the patrons were mainly those that frequented the Grave Maurice, Blind Beggar, and other pubs along Whitechapel Road. These people would bet on anything. The main hall of this club was dimly lit and if they had had smoke alarms back then I am sure that they would have been in constant use. There were a couple of smaller rooms along the right-hand side of the main hall, in time I would learn that these were used by the "mob" to both entertain guests and to interrogate people that had fallen out with them. I had noticed a lot of black cabs parked outside and would later find out that after working all night, these driver / owners would be at the club for breakfast, after which they would gamble away their hard-earned wages. On my first ever visit I hung around for a while, arousing suspicion amongst the clientele, in the East End certain people were always wary of strangers. I went back to the betting shop, where my job for the day would be to work out the bets and hand them to the counter staff, after which the winning bets would be paid out. It was now 12.45 pm and still the shop was totally void of punters. Pat quizzed me for a while as to why I had been sent from Head Office to help for the day, I could only tell him the truth, that there was no one else that could be sent. The first race of the day was at 1.15, at 1.13 every member of the club next door filed into the shop. All hell broke loose. Instead of writing out their bets and bringing them to the counter in an orderly fashion, which was the norm, punters just shouted out the name of the horse and how much they wanted to bet. The counter staff had to write out the bet, note the name of the punter on the betting slip and then ring it through the till. Each bet was then put onto the desk in front of me and I had the job of trying to make a book and work out how much I should lay off to Head Office. The money for these bets would simply be thrown from the back if the punter could not get to the counter. Almost every bet was taken either one minute before or one minute after the race had begun. It was manic, I had never seen anything like it. It transpired that a good percentage of the punters were illiterate and could not actually write out their own bets. This shop would sometimes take more money on one race than some other shops took all day. I hardly had time to work out a bet before the punter was there at the counter, demanding his winnings. My

A Life Like No Other

thoughts at the time led me to believe that it was absolutely without doubt that the staff in this shop had every opportunity to ring up blank slips and write out the winner after the race had run. Checking these bets in the security room, I would never have known whether a bet was genuine or not as the staff wrote out almost every bet. After a few races, I got used to it. There were several disputes during the afternoon, with punters claiming they had backed the winner when in fact the counter staff had written down the name of a loser. Most of the punters that backed a winner would return, back to the club, and bet the lot on the turn of the roulette wheel or chance their luck at, blackjack. I found my afternoon at Mile End to be overwhelming and fully understood why Ruggie had told me to be careful. In no time at all, racing had finished for the day, all the punters had left, some were back in the club whilst the cab drivers went off to the West End to earn more money for the next day. I worked at Mile End quite a few times after this and got to know several of the punters. One cabbie told me that he only went home to his wife and three children on Sunday's. Pat Brown and four staff were evicted from Mile End about six weeks after my first day with them. Someone had grassed them up, they were of course all adding to their salary by backing winners after the event. A lot of people within the company thought that it was something of a coincidence that it was not long after I had worked there that Pat, and his staff were removed. Pat was taken into one of the side rooms in the club by Harry Rose and Bob White and had confessed without the need of violence. Terry Bishop's twin Brother, Ron, was installed as manager, strangely, he wore his "combover" on the opposite side of his head and when the brothers stood side by side, in windy weather, their shadow resembled an aircraft! Ron Bishop lasted just a couple of weeks. He was not strong enough to handle such volatile clients. With his Bobby Charlton hairstyle, he took a load of abuse from the punters. Jimmy (hit man) Jones, one of Harry Rose's mates was the next manager. He was a bigger crook than most of the people in the club. Jimmy had many disagreements with the punters. Ten days after he had squared-up to one nationally known hard man, he was found hanging in his garage in Dagenham. The police suspected foul play but officially logged his death as suicide. Over £4,000 in cash was found under his bed, no one knew where it had come from. Eventually Johnny Young, Brother-in-law of Billy, was to become manager. I thought that his appointment was one of those, "better the devil you know, then the devil you don't" scenario's. Some three years later I found out that Billy owned the gambling club, he took the rent from the manager but had no part in the gambling or extortion that took place there.

Paul Lucas

The Kingsbridge Arms at 154 West Ferry Road, Isle of Dogs. Opened in 1869, demolished in 2004.

44 – 18 Years Old

On the 22nd, March 1969, I became eighteen. It was a Saturday. Peter Sarstedt was at number one with, "Where do you go to my Lovely", but more importantly, Marvin Gaye had reached number two with, "I heard it through the Grapevine", a classic, all-time hit. I had promised my parents that I would be home that evening, as they were going to throw a party. The party would be after our local pub, the Aberfeldy, had closed. My parents often had "ad hoc" parties after closing time. Most of the people in the pub were invited. They would carry crates and kegs of beer back; the manager of the pub would bring over the gas and optics and we would have a full-on pub scene. We already had the "decks" (two turntables), four 250-watt speakers, and a state of the art, Pioneer four channel stereo amplifier. All our neighbours were invited as they would not be getting any sleep. Janice Winterflood, also eighteen, had been invited by my mum, without my knowledge, and she was pursuing me all night. I got Brian Ellery (Herbie) to keep putting Vodka into her drink, she passed out at around 1.00 am and I was a free man again.

Soon after my eighteenth, I was charged with arranging our first overseas holiday, something I was to do for the next four years. There was no internet in those days. The set up was that you firstly went to your local travel agent, luckily, we had one just 50 yards from where we lived, I took loads of brochures away, and then decided upon where we all wanted to go. I then revisited the travel agent to arrange the booking. I was to become a regular at "Sharps Travel Agents" in Aberfeldy Street, yes, yet another Scottish name. A few days later, I decided that brother John, Brian Ellery (Herbie), Pat Ellis (Joe 90) John Duggan and me would all like to go to Cattolica, in Italy, for a fortnight, in July 69. I went back to Sharps to book the holiday. I was to find out for the first time that we, the UK, had strict controls on the amount of foreign currency that we could get for our precious GB Pound. At the time of booking the holiday I was told by Sharps that, in total, we would be allowed to exchange just £50.00 each, irrespective of the length of time that we were going to be away. The exchange was recorded in your passport, I still have mine. On the 6th, June 1969, I exchanged £19.00 for Lira. On the 11th, July, just prior to departure I exchanged another £31.00. That was it, no matter whom you were or how much money you had, officially your passport could not show more than £50.00 in exchange for foreign money. To be fair £50.00 back then was equivalent to £1,000 today. There was a famous story surrounding this restriction.

A Life Like No Other

Cilla Black and husband Bobby had bought a Villa in Spain and had to pay £1,000 to their builders but were not allowed to change up sterling, Bobby, a former baker, hollowed out a loaf of bread and hid the grand inside. If you were caught with more than your allowance of £50.00, firstly the money would be confiscated, and secondly you would be prevented from leaving the Country. So, you see, we were once a Communist State. This situation, known as a "V" form was introduced by Harold Wilson in 1964 to stop our currency from leaving our shores, however this had an adverse effect on the economy and many International Companies stopped investing in the UK as they were unable to get their profits out. Maggie Thatcher abolished this scheme in 1979. Whilst we only each had £50.00 to spend, less than £4.00 per day, we still managed to get pissed every day, eat as much as we liked, bring presents back for family and still have change out of a farthing. We liked it so much in Italy that I arranged the same trip in 1970.

The manager of the Aberfeldy pub, having been at my birthday bash, and having seen our twin decks and heard our massive speakers, asked if I would be interested in being a DJ in the pub on Friday-Saturday-Sunday nights, the reward would be £15.00 per night, nearly as much as my legal, six days a week salary. On good Friday, April 4th, 1969, I began my new career as a pub DJ. My dad and myself loaded all the equipment and records into his escort van and drove the fifty yards to the pub, unloaded everything, and set it all up in the pub in readiness for the night's entertainment, due to commence at 7.30 pm. My brother's, mum, dad, and friends always drank in the public bar, the music was to be played in the Saloon. That night everyone I knew was in the saloon, it was heaving. The usual clientele of the saloon bar would have been mum and dads age group, middle of the road music would have to be played. The likes of Dean Martin, Noel Harrison, Cliff Richard, Frank Sinatra, Cilla Black, Elvis, Englebert Humpback and even Donald Peers had records in the charts at the time and prior to arriving "on stage", I was pretty much set on having to play this more sedate of popular music. However, due to the influx of most of my friends and people they had told, there were more youngsters than old fogies, and I was able to play The Who, The Beatles, Hollies, Johnny Nash, The Beach Boys, Tremeloes, Cream, Kinks, and Love Affair, amongst others. The pub rocked, people, old and young were dancing. I was turning the volume up, the manager kept asking me to turn it down. I did requests for people, each time I did, I received a drink. By 10.00 pm I was out of it, volume was at maximum. I can still vividly remember that night. Mum and dad announced that there would be a party, back at theirs. Around 120 people crammed into my parents flat that night. The stronger patrons of the pub carried the disco-gear back on their shoulders. It was real old East End entertainment, there is nothing like it nowadays. The whole thing was repeated on the Saturday night and on Easter

Sunday I handed over the decks to my dad. My dad went on to help me every weekend, he loved it. By the way, "The Israelites", by Desmond Dekker was the number one record at the time.

45 - Welcome to Leysdown

On Easter Monday 1969, I was asked to manage the racing room, as Rosie, the nose on legs, Harry Rose and most of the other Rosie's had been called to a religious gathering in Israel. Rosie later brought in a photo of the gathering, for some reason they were all stood, looking at a wall, strange people indeed! After racing had finished TB called me into his room, Billy was also present. I was asked if I would go and manage the Leysdown branch for the summer. Momentarily I hesitated, as I was just about to find fame as a DJ and how would Radio One discover me if I were on the Isle of Sheppey? My hesitation probably went unnoticed as I of course said yes to this proposal. My dad was more than keen to be the East End's oldest DJ and he need not worry about his later life as he had no aspirations to work for the BBC. On Sunday May 4th, I took one of my eldest brother's cars, he had several, most of them stolen, and set off for Leysdown, pearl of Kent. I had no driving license and no insurance. I had been driving "illegally" for about a year. I had been stopped by two police motorbike riders in Leyton earlier in the year. They asked me where I would like to produce my documents, I told them that Limehouse Police Station would be convenient for me, knowing full well that I had no documents to produce. I had seven days in which to report to the Police Station. I walked into Limehouse Police Station on the third day, and shuffled nervously to the counter, a constable was there, looking down at paperwork, he did not look up when I said,

'I have come to show my documents.'

Before I could continue, the constable, still not looking up at me said,

'Yes, we have been waiting for you, now sod-off and think yourself lucky.'

The constable in question was none other than one of my old George Green school mates, whom, for obvious reasons I cannot name. The constable told me that he had nothing there appertaining to my incident. In fact, he had destroyed the paperwork when it had come in from the Leyton cops. No computers in those days on which to record everything just, good old bits of paper.

It took me about five hours to find Leysdown. I had never driven outside of London before. It should have taken about 90 minutes. I had simply forgotten to take my sat nav. I drove, without documents until I was 27 years old, I had over twenty cars during that time but never got stopped again. I even managed to sell my brothers mini to someone in Sheerness, as he had told me it was too hot to bring back to London.

Arriving, late Sunday afternoon at one of the two bungalows in Leysdown that were owned by Billy, I was greeted by John Long, I had never met John before, but I had heard of him, he was generally known as "Long John," so named, as one of his legs were missing, cruel but funny. John had hopscotched to the door as he had taken his right leg off as it had begun to chafe his thigh. John informed me that everyone else had gone to the Kings Club for Sunday lunch and that they were unlikely to return until after midnight. I did not fail to notice the stuffed parrot that stood, proudly, upon the mantle-piece.

I asked Long John why he had not gone along with the others, he replied that he was a bit pissed off with them because whenever they all went out, they would all be paralytic when they got back and when he fell asleep his leg would disappear. One morning he had found it, way up on the washing line in the back garden, everyone else had gone to work but he could not reach high enough up the pole to untie the rope and was therefore basically stranded. Poor sod I thought, although this did not stop me from burying his leg in the sand on Leysdown beach one Sunday afternoon.

Anyhow, I made him get ready and go with me to the Kings Club. We arrived at about 7.00 pm, the place was heaving, full of East End holiday makers, it was like home from home. The very first person that I noticed was one of the cab drivers from Mile End, he was known as "Chunky", yes, he was a fat, bald headed little git. He had previously told me that he only saw his wife and kids on Sunday's. Now he must have racked up a whole load of brownie points as he was spending a whole week (or more) with them, or was he? What do you want to drink he shouted, he had to shout as Alan Price was belting out "The House That Jack Built" a big hit for him in, 67. I took the pint from Chunky, he wandered over to his wife and kids, Long John pointed to the other side of the dance floor, towards an eight seater table and there sat half a dozen blokes, one or two of them I already knew, the majority I had never met before, but I had heard of them. There was Dennis Hampton, I had previously nicknamed him "Precious" as he laughed, in exactly, the same way as the cartoon dog. Next to him was Colin Scales, the raving poof, who dressed like an undertaker and had the limpest of handshakes, these were the two people that I already knew. Colin had been the manager for the first four weeks of the season, but I was now about to dispose him of that job. His nickname would become "Alf Alpha" due to his plastered down black hair, a few strands of which always pointed up to the sky. Long John introduced me to Keith Morgan, whom from that moment was always to be known as "The Captain". Morgan was more bent than Colin, and I wondered if the two of them were "at it" in the Bungalow. Alan Everett, a young version of Jimmy Saville, had his hand right up a fifty-year-old woman's dress. Sat next to Alan was David Francis, he so resembled Barney Rubble from the Flintstones, I was so surprised that no one had seen it before. David had now become "Barney". Making up the eight-permanent staff was the real weirdo of the group, Peter Fawkes, he already had a nickname, it was "Guy", I had no idea why. Guy was twenty-two stone, he constantly perspired, he always had sweat marks under his arms and stank like a skunk. However, he was a lovely bloke and good to have around whenever it kicked off in the shop. I had to move him from my bungalow to the one next door after we run out of air freshener. This was all eight of us, Long John, Precious, the Captain, Jimmy Saville, Barney, Alf Alpha, Guy, and me. God knows what they called me. We would be living and working together for the next four months. On Saturdays, our ranks would be added to, as three or four additions from London would arrive to cope with the sheer volume of business. I had the job, at just eighteen years of age of controlling this lot, it was not going to be easy.

I was introduced to Mr. King, he was the owner of the club and the single biggest punter that Massey's Leysdown had. The King's Club was a top venue back in the 60's and early 70's, on a par with the Circus Tavern in Essex. It attracted well known acts, such as Alan Price, Georgie Fame, Dusty Springfield, Madeline Bell, The Drifters, Tommy Cooper, and many others. Believe it or not, these household names lived in caravan's, within the grounds of the club. The captain, being the most extrovert of us, virtually had a free run of the club and was a regular visitor, after hours, to the temporary abodes of most of the acts. A few weeks after starting my stint as the youngest betting shop manager in the UK, the Captain told me that we were invited back to Danny La Rue's van after his show. What I saw within the confines of this caravan cannot be told in detail and I have resisted all further invitations.

46 - Leysdown (Part 2)

On Monday May 5th, 1969, I was woken by a red cheeked, plump, jolly lady. She had come into my bedroom, uninvited, to ask me what I wanted for breakfast. I did not do breakfast then and still do not partake today.

'I would just like some tea and biscuits,' was my reply.

'You cannot go all day without any food in your stomach, I am cooking a full breakfast, and you will jolly well eat it,' was the fat lady's response.

My god, this was like being at home, I thought.

Whilst Mrs. Jones was cooking, I found the bathroom, there was a shower, I took one, got dressed and walked into the kitchen. At the ten-seater farmhouse table sat my staff, they were all shit-faced. The captain was missing and when I enquired as to his whereabouts the answer, I got, was that,

'He has probably stayed with Danny.'

'How nice,' I said.

I felt quite nervous, after all, I was the youngest of all the staff working at Leysdown and they would no doubt look at me and think that I was there to keep an eye on them, which according to Billy, I was. Half-way through breakfast, another equally rotund lady appeared,

'Hello, I am Mrs. Smith,' she informed me.

'You must be Mr. Lucas from Head Office?'

it all sounded so formal. I later found out that the others had been winding her up, telling her that she must address me as Mr. Lucas and that I was the adopted son of the boss and that I would be checking her cleaning, washing, and ironing. So, there we had it. The original "Smith & Jones" eat your heart out Mel & Griff.

Before I left for the shop, Mrs. Jones enquired as to whether we would be dining in or out that evening, everyone looked at me, as apparently it was left to me to decide.

'In,' I think,' was my response.

'OK' I will get some steak then.'

The subsequent mornings would always be the same, but half of the time that Mrs. Jones went shopping for the evening dinner we never turned up as we had been invited to the Kings Club or we had earnt enough cash on the side to go there anyway. I much preferred eating at the Kings as Mrs. Jones cooking was shit, almost as bad as my mum's! Our two ladies would split the food that we never ate.

At 9.30 am, on the first day that I was to oversee the running of this ultra-busy gambling den seven of us made our way across the high street and into the shop, it was just 100 yards away from the two bungalows. Upon reaching the shop door, Precious handed me the keys and said,

'They are all yours now, boss.'

The inside of the shop was massive, about eight times larger than the interior of Mile End. In fact, on some afternoons there were more people in the shop than there were at a Leyton Orient home game. The counter was long and consisted of six tills, with five cameras sandwiched in between. There was a platform, with steps, to one side, these gave access to the chalk board, this took up the entire length of the counter area. The staff took it in turns to write up the results during racing. Unfortunately for me, Alf Alpha had to sit next to me in the back room as he was my "second settler". Every betting office in the UK had a sound system and this had to be turned on first thing in the morning, as announcements would be made in respect of the afternoons racing. At Leysdown they had added a microphone, for crowd control. A radio would be placed in front of the microphone and music would be played over the sound system, right up unto racing started. This was the only shop that ever did this, it created a party mood, and the punters loved it, after all, they were all on holiday. The back room, where four of us would continually work out bets on Saturdays, was enormous, bigger than most shops that I had worked in. There were two toilets, a kitchen area, a sofa and two chairs, four high back-office chairs for the staff, mountains of betting slips, pens, pencils, film for the camera and two spare tills. You could have lived there, and on some weekends, some of our invited friends would do just that. The back door of this room opened out onto a courtyard, beside which was the beer garden of the Rose and Crown Pub. Only a narrow alleyway separated the betting shop and the pub. At 10.00 am, when we officially opened the door to the public there was already a queue outside. There were no women amongst the large crowd of men. It would become clear to me, over time, that the men, on holiday with their families, would have breakfast at one of the holiday camps, leave the wife and kids to amuse themselves whilst they made their way to, firstly the betting shop and then at 11.00 am to the "Rose and Crown". On most days, the women and children would simply not see their other half's until after racing had finished, around 5.30 pm.

From the time we opened the door, at 10.00am, and until the first race of the day, there was a constant stream of punters, each one probably gambling more than they should have. If you were to walk into the Rose and Crown at mid-day, then you would recognise almost every patron as having been in the betting shop earlier. At 2.00 pm the first race of the day would be under way. I would estimate that there were over 100 punters in the shop. At 2.20 pm the first cartridge from one of the cameras was placed on the desk in front of me. It was my job to change the film and return it to its respective slot by the side of a till. The mountain of betting slips upon my desk was overwhelming and Alf Alpha had simply disappeared. The staff were already waiting for me to settle winning bets as impatient punters wanted to withdraw their winnings in order that they could lose it all on the next race. It took me a full fifteen minutes to return the cartridge to the camera, and in the meantime, firstly Precious and then the captain had deposited some money into a cardboard box at the edge of my desk.

'What's that money for?' I asked Precious, as he arrived with even more betting slips.

'That's our night out dosh guv,' he replied.

By the end of the day there would be over £45.00 in the cardboard box. I believed this cash was "tips" from punters that had won a few quid. In fact, this was the proceeds of winning bets, struck by the staff whilst the film was out of the camera. It was easy, just ring up a blank betting slip and fill it in after the race as there was no camera to record it at the time that it was taken. This happened every single day. Other scams constructed by the staff was the paying out of unclaimed winning bets. How did this work? Well, if a winning bet stayed in the pigeon-hole for a few days without being claimed then it was safe to assume that the punter who had struck the bet was either too pissed to remember which horse he had backed, or his holiday was over, and he had gone home. There were no duplicates in those days, the punter simply received a ticket when placing his bet, therefore the onus was on him to remember what he had backed. Having identified such a bet, the staff would simply place a blank betting slip on top of the unpaid bet and trace what was underneath, this was deemed to have been enough proof to pay-out a punter that had lost his ticket. It was as simple as that. On average, we managed to generate about £300 per week for the drink's kitty. On Saturdays, when additional staff were there, great care was taken to ensure that those people never knew what was going on. Misdemeanours were never committed if one of Billy's relatives happened to be there. When it was hot, the back door was always open, and punters would simply wander in with trays of drinks for us, it was nothing to have drunk four to five pints during the afternoon. I was always amazed that we never got held up as each time any till was full of money the staff had to count it into bundles of £100 and bring it to the back and place it on my desk. Most times it would just be thrown in and would end up on the floor, I was far too busy to gather it up. Any visiting punter to the back room could simply have shot us and legged it with the money,

When the shop finally shut at 6.30 pm, it was a mess. Two cleaners would come in and sweep everything up. Once they had gone, the next scam would come into operation. In the pigeon-holes, there would be several winning bets that had not been collected. As I have already said, it was rare for winnings not to be collected almost as soon as the race was over. All the tickets that were on the floor were now nestling in a large bin. Six staff examined each ticket to see if any of them belonged to any of the winning bets. Almost every day one or more winning tickets would, be found, on Saturdays sometimes several. The ticket would be stapled to the winning betting slip and the amount of winnings would go into the kitty. This was very much our day-to-day life. We, the eight-permanent staff, would eat, drink, and live like King's, never paying anything out of our own pockets. Most nights we would start drinking in the Rose and Crown and then go onto dinner and more booze at the King's. We saw some memorable acts and some not so memorable as well. Each Saturday, after racing, I would get the call from TB,

'How much are you sending?' he would ask.

Sometimes it would be as much as £5,000 (£100,000 today). I would be asked if I could drop it off at Billy's or Harry Rosie's. This was no big deal for me as I always returned home on a Saturday night in order that I could go out with my mates. Billy lived in a mansion at Abridge, Essex. In 1983 his house was sold for £1 million. He bought another one for £1.5 million. I much preferred going to Billy's with the money as he always gave me £50.00, Harry Rose gave me sod all. Billy once asked me if Harry had given me a tip, when I told him no, he was furious. Apparently, Harry had been pocketing my bonus himself. My new-found lifestyle continued in much the same way through to July when the famous five, John Duggan, Joe 90, Herbie, Brother John, and myself, headed off to Cattolica. I returned to Leysdown after my holiday and remained there until the end of August. If I could choose one period of my working life to replicate, it would be the time I spent at Leysdown.

The 'Beach' at Leysdown-on-Sea

47 - The Shotgun

For the first two weeks of September 1969, "Bad Moon Rising" by Creedence Clearwater Revival, topped both the UK and USA charts. I was seconded to the racing room, as manager, during Rosie's two-week vacation, which, on this occasion, he had decided to spend at Belsen, simply to tread in the footsteps of his forefathers. Leysdown had been left in the capable hands of just one man, he was Wally, from the shop in Sheerness. All Wally had to do was open from 10.00 am until 1.30 pm, take what few bets there would be and then drive back to Sheerness, where the winning bets would be worked out by the manager there. Wally would take the winning bets back to Leysdown the following day and pay them out to their respective winners. Masseys had to keep the Leysdown shop open every day, albeit for just a few hours, otherwise they risked losing their License. Every book-making firm in the UK was looking to get a License at Leysdown, none ever did. After racing had finished on my first Monday back at Head Office, the old man, shovel nose, who was never allowed into the racing room whilst Billy, his son, was there, was looking out of the window into Alie Street, when a brand-new Ford Capri Ghia pulled up, and out stepped none other than Alan Everett, alias Jimmy Saville. Old shovel nose could not contain himself,

"Where the fuck did that bastard get that brand new car from?"

His old and lined face turning as red as Arsenal's shirts. Looking at me, he then said,

'You have been at Leysdown with him, has he been nicking money?'

Now I knew the real story behind Jimmy's new car, his dad was a car dealer, he would have wiped the floor with Arthur Daley. Jimmy's dad had got the car for him, through the trade, however Jimmy's take from the scam's at Leysdown was nearly a grand and having a dad as a car dealer was a bloody good cover story. Alf Alpha had bought a racehorse with his cut, yes, a real thoroughbred which won its first three races at Fontwell Park. We all made a nice few quid from backing this horse, named by the gay boy as "Lamb Chop". I had come away from my four-month stint by the sea with nearly £1,500, this equated to one and a half years salary. Did I want to be at Leysdown in the summer of 1970? Only an ingrowing toenail would stop me.

I spent the rest of 69 managing a brand-new shop, this shop was not under the Massey brand, the sign on the outside read, Terry Bishop, Bookmakers. There were two other additions during this year, they were both called H J

Rose Bookmakers, all three were owned by Billy and Peter but under other names for tax purposes.

The shop I managed for the next four months was in Hackney, it was tough. One afternoon a disgruntled West Indian punter came in with a very nasty Alsatian Dog, which he lifted over the glass of the counter, the dog promptly sank its teeth into the leg of Jack Beanstalk, a giant of a man, Jack was off work for six weeks. The police came, and then the fire brigade, the ambulance service and finally some old ladies from the Women's Institute. The dog, aptly named 'muncher' was destroyed. Legend has it that its West Indian owner was also destroyed, as he was never seen in Hackney again. On boxing day 1969, "Two Little Boys" by the now known pervert, Rolf Harris was the Christmas number one. On this day at 6.00 pm, I was alone in the shop, waiting for the clock to strike 6.30 when a young man, sporting a black balaclava and holding a sawn-off shot gun presented himself to me as I was sweeping the shop floor. The shotgun was placed firmly against my temple, the gunman was shaking. I asked him not to be silly, he kicked me, told me to get behind the counter and pull out the telephone wires. Now I had never attempted to pull telephone wires from their socket before and the old-fashioned telephones were extremely difficult to dislodge, I never managed to do it. By then, my would-be assassin was also behind the counter, he had opened the till and was disappointed to find only a tenner and some loose change in there. I explained to him that the days winnings had been taken to Head Office over an hour ago, he did not seem to believe me. By now I was getting very anxious as he wanted money, and I did not have it to give to him. He made me turn out my pockets, I had about £35.00 which he took and then scarpered out of the door. I watched him disappear down the road. I rang 999, the police arrived about five minutes later. I was asked as to how I was getting home and when I told them by car, they duly turned my car over, despite me having told them that shotgun man had only nicked my own money. From that day on it became company policy that two men had to be in every shop until closing time. I was not offered any counselling or time off. Back then, men were men. Six weeks later, a man with a shotgun was arrested during a bungled robbery at a William Hill shop in Dalston, I was asked to attend an identity parade. Eight men were lined up in Dalston Police Station and I was asked to "walk down the line". What any of the nice officers had failed to realise, until I pointed it out to them, was that,

'He was wearing a black balaclava", so how the hell,' could I pick him out?"

To my great surprise, two days later I had to go back to the Police Station, eight men were again lined up, this time they were all wearing balaclava's. Now I was only eighteen years old, but I had a bloody good idea that I would not be able to identify the hooded man who may have snuffed me out that day. This would not be the only time that a shotgun was held to my head. I just seemed to attract men with guns.

48 - The First Football Dance

By January 1970, I was still a massively overweight seventeen and a bit stone, a legacy of my days working at the head office. My trousers were enormous, the tale of the tape showed my waist to be a bulging forty-four-inches. I was drinking up to ten pints of beer a night, my brother John normally drank a lot more than me, but he was quite a normal size. All those years of drinking and eating three meals a day had taken their toll. I had not been able to play football since I was fifteen, now I was approaching nineteen years of age and my brothers and friends were all playing on Saturdays and Sundays, and I could only stand and watch. Something had to be done, and only I could make it happen. There were no weightwatchers or alternatives for overweight fat gits like me. I decided that I would cut out drinking altogether and that I would not have a whole packet of biscuits for breakfast or lots of snacks during the day. I would eat only fishfingers or filet steak for dinner. My brother John was now working in Leadenhall meat market, and he got me all the filet steak that I could eat. My mum kept cooking me dinners, I kept leaving them. One evening at home, mum had had enough, she had cooked liver, sausage, and mash for the whole family, when I refused it, she whacked me hard on top of the head with the copper-bottomed frying pan. I was out cold on the kitchen floor, my mum was beside herself, which is very difficult to do, as she thought she had killed me. She never cooked me another dinner for some eighteen months.

My friends just thought that my self-induced dieting was a passing phase and that I would soon start drinking again, how wrong they were. I would only drink orange squash. I drank pints of the stuff and I used to spend half of the night getting rid of it. My goal was to be able to resume playing football when the new season began in September 1970. Being, a born organiser, I formed the basis of a team from my close friends and two of my brothers. We added a cousin and two ex-professionals, old school chums, that had played for Orient and QPR, but had never quite made it. I went to see Wally Reardon, the landlord of the Aberfeldy Pub and informed him that he would need to come up with some dosh in order that we could rent a pitch for a whole season, buy a brand-new kit and some footballs. He asked what was in it for him, I explained that all the players and supporters would come back to his pub after the game on Sunday's and that his takings would improve drastically. The tight sod, whose trouser pockets had been sewn up, declined. Now I could have funded the whole thing myself, but I thought why, do that, as I could just go and play

A Life Like No Other

for another club and not have any of the aggravation of running a team myself. I then came up with the idea of putting on a dance, to raise money to cover the expense of running a football team.

With the help of my dad, I managed to get St. Nicholas church hall in Aberfeldy Street, they waived the fee as my dad had given his time to them free of charge when they needed music at a couple of functions, we were rolling. I sat down and did the maths. If we charged £5.00 per ticket and sold 150 tickets, our revenue would be £750.00, easy, that one. We would get all the beer from the pub without Reardon's knowledge. We would have bottled beer and kegs of draught all we would then need was the gas and fittings to keep the beer nice and cold. We would buy the spirits and mixers from Makro, my dad had a van, therefore the logistics were quite easy. Dad would be the DJ, so this would cost zilch. At the time, my mum was working as a caterer in the city, and she would commandeer some of her colleagues to sort out the food. We would require three to four bar staff, several people volunteered when I let it be known that they could drink all night, in lieu of salary. This was known as community spirit, the East End loved a knee's up, and so many people were willing to chip in.

I had now signed up thirteen players and I told each of them that they would have to take ten tickets, I was confident that I could easily sell the remaining twenty myself. For the £5.00 entry fee, there would be unlimited drink and unlimited food. There would be shellfish available from the fish man that had a stall outside the pub at weekends, this was included within the £5.00. The date was set, the dance would take place on Saturday 25th April 1970. All 150 tickets were sold, well in advance of the dance. We therefore had no cashflow problems. I had booked the day off via TB, but unfortunately at 9.30 on the morning of the dance TB phoned me at home and insisted that I came in as Rosie's father had, passed-away, the previous night, and Rosie was needed, as it was, he, as the eldest Son that would be extracting all his dad's gold teeth. Billy would not let anyone else take control of the racing room. He agreed that I could go into work at 1.00 pm and leave straight after racing finished, I left it to my dad to organize everything until I got back from work, so I had no real worries. On the 25th, April 1970 at 7.30 pm, our first football dance was under way. "Back Home" by the England World Cup Squad was at number one and I can assure you that it got played several times during that successful evening. My weight was down to thirteen and a half stone. We made a profit of just over £300, which was more than enough to pay all the expenses of Aberfeldy FC, for the coming season.

Aberfeldy FC (1971-72) showing off their brand-new strip – There are three sets of brothers here. I am the one with the long beige coat (third from the left).

49 - Nijinsky

I had now started to gamble heavily. Being a bookmaker, I should have known better, but the buzz and the ease with which I could gamble was far too attractive. In 1970 the single most famous horse in the world was, Nijinsky. Trained by Vincent Price and ridden by Lester Piggott. I had almost adopted Nijinsky.

After being undefeated as a two-year old in 1969, Nijinsky was entered, into all three English Classic Horseraces. The 2000 Guineas at Newmarket, The Epsom Derby, and the St. Ledger at Doncaster. Collectively these three races were known as the "Triple Crown". No horse had won the "Triple Crown" since 1935. Nijinsky had won his first race as a three-year old at the Curragh, in Ireland, in a canter. Next on the schedule was the 2000 guineas at Newmarket, in April 1970. I placed my single largest bet, (at the time) of £600 at 4/6. I did not have the money, I simply rang up the bet in Massey's shop at Victoria, which I was managing for a week. I would take £400 from the till should he win. He won, unchallenged. I now had £400 in my Nijinsky kitty. On Derby Day in June, I wagered £400 at odds of 6/4. I believed that this horse would never lose. The wonder horse did the honours for me. My Nijinsky kitty had risen to £1,000. To put that into perspective, it was roughly a year's salary. Three weeks after winning the Epsom Derby, Nijinsky would run in the Irish Derby at the Curragh. The odds were 4/11, I had to add £100 of my own money to strike the bet. I wagered £1,100 to win just £400. The result was never in danger, Nijinsky by two lengths, un-extended. I now had £1,500 in the pot. To everyone's surprise Nijinsky was to run in the King George and Queen Elizabeth Stakes at Ascot in July. The King George is a race for horses of all ages and the "greatest" was to take on former, older Derby winners. There was concern amongst some of his connections that this race was much too soon after the winning of two Derby's. I also had my doubts, I did not back Nijinsky that day, I was punished for this, as he won without ever being pushed. Next up came the St. Ledger, the final race in the triple crown trilogy. Nijinsky was bidding for his tenth straight win. Should he win the St. Ledger he would surely be known as the best racehorse ever. His value at stud would be colossal, unprecedented. I bet the whole £1,500 at 1/3. I would only win £500. There was never a moment that I thought I was going to lose. Nijinsky duly obliged and was now being touted as the "greatest." My one-horse kitty now stood at £2,000. After winning ten straight races, Nijinsky was sold by his owners for USD 5.44 million. Thirty-two individuals paid USD 170,000 each for just one

A Life Like No Other

share in him. It now made no difference to his stud value, should he race again and lose. In October 1970, Nijinsky was to run in the Prix de Arc de Triomphe at Longchamp in Paris. His opponents would be some of the World's greatest racehorses. Before the race, his jockey, Lester Piggott, had made it known that he thought that "the Arc" could be one race to far for him, adding that having won ten of the most prestigious races available to him, he should be retired. The owners did not agree, and Nijinsky took his place in the starting line-up. Whilst I had my reservations, I could not see anything in the field beating him. I placed my bet, £700 at 4/7. I would only win £400 but it seemed like easy money to me. With two furlongs to race Nijinsky produced his trade-mark sprint finish, he went past the leader Sassafras and looked to have the race sewn up, but somehow Sassafras managed to get her head back in front on the line. Nijinsky had lost by a few inches. I had lost £700. The race was on a Sunday, we were watching it at home. My mum, hidden behind the sofa, was crying, my dad made the tea. I said,

'Oh well, all good things must come to an end.'

I still had £1,300. Nijinsky was to run one more time, in the Champion Stakes at Newmarket, in November. This time, Lester Piggott was joined by his trainer, Vincent O'Brien, in publicly voicing their opinion, that they thought the greatest had done enough and that he should not run. The owners had a different opinion. I did not back him that day, he lost to Lorenzacio, a horse he would have beaten "out of sight" a few months earlier. Nijinsky went off to Kentucky and made love to hundreds of horses for the next fifteen years or so. His stud fee was more than USD100,000 a time. He sired over 150 Group One winners and remains the only horse ever to sire Epsom and Kentucky Derby winners. Nijinsky was, "Sports Personality of the Year" in 1970, showing how highly he was regarded amongst the sporting public. Sadly, he was Euthanised in 1992 at the age of 25. There have been others since that have laid claim to being, the greatest racehorse of all time, however if you watch his races on YouTube, you might find it hard to agree with that. Nijinsky bought me a brand-new Ford Cortina 1600E, six months later, I lost it, after just three months, gambling of course.

50 - Job Offer

At the end of June 1970, I informed my newly assembled players that football training would begin in late July, and this would take place at Victoria Park, Bow. I had successfully applied for entry into the Hackney and Leyton Sunday League, which consisted of six divisions. Being a newly formed club, we were told that we would start life in division six. I managed to convince Roy Janes, a former coach at Orient to take charge of the training for us, in return, he could play, should he wish to. He was very keen and subjected our players to a fitness regime that, apart from the two-former pro's that had signed for us, they could not have imagined was possible. At this point I knew that I, myself would not be taking part in matches. My weight, by the time training began in July had fallen to eleven and a half stone, a loss of six stone in just six months. I could not sustain a run. I had no stamina. All my efforts had been based on the hope that I would be able to play in the team that I had formed, it was not to be, I was stuck with being a manager.

Just prior to the commencement of training, the famous five returned to Cattolica. I was as skinny as I ever would be. I resumed drinking and I was sick. I stopped drinking. I met a girl, in fact she was about as old as my mum, so not really a girl. I was nineteen and a bit, I had never had time for a girlfriend, neither did any of my mates or my brother John. This woman came from Streatham in South London, a totally alien neighbourhood as far as an East Ender was concerned. When I showed her photograph to, Ray Puxley, he named her "Nijinsky", after my hero. In fact, the champion racehorse was better looking than her. I went, just the once to Streatham, after we had returned from Italy. The girl, Ethel, lived with two friends in a stable on a run-down council estate, I turned up, well dressed, thinking we would be going out for the evening. In fact, I was given a pair of overalls that must at one time have belonged to Cyril Smith and was asked to join in with the painting of the stable walls. I left at around 10.30 pm, never to return. Whenever I watch horse racing on the TV I almost always think of that girl.

Although I did time at Leysdown during the summer of 1970, it was not permanent, and Johnny Young had been installed as manager. He was Billy's wife's relative, and always seemed to be installed into a shop where the staff were under suspicion of being dishonest. Young could not work out bets and was therefore managing the counter staff. I was told by both Precious and the Captain that the scope for making money on the side had diminished considerably. I knew however that at the end of the season Mr. Young had purchased for himself a nice little permanent home on a site at Whitstable. I always wondered as to how he was able to afford a second home.

Just before Christmas 1970, I was summoned to Head Office by TB. Entering TB's office, I was quite taken aback. Present were Billy, Peter White, TB, and Jim Rainbird. My heart sank, I believed I was in big trouble. I had been betting large sums of money by this time and I thought that Bob White had bubbled me for this. Nothing of the sort, in fact I was asked if I would take a job as assistant to TB, job title, "assistant general manager". I was just nineteen years old. It was explained to me that I would only be answerable to TB, Rosie would be below me and that I could even tell the old man to "fuck off", if I so desired. TB told me that I was the one person within the firm that had covered almost every position and as such was the most knowledgeable and that there was no one else being considered for the job. Even though I was a more than confident nineteen-year-old I could not muster the words that were needed to ask about salary. I did not have to wait long before Jim Rainbird told me that I would receive £35.00 a week. This was £12.50 more than my current salary. Whilst it seemed great to have been offered more than a 50% pay rise, I would not be able to bet, and I would no longer be able to supplement my income by other means. Most weeks I was clearing over £60.00, via foul play. At the end of the discussion, I asked if I could think about the offer and let them know, they agreed.

Three days later I informed TB that I did not want to take the job as I had fought long and hard to get away from the Head Office and I really did not want to end up at a desk all day. He understood, adding that Billy would be quite upset as he wanted me to take over from him (TB), one day in the future. This could be deemed to be one of those "corners", where I should have taken the other route, instead I chose not to. My future years at Massey's would surely have been a lot different had I taken this job offer. On the bright side Dave Edmunds with "I hear you knocking" was at the top of the charts.

Aberfeldy FC had enjoyed a monumental start to their first season in Division Six of the Hackney and Leyton League. We had played eleven games and had won them all. I had been a player manager but had never kicked a ball in anger. One of the patrons of the Aberfeldy was a strange man who went by the name of Alan Straughn, he was also the Chairman of the East London Floodlight Football League, a seven a side league that played its matches at night-time on Mondays through to Thursdays. One evening in February 71 Straughn asked me if I would be interested in entering a team into his league for season 1971-72, I stated an interest, and he subsequently gave me an application form. Our application was successful, and we were put into Division Two, the first game would be in September 1971.

Once again, I needed to raise money, another football dance was pencilled in for April 1971. Most of the players for the pending midweek games would be the ones that were playing on Sunday. When I announced that we would be holding another dance, several of the players asked if they could have twenty tickets each. Such was the success of our previous function, that it looked as though we could double the number of sales to around 300. The church hall in Aberfeldy Street would be too small. My dad had done the disco at a wedding at Vernon Hall in Bow and had got to know the manager, he drove over to see him and was able to get us this hall, which could hold 300+ people for just £50.00. The hall was booked for the 10th, April1971, the Saturday after Good Friday.

In the summer of 1970 the former British & Commonwealth Heavyweight Boxing Champion, Henry Cooper visited Aberfeldy Street, he was there to open a new betting shop and whilst there he was enticed into the Aberfeldy. I managed to snap this photo. I am sure there a few people still around that will recognise themselves.

Henry Cooper at the Aberfeldy, summer 1970.

51 - The Kent Arms, North Woolwich

By March 1971, the month of my 20th birthday, my life was a constant roller-coaster, I cannot remember ever staying in and watching TV with my family, I was always out. On the evening of the second week of March I was playing cards in the Aberfeldy when Pete Dillion, a former relief manager of the pub that was almost my second home asked me if I would be interested in bringing my disco gear over to his pub in North Woolwich, the pub in question was known as the Kent Arms, apparently it was already notorious for a certain type of clientele, however my brother John and myself had never heard of it, we tended to stay well clear of the notorious Custom House area of East London. Initially Mr. Dillion wanted us for Thursday nights only, this suited us, as the disco gear was only being used Friday – Sunday in the Aberfeldy. Our opening night would be on Thursday 25th, March, three days after my birthday. I managed to get away from work in time to help load up my dad's van, the poor sod was always doing something for us. We headed off to North Woolwich at 6.30 pm and were set up by 7.15. The Kent Arms was one of those, big, imposing buildings, with high ceilings and Del Boy chandeliers. We were going to be playing our records in a large room known as "the cave". The cave had been purpose built, it was formerly the public bar, but now the inside really was like a cave that had been made from Paper-Mache, painted black, with thousands of small twinkle lights embedded into it. The bar was "retro style" with a stainless-steel top, it was lit by those blue florescent strip lights that made it look as though you had dandruff when stood underneath.

It was noticeable that there were only a couple customers at the main bar when we first entered, brother John said that our days could be numbered, I could not disagree with his observation. At 7.30 we played our first record in the "cave", we had to use a torch to see the titles on the records, it was that dark. The first ever song to belt out over our very loud sound system was the number one single of the previous month, "My Sweet Lord" by George Harrison, followed by "No Matter What" sung by Badfinger. We should have played "Silent Night" as there was nobody present to appreciate what we were playing. Half-way through Badfinger, a stream of people entered the cave.

"Where did all these queers come from" asked Brother John.

I had been, knelt, with my back turned, trying to read the title of the next single to be played at the time and had therefore not seen them troop into the bar. A bloke wearing a tight, Pink T-Shirt and matching pink leather trousers came over to us and said, in the most effeminate voice I had ever heard,

'Hello ladies, I am Raymond, Mr. Teasy-Weasy,'

My brother withdrew, picking up a small club hammer that our dad had given to us, "just in case". I heard John mutter under his breath,

'If you come anywhere near me, you will get this on your bonce.'

The suspect looking hairdresser looked at me and said,

'Who rattled his cage?'

We knew of Mr. Teasy-Weasy, he was probably the most famous hairdresser in the world at the time. Vidal Sassoon worked for him and although Vidal was not present that evening, he did "join the party" on subsequent occasions.

'Anytime you want your hair doing properly, just come and see me. I have a lovely little room above the salon in Mayfair.' I could feel my brother getting tense. Trying to diffuse the moment, I scanned the bar and then said to John,

'Look, that's Dusty Springfield over there.'

Dusty was clearly with a certain well-known black, female singer, in fact, we had some of her records with us and made a point of playing them. Lionel Bart stood at the bar, he was, of course a household name. There were other's that we recognised but could not fit names to. Mr. Teasy-Weasy was the first hairdresser in the world to have had his own TV show, he owned salons in Mayfair, Kensington, Soho, and other expensive locations around West London. In 1956, he had famously been flown out to the states to cut and blow-dry the hair of Diana Doors, it had reportedly cost the blond bombshell £2,500 or £70,000 in today's money. Some may remember that old Teasy-Weasy had been the owner of two grand national winners, Ayala in 1956 and Rag Trade in 1976, I personally had heard of him because of his equine connections. Lionel Bart had been born in Stepney, the son of a Jewish tailor, that specialized in the making of 24-hour suits. He had written many a musical, the most well-known of which was "Oliver", he had been known to have earnt and lost a fortune several times over. Lionel also wrote, "Livin' Doll" for Cliff Richard. During one of his lean spells, he had sold the rights in Oliver to Max Bygraves for £350. Max subsequently sold them on, to Rolf Harris, for £250,000.

Max needed to buy quite a lot of "Tulips from Amsterdam" at the time. Lionel Bart was made bankrupt in 1972 and died penniless in 1999, aged 69.

Now, it is not for me to cast aspersions or point fingers, however the clientele at the Kent Arms each Thursday night was very much of the gay variety. It was a well-known secret that Dusty and her fellow singing companion were a couple, Lionel was married, with children however he dressed and behaved in a manner which belied his public persona. One should remember that being a homosexual in public was still very much frowned upon by the public at large. Being homosexual at all was, in my opinion, quite scary at the time, my brother shared that opinion, we were concerned, but here we were, amid some of the gayest people in London. We were not happy. There was a large crowd of young men, under-age most of them, accompanying the older, more well-known men (and women). Some of these young studs would come over to us, put their arms around our shoulders and pretend to blow kisses at us. It amused me, but brother John could not handle it and would pick up the hammer until they moved away. They would request records that they could dance to, they were all fantastic dancers. We must have played, "Resurrection Shuffle" by Ashton, Gardner & Dyke at least ten times during that first night. "Ride a White Swan" and "Hot Love," both T-Rex classic was high on their request list, along with "When I'm dead and gone" by McGuiness Flint. This song had a certain meaning to them, we failed to understand why. As the weeks went by, the "cave" was attracting more and more people. Two coach loads, arranged by Teasy-Weasy, were now arriving every Thursday night. A circle of transvestites was now among the regular celebrities. One Thursday evening, our eldest brother came over to see all of this for himself, we watched as he chatted up one of the trannies at the bar, he really had no idea that, "she was he," he went for a leak, the trannie followed him. He came back from the loo, waved to us, and left. The trannie was carried from the loo and revived before taking up her/his position at the bar. Fights would be a regular occurrence amongst these normally gentle gay people, they were completely jealous of each other and would scratch, bite, and slap one another should one of them even look at another's young partner. We survived ten weeks before it all became too much for us, the police had served notice on the pub that its licence would be revoked unless these gatherings ceased. It transpired that Peter Dillion had not applied for a music licence. I have never revisited the Kent Arms in North Woolwich again. As an afterthought, we would play "Sweet Caroline" by Neil Diamond, nobody sang along. Fifty years later this song had become a worldwide anthem.

52 - Goodbye to Bookmaking

On Saturday, April 10th, 1971, our second football dance took place. All 300 tickets had been sold. This time the logistics of the venue, being three miles away from our home, proved to be a bit more challenging. We had to double the bar staff and this time we had to pay them. I was worried that with so many people we might attract "chancers", blokes that would turn up without tickets and say that they were with one of our players but did not have their ticket with them. I had to spend much of the evening stood at the door to weed out these non-payers. Most of those that had paid, turned up in groups together with the player that had sold them the ticket, however there were a few that did not. More than once, I had to call for my brothers to help eject those that were trying to gate crash. It was a long night, the dance finished at 1.00 am, mainly because there was still a lot of booze to be consumed. We had to bung the hall manager a few quid for the extended time, as officially we should have shut down at 11.30 pm. As they left, almost every patron that was still standing, came to me and told me what a wonderful night they had just had and how on earth were we able to provide so much for just a fiver. To be honest I never really knew the answer to that. We cleared £600, ensuring that I would not need to collect any monies from my players for the coming season.

For the third year running, I was again charged with booking our annual holiday. We had done Cattolica to death. This year it would be Arenal, Majorca. In 1971 there was an addition to the famous five, this was Steve Richardson. Steve was slightly younger than the rest of us and because of this he had not joined with us on our trips to Cattolica. He was now 18 years-old, and his mum said he could go.

In July 71, a major incident occurred in my life. I was once again the manager at Leysdown but had been summoned to the head office, for reasons unbeknown to me at the time.

On Monday July 11th 71, feeling rather worse for wear, after getting slaughtered at my brother Johns nineteenth birthday bash the night before, I arrived at the Head office. Before climbing the stairs, Ruggie took hold of my arm and said,

'Don't worry Son, I will look after you.'

I remember thinking, "what the hell" is going to happen to me? I went upstairs, expecting to meet with Billy, Peter, Harry, and old shovel nose. In fact, my relief must have been evident to TB and Micky Embrey (Micky had taken

A Life Like No Other

the job that I had been offered and subsequently turned down) as they were the only two people in the room. TB started the conversation,

'We know what is going on down there,' meaning Leysdown.

'Just tell us who is involved so that we can act and then you can go back tomorrow.'

They did not seem to think that I was involved, or were they being very cagey? I would never "grass" on anybody and since I was as guilty as anyone else, I just stuck to story, that I knew nothing of anything untoward happening in Leysdown. TB produced a large wad of betting slips, all were winning bets, all had been worked out by me.

'So, you do know that these bets were rung up after the race had finished?' I was asked.

'How would I know that? I am sat out the back and cannot see what is going on at the counter.'

'Well, we know that Hampton (Precious) Morgan (the captain) Long John and Everett (Jimmy Saville) are all ringing up blanks and putting them through and then getting punters to fill in the winner's'.

"Good God, I had no idea."

Now, for the first time, Micky Embrey spoke,

'Come on Son, we know, you might not be involved but you must have known?'

'There are no losing bets written out in this handwriting, this punter must be a bloody genius as he only backs winners.'

I remember thinking that this was a flaw in our system, I had told the lads many times to put through some losers, had they done so we would not now be exposed in this way. As I did not wish to be interrogated any further, I told them that I was walking. I got up from the chair, opened the door and walked down the stairs. As I entered the shop Ruggie said,

'Hold on, I'll walk back to your car with you.'

My answer to Ruggie was that he would have a long walk, as I had come by train.

We ambled, side by side, to Aldgate East Underground. I informed Ruggie, word for word what had happened, he told me to ring TB later and tell him that I was prepared to go back to Leysdown tomorrow.

'No, that's it, I have left.' I replied.

I did not return to Leysdown, after six years I was no longer in the employ of William Massey Bookmakers. One of the worst songs in living memory "Chirpy Chirpy Cheep Cheep" was at number one.

That evening Ruggie rang me at home, in his broad East End accent, he said,

'Alright son, I have sorted everything out, you are going to be a grocer'.

"What are you talking about.' I asked.

'Come and see me tomorrow night and I will explain.'

The following evening at 7.00 pm I knocked on Ruggie's door. Vikki, his gorgeous wife, whom I had fancied from the day that I first saw her, when just fifteen years old, answered. I would have taken Vikki away from Ruggie at the drop of a hat. Ruggie was forty, bald and had a long narrow nose, he was more like a cartoon character than a bloke, and he looked to be nearer to fifty. Vikki was blonde, vivacious, aged about thirty, but looked only twenty-two. I had continually fantasised about her, how on earth she had ended up with Johnny Rugg I could never understand. Twenty years later, I still wanted to take her away. I was shown into the living room, Vikki went and slipped into something more comfortable and came back and placed her right nipple into my mouth. There I go, fantasising again. Looking around the Rugg's living room I got the feeling that his meagre salary would not have paid for the quality furniture and fittings that were so evidentially expensive. I concluded that Ruggie was also "at it", and right under the gaze of every-one at head office. Ruggie began to explain,

'I know someone in wholesale grocery, you can buy from him.'

'I have a mate that has two stalls that he wants to sell, market licence included.'

'Good for you.'

To cut this story very-short, I was about to become a stallholder in both Roman Road and Whitechapel markets, in the heart of London's East End. Ruggie informed me that he was having the following week off, and that "we" would be able to get everything set up.

True to his word, the following Monday, Ruggie turned up at my mum and dads in a large, battered old van. We drove to Brighton and arrived at a massive "cash and carry" warehouse. I watched as Ruggie picked boxes of groceries from the shelves, two blokes carried and loaded them into the van. Once the van, which had no number plates, was fully loaded, we left. We drove back to Bow, London E3, arriving at a lock up at the back of a row of shops, the fronts of which were in Roman Road, one of the East End's largest markets. The two of us unloaded the contents of the van into the lock up and once finished, an hour or so later, we padlocked the lock-up door. There were two market stalls parked outside the lock-up,

'These are yours,' Ruggie announced.

I was lost, I felt vulnerable. For the last six years I had been cocooned in the sanctuary of William Massey Bookmakers, now I was having to fend for myself. The next day, Tuesday, was market day in Roman Road, Ruggie told me that he would pick me up at 6.30 am.

'Six thirty in the morning, are you barking mad, I don't normally get up until nine.'

"Those days are over, son.'

53 - Market Trader

At 6.30am on Tuesday 19th, July 1971, Johnny Rugg collected me from No. 5 Athenia House, Blair Street, Poplar. At 6.50 am, Ruggie opened the door of the lock-up that was located to the rear of the shops, in Roman Road. He then took out some terraced shelving and placed it onto one of the stalls, I then helped him to load at least one carton of everything that we had purchased the previous day onto each of the market stalls. I was still unaware of what would happen next. Ruggie then told me to start pulling one of the stalls, whilst he pulled the other. We left the area of the lock-up, I was struggling to pull my stall as it was now heavily loaded with goods, and I had never done a day's work in my previous twenty years of life. Thankfully, we were as close as we possibly could be to the two pitches that Ruggie had secured (on my behalf) and we parked up at the side of the road, right in front of Mr. Byrites clothes shop.

Momentarily, my mind wandered back to July 1966. My fellow truant, George Downey and I had both been employed by the owners of Mr. Byrites, they were twin brothers, both of Jewish extraction and both had yellow tinted skin. My mum said that they must have yellow jaundice. We had worked on Saturdays for these horrible look-a-likes since the beginning of June and were paid the princely sum od £1, ten shillings for giving them ten hours of our lives (8am – 6pm). We took the job's simply to get some spending money for our holiday, which would begin on world cup final day, the 30th, July 1966. On the 23rd, July, Portugal was playing North Korea in the quarter final of the world's most prestigious football competition. There was a small black and white TV upstairs, and the brothers were watching the game. The shop was void of customers. George and I quietly climbed the stairs and peered around the corner. Herman Levy caught us and marched us back down. There was still not a sole in the shop and North Korea were winning 3-0. We could hear the sound, Portugal, were staging a remarkable comeback but, still the brothers, who had missed the train to Belsen by just a couple of days, would not let us up to watch. Unbeknown to the "custard twins" as George had named them, we loaded about forty shirts into cardboard boxes, opened the back door and placed the boxes alongside the large pile of rubbish. At 6.05pm, having been dismissed for the day, we left the shop, walked around the back, and retrieved our stolen goods. We made more than enough for our holiday from the sale of

A Life Like No Other

the shirts to our friends and neighbours. We never returned to Mr. Byrites and we had given false addresses when we had started our employment with them.

As I stood dreaming of days gone by, I was rudely interrupted.

'Right' said my new boss.

'We have to unpack this lot and display it.'

From the handwritten message on the outside, the first carton that I unpacked indicated that it contained 24 cans of Smedley's peas. It did contain 24 cans however, there were no labels on any of them.

'Right' Ruggie had a habit of saying 'right' just before he barked out an order.

'Go to the van, get the paperwork, labels and pens.'

When I returned, Ruggie was a little perturbed,

'We have been well and truly had over' he exclaimed!

I thought, no, we have not been, had over, you have!

You see, none of the cans that Ruggie had unpacked had any labels on either, they were just shiny cans, half of which were dented. Before we could line them up neatly on the stalls, we had to mark the top of each can according to which carton they had come out of. When we had finished the display, at least fifty percent of the cans were label less. On the top of these cans, we wrote "Peas", "Beans", "Peaches", "Butter Beans", whatever it had said on the outside of the carton was what we wrote on the tops of the cans. In addition to the cans, we had biscuits, custard powder, peanuts, crisps, and a whole host of other groceries that you would expect to find on such a stall. We even had Sausage Rolls in a tin, neither of us had ever seen this before. There was just one can with a label, this showed that the contents were 6 Smedley's Sausage Rolls. The rest had labels that were plain white and printed around the middle of the can were the words, "Sausage rolls in a tin."

On these tins there was no indication as to whom had made them and no reference as to how many were inside. I took a tin home to my mum, she put the whole tin in, the oven. Twenty minutes later there was a loud bang as the tin hit the inside of the oven door. Thankfully, the oven door was not glass. The sausage rolls were quite nice. I took six tins home the following week and a further seventeen later, as we failed to sell a single tin to any of our beloved customers. On that first day as a market trader, I also had to work out how much we were going to charge for each item on the stall. I had no idea of how, to price-up groceries. I had never been grocery shopping and Ruggie was in the same boat. We had shot ourselves firmly in the goolies. We were totally unprepared, but this was Ruggie's way, everything he did was on impulse. I looked at the price sheet that we had got from the cash and carry in Brighton and tried to figure out how much we should mark up. As we both had no clue, we decided to add fifty percent to our cost price and see what happened. At 8.00 am we were officially open for business. We had overlooked many things, having change was one of them. Our very first customer spent 80p and gave me a £1.00 note. We did not have 20p to give to the kind old dear, she was reluctant to part with her pound unless we gave her the 20p. She took the £1.00 back from me and said she would change it up and come back with the right money. We never saw her again. As time went by, on that first day of being a "market trader", I learnt from Ruggie that on Tuesday's, Thursday's & Friday's I had to be at Roman Road and on Saturday's we transferred to Whitechapel market, which was about a mile and a half away. This meant that I had to go to Brighton on a Monday or Wednesday to purchase more stock. I asked Ruggie several questions,

'Why go all the way to Brighton to buy cans with no labels?'

'How do I get to Brighton, as the van had been borrowed from a mate and I only had a two-seater car.'

'How do I pull a fully laden stall from Roman Road to Whitechapel on my own?

'What are we going to do about our pricing as it was already quite apparent that most of our items were overpriced? Ruggie, a man that never ever got fazed, simply said,

'Right, don't worry, everything will be OK.'

I really did not want to be doing this business, but I now seemed locked into it.

That evening, after explaining everything to my dad, he said he would help where he could, until I could get things sorted. Later, I spoke to Brian Ellery (Herbie) on the phone, low and behold his dad had a Ford Thames Van that he wanted to see the back of. The Thames van was a tiny little thing, it would hold about twenty percent of what a transit could hold, but it would have to do, for now. That same evening my brother John announced that he had had a bust up with his boss at Leadenhall meat market and had left. Brother John was now going to help me pull the market stall to Whitechapel. I sat with my mum, and she guided me as to how much everything cost in a supermarket. Some of the items that had been bought from the cash and carry would only warrant a twenty percent mark-up, which would be more than useless, as far as profit margins were concerned. I rang my eldest brother and asked him where I could get a cheap transit van from. The next day he delivered one to me, stolen of course but fitted with fake number plates. No ANPR in those days. You could drive a stolen vehicle for years, with no problem, unless you were stopped. The next morning the transit van had vanished, big brother had taken it back as I had not immediately paid him for it. I took the underground to Upton Park and drove home in Herbie's dad's Thames's van. My dad told me of a cash and carry in Bow, I went there the following day. Everything was much cheaper

A Life Like No Other

than Brighton and it all had labels. They would even deliver to the lock up if we bought enough. We said goodbye to Brighton. On our first day of trading most of the old dears were asking for Anchor Butter, we did not have it. Again, dad to the rescue. He knew of a cold store, again in Bow. We visited and bought four cartons of Anchor Butter each carton contained forty-eight packs. By 3.00 pm on the second day of being a "barrow boy", we had sold just over two cartons of butter. When we reached under the stall at the end of the day, we found that eighty packs of butter had become two puddles of oil. Well, it was the middle of summer. Subsequent purchases of butter had to be executed based on actual demand.

Saturday, 23rd July arrived. Our first day of trading at Whitechapel, the market was known locally as "The Waste" and it certainly lived up to its name. It was a complete "waste of time". Brother John and I arrived at the lock up at 6.45am, after firstly collecting the butter. By now, Ruggie had excluded himself from further involvement. We loaded the Thames Van and the market stall. John pulled the stall out onto Roman Road and proceeded very slowly until we reached the Aberdeen Public house. I was in close attendance, holding up all traffic behind at about 5 mph. After crossing into the second part of Roman Road there is a bridge over the Regents Canal, this proved to be too much for John. I had to park the van at the side of the road, get out and run over to the back of the stall and push whilst John pulled. We managed to get over the bridge, but we were still only half-way to our destination. John, now on a flat stretch of road carried on pulling. I made my way back over the bridge, there was no van! In my haste, I had parked the van and left it running, keys still in the ignition and some "chancer" had taken it. Might have been my eldest brother, I thought. I sat on the kerbstone at the side of the road and briefly considered suicide by means of the river, which was just yards from where I sat. I quickly dismissed that idea as I could not swim.

In today's world, I could have rung the police, reported the theft and they would have reacted, well possibly. In 1971 there were no mobile phones, and I could not even remember the registration number of the little Thames Van. I had to accept that the van, the stock, the aprons, with the money in the pockets, and a lot of paperwork would never be found. They never were. I caught up with John, now sweating profusely in the July heat and helped push the stall to the waste. We still had half of the stock on the stall, this was the main reason that John could not get it over the bridge on his own. We arrived at our pitch at 8.15 and were promptly told off by the market inspector for being late. Just why he was so anxious about our time keeping I would never know as we did not have a single customer until 10.10. Our first half a dozen customers all wanted to buy Anchor Butter and that had disappeared with the van. At 1.00 pm I left John and walked into the Grave Maurice pub, as I knew that Ruggie would be in there to buy the ham sandwiches for Billy and the rest of the staff back at Massey's Head Office. How I wished I was still one of them. I explained to Ruggie what had happened and as usual he simply told me not to worry, he would come over on Sunday and sort everything out. So far, my only investment had been to buy the Thames Van. I paid Herbie's dad £50.00 for it. It was probably worth £25.00, what a shrewd geezer I was! The second-hand car business was not for me. Ruggie came over on Sunday morning and gave me £200, telling me that this was all that I was going to get. I paid John £20.00. So now we had to make it work, I felt obliged to get Ruggie his money back, even though it was not my idea to do this business.

54 - Back to Bookmaking

On Saturday August 14th, 1971, the gang of six left for Majorca. The two weeks we spent in Arenal were superb. We had thought that Cattolica was good, but Arenal was so much better. Steve Richardson was the new addition to our holiday gang. On the second day brother John and I took the mattress from his bed and threw it from his eighth-floor room, he struggled to get it back into the lift. John and I dangled him over the balcony by his ankles then John let go. I was left holding him by one foot as he screamed in desperation. We managed to get him back to safety, but he never let John and I back into his room. On the street touts were handing out vouchers for free drinks just to get people into the bars and discos. It was possible to get very drunk for nothing if using the vouchers correctly. We took a boat trip from Arenal to Palma, it cost £2.00 each. For this meagre sum, we were rewarded with food and drink on the boat and three free drinks when we arrived at Palma's newest and swankiest night-club. The entertainment that night was Johnny Johnson and the Bandwagon and James Brown. These were never to be repeated offers and we were all fortunate enough to have been, "in the right place at the right time".

During our time away, the market stalls did not trade, and this had noticeably affected business upon our return. We kept it going though. Summer turned to Autumn and then to Winter, the butter was no longer melting. On most Saturday's Micky Embrey, assistant to TB at my old firm, would accompany Ruggie on the sandwich run to the Grave Maurice. Each time Micky would come and see me at the stall along Whitechapel waste. Each time he would ask me to come back to Masseys. I wanted to return but felt that I had to keep going for Ruggies sake. By December it was all too much, I told Ruggie that I was, turning it in. He simply said,

'Right, no problem, don't worry about it.'

I agreed with Micky to go back to Masseys on the condition that they gave brother John a job, they did. He also told me that no one had been sacked in respect of the investigation at Leysdown, I did find that strange, after all, it was that very issue that had ended my employment. On Monday, 6th December 1971 I returned to Masseys as a relief manager. "Ernie" by Benny Hill was number one and remained there throughout December. Brother John was lucky enough to be given a job as a counter hand at Mile End, he loved it. Ruggie probably lost around £400 setting me up in business, soon after he bought a newsagent's, in Roman Road, which Vikki, his adorable wife ran. I would pop in from time to time and Vikki would give me a treat. Ruggie continued to work for Masseys. My dad did a lot of shop conversion work for him, for which he never got paid. I guess Ruggie felt it was, tit for tat, for the money that he had lost supporting me. I was back earning at Masseys, so I made sure my dad was OK.

Having won division six of the Hackney and Leyton League at our first attempt, Aberfeldy, my one and only Sunday football team, had been promoted to division one. Such was the demand by players old and new to take part in the midweek East London Floodlight League that I was forced to enter two teams. The "A" team would play in the first division, which was the top sector back in 71 and the "B" team was put into division three. It had been agreed with the league that the A and B teams would always play on different nights in order that I could be at every game. Soon I would be working six days a week. Running a Sunday football team and two other teams on Tuesday and Thursday evenings. All of this had to be funded and I started to think about the next football dance. By the Christmas break, all three teams were top of their respective leagues. In addition to the football, I was still doing the disco in the Aberfeldy every Sunday night and filling in for my dad on a Saturday if he had a wedding, birthday, or anniversary to do elsewhere. By now we had two sets of disco equipment. Whilst working in the Masseys shop at Ludgate Hill, I had seen a Pioneer 'state of the art' stereo amplifier, it cost me £300, (six-grand in today's, marketplace). It was fantastic and made life so much easier when doing a disco. My dad had built a second set of turntables.

1972 had arrived, the first number one of the New Year was, "I'd like to teach the world to sing" by The New Seekers. I seem to remember that this was the theme tune for a Coca Cola advert. I was now managing the shop at Ludgate Hill after Brian Moss had been caught with his hand in the till, by yet another "secret shopper", things seemed to be tightening up as far as security was concerned, which, in a way was my own fault, as I had introduced several of the new systems for weeding out fraudulent transactions. Moss had been betting heavily but did not have the money to put in the till at the end of the day, so he started slipping bets through after time, but they were monitoring him. I was blamed by some for his dismissal as everyone attributed the new level of security to me. I was amazed at the amount of City Gentlemen that managed to escape from their offices to have a punt during the afternoons, the shop was always full. As not much went on at Ludgate on Saturdays I was always moved to a much busier shop.

It was nearing 22nd March 1972, my big day, twenty-one years old and already a veteran of so many situations. As ever, my Mum and Dad would be throwing a party. My birthday fell on a Wednesday, it seemed that everyone at Masseys knew of it. TB had told me to meet in the Grave Maurice in Whitechapel, he even allowed me to shut up shop at 6.00pm, half an hour early. By 7.00pm the long narrow pub was packed. Billy had put the money behind the bar. Micky Embrey put his arm around my shoulder and told me that in all his time at Masseys, some eleven years, no one had ever been treated like me. I was consumed by guilt. Harry Rose got very drunk and decided that he could take on anyone in one of the most notorious pubs in the East End. Unfortunately for him, he picked on a mountain of a man, the man was a little slow in the brain department, but he knew how to fight. He landed one, square onto Harry's jawbone, it was goodnight, Harry. He spent three days in Hospital, unconscious, and a further week recovering. The man that hit him gained notoriety as a double murderer later that year. Harry was never the same after this.

My birthday party was extra special, it was held in the hall above the Aberfeldy and took place on Saturday March 25th. The hall was packed. John Duggan, also twenty-one on the same day was there. All my players were there. Most of my family too, including my Nan. She had no idea where she was, but people kept giving her double vodkas, she took her teeth out and laughed a lot, she even managed a dance. Halfway through the evening, in walked a very voluptuous, but facially suspect girl. She came straight over to me, got her thruppenny bits out and invited me to kiss her nipples. I was wetting myself. She opened her handbag and showed me a packet of Durex, took my hand, and led me out of the room.

'I want you to take me home and use up all of these for your birthday.'

I could not help but laugh.

'Don't, bloody well laugh at me', she shouted.

Her shouting coincided with the lull in between one record finishing and the other one starting. Everyone in the room fixed their gaze upon us. I said,

'Come on then, let me take you home.'

The room was silent when she loudly replied,

'Are you going to do it to me then"?

My face must have resembled a post box. My nan pushed a small envelope into my mouth. I could have toasted bread upon my cheeks. I ushered the large breasted tart out of the door, there was a loud cheer and clapping from the gathering crowd. I led her back to our flat, which was just one hundred yards from the Aberfeldy, asked her to wait in the hall whilst I went into the bedroom. I reappeared and handed her twenty pounds.

'There is no need to pay me, your friends have already done it, don't you want to sample my delights?'

'No thanks, you are not my type.'

A Life Like No Other

The Barbara Windsor lookalike left. I returned to my party half an hour later, to great applause from my friends and family. Of course, the girl was a boy, but his boobs looked quite genuine.

On Saturday, 8th April 1972, our third football dance took place. I had decided to return to the Church Hall in Aberfeldy Street, as firstly, it was not very convenient for our volunteers to go all the way to Bow and secondly, I did not want things getting out of hand, as they very nearly did the last time. I managed to convince the church to allow us to invite 250 people by opening an adjoining room that was not available to us the last time. All tickets were sold within a week of printing them. I could have sold 400, the price was still £5.00, all in. I was to later find out that our dance tickets had created a black market and that some of my players were charging £10.00 a ticket, such was the value. We still cleared £675.00, and had quite a lot of booze left over, which would be used at the next dance, which, for various reasons would be our last.

55 - The Blind Date

Apart from the Nijinsky look alike that I had met whilst on holiday in Cattolica the previous year and some brief encounters with Janice Winterflood, I had never really taken much interest in the opposite sex. At the football dance however, I noticed a girl that I found my eyes following every time she was in view. As the organiser of the dance, I was extremely busy most of the evening and she was flitting in and out of my mind. Eventually Donna, the new girl-friend of Stephen Richardson, introduced me to her as being her best friend. Her name was Barbara, and most of the night she had been talking to and dancing with another Paul, he was Paul Jefferies. He had once or twice played football for us and was often in the Aberfeldy Pub. Barbara agreed to have the last dance with me. My dad, as he always did, played The Last Waltz by Englebert Humperdinck and I proceeded to spend the next three minutes treading heavily upon Barbara's toes. I was a crap dancer in my early years, I am profoundly worse now. The music stopped, we parted, Barbara left with Donna and Stephen, and I had a good three hour's work in front of me, clearing up the hall.

Two days later, Steve Richardson informed me that he had obtained some tickets for a dance at Standard Cables in Silvertown, E.16 and that he had arranged a "blind date" for me. I immediately pooed my pants. Although I had done more than most men of my age, yes, I was officially a man now, I was still very shy around girls and maybe this was one of the reasons I had never pursued a relationship. On Saturday 22nd April 72, Donna and Stephen came to my Mums house and together we walked to my impending doom. Donna then knocked on the door of number 53 Oban Street, yes, yet another Scottish street name. Who opened the door? It was Barbara, looking quite stunning, apart from the bandages on her feet. Work it out!

'Oh,' she said, in a somewhat disappointed tone.

'I was expecting the other Paul, the one with the White Capri.'

'Well, I have a red route-master bus waiting up the road.'

We walked from 53 Oban Street to a bus stop in Canning Town, a good mile away, we took the bus to the Dance Hall in Silvertown. "Without You" by Nillson was at number one. It was noticeable that Barbara loved to dance, as did Donna and most of the other girls. It was also noticeable that whilst the girls danced, the men loved to stand at the bar and drink. I did partake in the slower dances and managed to add to the bruises on Barbara's feet. We took a taxi back to 53 Oban Street and as I prepared to give Barbara a goodnight kiss in her porchway, an extremely large man, sporting a string vest and matching Y-fronts opened the door and said,

'What time do you call this?',

The overweight man in his undies was Barbara's father, Bill, a man I had seen many times in the Aberfeldy but had never spoken to, I had no reason to.

I legged it, after all, his daughter was only sixteen and I was twenty-one, almost a pensioner. At the corner of Oban Street, I met Steve Richardson, and we strolled down to the House of Wan, Chinese Restaurant in East India Dock Road. I remember spending most of Sunday thinking about my date from the previous evening. Due to the intervention of her string vested father, I had not been able to ask her out again, in fact, I did not even know if she might be interested. This problem was solved when I met Steve and his girlfriend, Donna, in the Aberfeldy on Sunday night. Donna informed me that Barbara had liked me, I asked her to get me Barbara's telephone number, this proved to be difficult as there was no phone in her house. The following day Donna gave me Barbara's work number, asking that I only call at lunch time as she would be manning the switchboard at that time. I called on Tuesday lunchtime, a very posh voice said,

"Cunard Brocklebank" I asked to speak to Barbara.

'This is Barbara,' was the response.

Barbara had a distinct "telephone voice", she always did.

Much to my delight, she agreed to go out with me the following Saturday. I remember having the kind of palpitation's that most people have only once in their lives, it was the heartbeat of love.

This meeting of Barbara would prove to be my fourth most significant "corner" as, had I not arranged the dance, had Barbara not been there, had Donna not arranged the blind date, then my life would not have turned out as it did. Still, you cannot have everything!

The following Saturday the gang of six would become the gang of ten, as Herbie, John Duggan, Steve, and myself all now had girlfriends. Our collective worlds were changing. Only Joe 90 and brother John were now "single". We had all met up at the Rose and Punchbowl in Stepney, an early seventies disco pub. Barbara was under strict instructions to be home by 10.30 pm. At 11.30 we came out of the Punchbowl; we all drank doubles back then. Barbara was sloshed, she had been drinking double Port and Lemonade all night. I got her home at 12.15. Big Bill Harrison was waiting, food stained, stringed vest and off-white Y-fronts. I scarpered. I saw Bill in the pub the following day, after we had finished playing football. I mentioned to him that he looked quite different with his clothes on. I got on well with him after that and I think he was OK with his daughter getting home late as he now knew who she was going out with. Bill was a commissioner at Tate and Lyle Sugar Company, he wore a uniform with three sergeant's stripes on the arm. He had been a Sergeant Major in the Army, and he certainly played the part. The first time I was invited into the Harrison's home, which was a carbon copy of our previous house in Venue Street, I was sat in a chair in their tiny living room when Bill arrived home from his shift. He stood bolt upright by my side and coughed several times. I could see both Barbara and her mum becoming a little nervous, Barbara then said,

'You are in my dad's chair.'

I looked up at the six feet, four-inch, eighteen stone sergeant-major and said,

'There are no special chairs in my house, my dad sits on the floor sometimes.'

Bill looked down at me and simply said,

'Out.'

I did what I was told. Barbara's mum got up, put the kettle on and brought Bill a kipper sandwich, it stank. He offered me half of his sandwich, I declined. By now, Barbara and I were officially courting. We would spend a couple of nights each week in the Aberfeldy, her mum and dad and mine became friends. Barbara was introduced to my extended group of friends, amongst whom was Johnny Skeels and his lifelong girlfriend Christine Wilmore. Johnny was another boyhood friend from Venue Street, he was my eldest brother's age but as big brother had moved away, Johnny and Christine were always with us. Barbara and Christine became good friends and remained so, throughout their lives.

On Saturday June 3rd, 1972, the love of my life, Barbara Harrison became 17 years old. In time honoured tradition I arranged a little get together in the public bar of the Aberfeldy Pub. We had been dating for just under two months, but I already knew that she was going to be the one for me. I walked to her house and escorted her to the Aberfeldy. I can still see the look of surprise upon her face when she saw a pub full of friends and family. 50 years later, life had taken its toll and many of those attending that night are now, sadly gone.

At the back: Peter Lucas – Stephen Aldis – Johnny Skeels – Reg Hale – Bungy – John Lucas – Me
At the front: Betty Dorney – Jean Lucas – Christine Skeels – Barbara Harrison

56 - Sunny Beach – July 1972

I had been working back at Leysdown from the beginning of May. I needed to add to my income now that I had two mouths to fill with drink. I would drive all the way home to be with "Babs" at least one night during the week. I would also come back home on a Saturday evening and not go back to Leysdown until Monday morning. For the fourth year running it had befallen upon me to arrange our annual holiday. This year there would be brother John, Herbie, Joe 90, Precious and myself. A different famous five. John Duggan had fallen by the wayside, as his girlfriend wanted him all for herself. Steve Richardson could not go as Donna did not trust him. Vinnie Steel really wanted to go with us, but he was committed to go to Ireland to visit his family. Barbara had already booked her holiday, long before I had met her, she was going, with two friends, to Skegness, that utopia of the East Coast, that for one day a year bathed in the warmth of the North Sea breeze. I had been charged with finding somewhere to go that no one else had ever been to, and I did just that. I booked us two weeks at Sunny Beach, Bulgaria. I must be honest and admit that I was not considering the other four members of our party when making the booking. It was purely a self-indulgent decision, you see I was always an adventurer, and Spain, Italy and Greece did not seem like much of a challenge to me. When informing the others of our holiday destination I was not surprised to learn that none of them had the faintest idea as to where Bulgaria sat, geographically.

Barbara went off to Skegness on Saturday 15th July. I was working at Leysdown and was not there to bid her farewell. We were leaving for Varna the following day. As usual, I dropped off the week's winnings from Leysdown at Billy's house. He handed me £100, telling me that this was for my holiday. This generous tip doubled my spending money. I soon wished that I had not taken it with me. Johnny Skeels had volunteered to take the five of us to Heathrow in his van. By now Johnny Skeels was working for my eldest brothers roofing company, he arrived at my mum's house on Sunday 16th July without bothering to clean out the back of his van. Whilst I did not care too much as I was first in, taking the passenger seat before anyone else could, the others were less fortunate. Inside the back of the van there were gas bottles, a large bitumen pot, rolls of felt, various tools and a single mattress. We all knew what the work-related objects were for, but we quizzed Johnny in respect of the mattress.

'Well, he said,

'I can't have sex with Christine in her house (they had been courting for thirteen years) so I to get her in the van, whenever I can.'

'Do you dip your John Thomas in the tar pot first?' asked Precious.

After a lot of re-arranging, four of the famous five, plus all the luggage, managed to get into the back of the van, and we set off for Heathrow. Our clothes would smell of tar for the whole two weeks of our holiday. We bid Johnny farewell. Precious had a large sticky black patch on the seat of his white trousers, we did not tell him though. The Aircraft we boarded was a Tupolev TU-114 flown by Aeroflot. It had four Turbo Prop engines and was without doubt the noisiest plane I have ever flown on. In its prime it had been the fastest and longest-range Aircraft in the World. Unfortunately, by the time we boarded it in July 1972 it was way past its best.

We landed at Varna Airport at 7.45 pm. There were over 200 passengers on board but only a dozen or so of them alighted at Varna, us five included in that total. The rest, we understood, were ultimately bound for Sofia, the Capital of Bulgaria, we had flown over Sofia forty minutes prior to landing in Varna. We had been given several forms during the flight, one of them was more akin to an SS briefing, as opposed to something a holiday maker should need to fill in. It asked, amongst other things,

'Have you had polio, smallpox, leprosy, an ingrowing toenail (guilty) do you suffer from, allergies, depression, sea sickness, homosexuality (Joe 90 put yes to all) have you ever been convicted of rape, murder, drunk in charge of a donkey or the illegal tampering of a cricket ball?' (Precious put yes to all). After surrendering all these forms, we presented our passports at Immigration. There was a single man in a hut the size of a cigar box, he had a scar from one ear to the other side of his face, he only had the one ear. He wore an eyepatch with a hole in it. I could see his dark brown eye. His other eye was closed. He beckoned me over; I handed him my passport. He looked at me, he looked at my passport. He called my brother over, took my brothers passport and then gave my brother my passport. He held up my brother's passport against his closed eye then turned the passport upside down. He murmured something in Arabic, stamped my brother's passport and waved me through. I was now officially in Bulgaria. My brother held his hand luggage up, in front of his face, the man looked at the bag, looked at *my* passport and then stamped it. Brother John was now also in Bulgaria, how lucky was that? Joe 90, Precious and Herbie, not wanting to be outdone, all swapped passports. Herbie was next to be called, Herbie is black. He had Joe 90's passport. The man seemed confused, I tried to go back to the cigar box. A guard with large machine gun stopped me. I said,

'Come on then, make my day, punk' he took aim.

I thought, sod this for a game of soldiers. In the end, the Immigration official saw the funny side and left his post, leaving the seven other passengers stood on the wrong side of the border. We were then ushered over to a small kiosk that had the words "Money Exchange" written upon it. Now we had been unable to change our sterling into "Lev" (Bulgarian Dosh) in the UK because Thomas Cook had never heard of it, adding that they had never sent anyone to Bulgaria before. I should have known then and aborted our trip. Well, we were here now so we just had to enjoy it. We were asked to hand over our currency exchange forms. We had to enter, into the appropriate box, exactly how much sterling we had. Unfortunately, I had told the truth and had entered £200. I was now given a stack of vouchers, yellow, red, blue, and green in colour. I asked where the monopoly board was, I was moved on. The others surrendered their money, they also received similar coloured vouchers, in exchange. We followed the arrows that indicated where the baggage reclaim was, we ran out of arrows, John Wayne arrived with a wagon train and told us not to worry. There was no sign of a baggage hall. There was, however, a board, on a stand that read "Heathrow". As I knew we had not yet flown back home I assumed that this was where our bags should be, would be, might be. We stood there for forty minutes. Not a sole came over to us. The other seven passengers had not turned up either. Finally, a man in a uniform came over. 'Heathrow, Heathrow,' he said.

'No, "Mongolia",' I replied.

He shook his head,

'No Mongolia already left.'

Precious, a keen Muhammed Ali fan was now dancing around me, throwing punches my way, he screamed,

'Why have you brought us here Lucas?'

A guard stepped over and whacked precious squarely between the shoulder blades with the butt of his rifle, Precious went down.

What appeared to us to be a senior guard came over and had an almighty row with the guard that had just whacked Precious. We hoped that he would face the firing squad the following morning. A small, tubby old lady appeared, she was carrying the smallest first aid kit I had ever seen, it was the size of a cigarette packet. From this, she produced a small bottle, which she then proceeded to shove up the nose belonging to Precious. Had he been Ray Rose, the nose on legs, then the bottle would have disappeared! Precious immediately came around, got to his feet, and once again started to dance around me, throwing punches as he did. This time he received a standing ovation from the gathering crowd. The seven other passengers that had disembarked from the aircraft with us two hours previously, were still nowhere to be seen. Finally, an English-speaking gay Bulgarian, dressed entirely in pink National dress, came over and informed us that our luggage had unfortunately left with the plane and was now in Sofia. He assured us that we would get our bags the following

A Life Like No Other

morning. With hand luggage only, we left the splendour of Varna Airport, the total size of which was about 800 square feet. Outside there was an army van parked up, we knew it belonged to the army as seventeen soldiers climbed out of this eight-seater vehicle. We were beckoned over by a very suspicious looking bloke; he held up a board with the words "Sunny Beach" written upon it. I think he was Bulgaria's equivalent of our own Derek Trotter. We climbed in, I was sat in front of Precious, he was still swinging punches to the side of my head. The van moved off, then stopped. Del Boy got out, lifted the bonnet, scratched his arse, picked his nose, and then left on a donkey. It was sweaty, there was no breeze, we all just wanted to get to our hotel and get our heads down. I left the van and walked back into the Airport building, there was nobody around, it seemed that our fight had been the last one in and the arrivals board, which was just a blackboard, had already had its chalk writing cleaned off. As I returned to the van, a small guy dismounted from a camel, stuck his head into one of the van's windows and said,

'Sunny beach.'

Now we were not sure if he was going to drive us to Sunny Beach or whether he just wanted a lift. He closed the bonnet, tied the camel to a pole (there were no Bulgarians around) and jumped into the driver's side. Two minutes later we turned out of the tarmacked Airport Road and onto a dirt track. We had to immediately shut the windows as the dust coming into the van was just too much. We drove for about an hour, passing run-down houses and run-down people. They really had been run down and just left by the side of the road. This was not Cattolica. This was not Majorca. This was like no other place any of us had ever been to before, and I had been to Peterhead. The abuse that I was getting from the other four was about as bad as it could be, and I probably deserved it. I did point out to them that this trip would broaden their horizons and allow them to see the World in a totally different way. Three of them kept quiet but Precious remarked that,

'He would broaden my nose when we got out,' Precious had a way with words.

At 11.35 pm, nearly a full four hours after arriving at Varna Airport, we had pulled up outside the Sunny Beach Hotel. I had chosen Sunny Beach in preference to the supposedly much busier Golden Sands. Herbie was the last one out of the van and he gave the driver one of his yellow vouchers. The driver gesticulated in a manner that needed no interpretation. He was basically saying,

'What is this,

He did not want a voucher he wanted some English money. At the Hotel reception, we were asked to hand our passports over. I handed over Johns, he handed over mine, Precious gave Herbies and so on. The receptionist laughed I think she had seen this trick before. She then asked,

'Where is your luggage.'

Precious butted in.

'We don't need any luggage because we are not staying,' she laughed again, as she knew that we "were" staying.

'Where can we get food? I asked?

'Ah food, food finished,' she laughed for a third time.

Precious could take no more. He fell to the floor, punching and kicking like a small child having a tantrum.

'I want to go home.' he repeatedly said.

'How about a drink then?' I enquired.

Yes, another laugh, followed by,

'Sorry the bar is closed now, but breakfast is from 7.00am until 9.30,'

Looking up from his position on the floor, Precious shouted,

'Thank God for that then.'

'Is your friend, OK?' enquired the receptionist.

'He is not our friend, he just follows us, wherever we go,' replied brother John.

'Oh, such a sad person,' said the receptionist.

We all now had keys and just wanted to go to our respective rooms. John was sharing with me. Herbie and Joe 90 were together, and Precious was alone. That was planned, as no one wanted to share with this mad man. I asked if it was OK to drink the water from the tap. Yet one more laugh, followed by,

'Only if you want to die.'

The laughing receptionist opened a fridge door behind the counter, took out five bottles of Bulgarian tap water and asked us to part with one yellow voucher each. No wonder the van driver behaved as he did.

The following morning, I had the job of waking everyone up, it would be the same every morning. I managed to rouse Precious by 8.45 and at 9.00am we filed into the dining room. We need not have bothered. The eggs, bacon and sausage containers no longer had heaters underneath them. Whilst this did not particularly bother me, as I did not eat breakfast, the others were fuming. There was some cheese that was curled up at the edges and some ham that looked as though it had gone off several weeks before. The cereal was stale, and the bread was hard. I was in for a really bad day. Even the pre-brewed coffee was stone cold. Herbie said,

'Shall we just go out and eat?'

John was up for it, as he normally ate a horse for breakfast, and I thought that maybe he would do just that. We made our way to the outside, right in front of us was the beach. Not a soul was on it. To the left, there was nothing, to the right there was even less. John went back to the reception, laughing girl was not there, he asked a man that was taking a leak in a bucket,

A Life Like No Other

'Where can we get something to eat'? He was told,

'Tonight, everything will be open tonight.'

I feared for my life. We turned our attention to our lost luggage; I asked reception if it had arrived. Wiping the end of his willy with the back of his hand, the receptionist looked puzzled, he had not a clue what I was talking about. From nowhere seven people arrived in the reception, they were the missing party from our flight. They were all from Manchester. Joe 90 started a conversation with them. This was the first time that Joe had spoken since we touched down last night. In pidgin English Joe was asking them,

'Where you from? Have you been here before?'

'For God's sake Joe, bellowed Precious, they are from England', not Mars.'

The Mancunians let us know that they had collected their luggage from a place other than where we were standing and that there were other cases there. They then boarded an airconditioned coach and arrived at the Hotel twenty-five minutes later. They had enjoyed a lovely, hot breakfast at 8.00am and had just returned from a stroll along the seashore.

'Clever gits, aren't you?' said Precious.

The Northerners consisted of three couples and a girl, aged about seventeen, she was not that attractive, and we were not going to be fighting over her. As we stood, passing the time of day with the Mancunians, five suitcases arrived, we each took one and retreated to our room to don our Hawaii Five O attire.

After changing, we headed for the beach. We simply had to cross the road, a car would poodle by every five minutes or so. An army lorry would pass far more frequently than that. Joe 90 had his camera, he stood in the middle of the road, poised to take a picture. Two guards, stood on the pavement, shouted at him, and pointed to signs that were fixed to lamp posts. The signs indicated "no photo's", Precious was incensed,

'What do you mean, no photos?

'We are on our holiday's'.

The guards drew their rifles from their shoulders and pointed them at Precious.

'Oh, go on then, you stupid commies, who do you think you are, Hitler?'

John and I lifted Precious by his elbows and deposited him onto the beach.

Herbie spotted an oasis in the distance.

'There's a bar up there,' he exclaimed, in a tone which suggested that he had won the pools. (The lottery did not exist in 1972). We moved at a brisk pace along the beach, our aim, a nice cold beer. We reached the circular kiosk, on top of which was a thatched roof, made from, as we found out later, camel dung and straw.

'Five cold beers, geezer,' an excited and puffed-up Precious said.

'Sorry, no beer today, today is Monday, there is no beer on Monday,'
'You're having a "bubble", Precious retorted.
'No, sir, beer tomorrow.'
'What have you got then?' asked John.
'We have coke cola, Pepsi, orange juice, coconut, milk, coffee and of course vodka.'

Without warning, Precious landed one right on the side of my head, I went down, dazed but not out for the count. John had ordered Vodka, the barman lined up five glasses and put a bottle of vodka on the counter.

'One yellow voucher' was asked for.
'Give us four more bottles of vodka,' said John.

We each handed over one yellow voucher. We did not have a clue how much a yellow voucher was worth or even what it could buy but we had ten times more yellow ones than we did any other colour. From 12.30pm until 3.30pm we drank vodka. In between we staged mock boxing matches, we drew quite a large crowd. At 4.00pm we were all drunk, soon to be out cold on our respective beds. At 7.30pm I awoke and managed to get the others up.

'Come on we have to go for dinner, or it will all be gone.'

I went down to reception, alone. I had to find out about the vouchers. Laughing girl was behind the ramp, I asked her to explain. She told me that the yellow vouchers could buy most things, beer, (what beer, I thought) vodka (we already knew that) cigarettes, ice cream, sandwiches, prostitutes, and other cheap items. She went on to say that if we went to the back of the Hotel, we would find quite a few restaurants. These restaurants would have a coloured sign above them. The signs would be green, blue or red. Green is a cheap café style place, blue is a bit better, and red is the best. My four comrades had been given fourteen green, seven blue and four red vouchers for their £100 sterling. I had been given double what they had. We each had stacks of the yellow ones, I did not think we could possibly get through them all. We all left the Hotel. Walking around the back, as instructed, there were a series of paths, most of which were uphill. At various points along these paths were eating establishments. We settled on a blue eatery that night. John asked for five beers, only to hear the words that we would hear again and again.

'No beer tonight, it's not Tuesday,'

So, it was another five bottles of vodka, I hated the stuff. But it was OK mixed with orange juice. We had a three-course meal. The only memorable thing were the chips. The steak was without doubt, camel's butt. At 10.30pm everything shut, and I mean everything. We headed back to the Hotel, there was nowhere else to go and nothing else to do. In the lounge, the seven Mancunians were playing chess.

A Life Like No Other

'Oh, how exciting, can we play chess instead of going to a club and getting off our heads.'

No prizes for guessing who came out with that.

Along one wall of the fairly, large lounge, there was a radiogram with a large stack of 78 records on top. John and I, being the music buffs, went over to investigate. All the labels were in Bulgarian. John put one on, Precious did an Irish Jig. Our friends, "from up North" were not impressed. They all left, apart from the seventeen-year-old, she thought we were a laugh, unlike the miserable gits she was with. Herbie went outside, for a fag. He came back ten minutes later with a bucket full of frogs. John took one and put it onto the turntable of the radiogram and turned it on. The frog was fine at 33 rpm, a little worried at 45 rpm and flew off into the room when John turned the speed up to 78 rpm. The girl was in hysterics. This was to be our only source of amusement for the next thirteen nights.

Just before our first week was nearly up, we had a visit from the Thomas Cook rep. We begged to be sent home early. We had no joy there, as our tickets could not be changed. With little to do, I decided to buy some postcards and send them back home. I bought thirty, just to use up time. As I write this chapter, in 2020 not a single postcard, nor any of the three letters that I sent to Bab's were ever delivered.

Precious – Joe 90 – Herbie – Brother John – Bulgaria July 1972

57 - Goodbye Stan

One of the undelivered letters that I had posted from Bulgaria had informed Babs that I would be home on Sunday and that she should call me at midday so that we could arrange to meet up. I did not get the phone call and therefore presumed that Babs had met someone else in Skegness. I returned to Leysdown the day after I arrived back from Bulgaria. We did not resume our courtship for over two weeks, each thinking that the other had been dumped. Babs had thought that I had ditched her, and I thought that she had done the same. Donny Osmond, singing "Puppy Love" was at number one throughout July. What shit judges of music most of the UK public were.

After the season finished at Leysdown I returned to Ludgate Hill. Cunard, Babs's employer, had moved from Silvertown to Marble Arch, we were only a few stations apart on the central line. Babs and I would meet for lunch at St. Paul's a few times a week. Our relationship blossomed.

At Christmas 1972, I asked Barbara Harrison to marry me, but firstly, of course I asked her father, but he said he was already married, otherwise he would have been delighted to have done so. We planned to have an engagement party early in the new year, 1973, but we would not marry until we had saved up enough. You were unable to pay for anything by Credit Card back then. Chuck Berry ruled the Christmas roost with "My ding-a-ling". One of the worst records in living memory was at number two, Little Jimmy Osmond with "Long haired lover from Liverpool" which took over top spot for the whole of January 73. At the Christmas break, the Aberfeldy Sunday team topped the first division of the Hackney and Leyton league, and the midweek teams were first and second in the top tier of the East London Floodlight League. My newly formed representative team, East London, won their first two games 8-0 and 7-0. 1972 was one of the best years of my life.

I can remember that by March 1973, my wage at Masseys had reached a staggering £25.00 per week. I was now gambling very heavily on most occasions I was simply chasing my losses, occasionally I did win large amounts but invariably, I gave it all back. I was more than aware of the fact that I needed to save money. Firstly, to get engaged, secondly to buy another car, and thirdly to save enough dosh to enable me to marry the only love of my life, Barbara Harrison. My eldest brother's car stealing days seemed to be over, as he, along with our cousin, was running a very lucrative roofing business and was now almost legit. Both Johnny Skeels and Ray Puxley were working for them.

A Life Like No Other

After ten years of working as the settler at the Head Office shop in Alie Street, of which Ruggie had been the manager, the best dressed of all of Massey's staff was finally caught out by Bob White and Co. Stan Romaine, a compulsive joker and wearer of a brand-new suit almost every day, had been tumbled. As mentioned earlier, Stan had always maintained that his father was a Director of Dunn & Co, broadly recognised as London's best, multiple tailors. There was probably not a single City Slicker that did not wear some form of clothing that had come from one of Dunn & Co's outlets. Everyone at Masseys, me included, had taken it for granted that because of Stan's close affiliation with his father's employers he was very well off. I always wondered why Stan, who was proud to inform everyone that he lived in Great Portland Street, had chosen to be a mere settler in a betting shop when he could easily have been the next Tommy Cooper, he was that funny. For ten years, Stan had kept to himself the fact that he was "skimming" on almost every bet that he worked out. He did not take much from each bet, it would be 25p here, 50p there and occasionally £1, or more. His scam had been fool-proof for over ten years, simply because such small mistakes would go unnoticed. How did it work? I knew, for I had been doing the same thing. Stan would settle a bet and should the amount to pay out be £4.50, Stan would write £4.50 on the bet and the counter staff would pay this to the customer. If it were £5.00, he would write £5.00. After paying out the customers, the betting slip would be placed in a tray upon Stan's desk. He would change £4.50 into £4.80 and £5.00 into £6.00. Stan was mathematically very clever, he would add all the amounts of the amended betting slips in his head, and at some point, when no other staff were there, he would simply take the accumulated amount from the till. The till would still be correct as he had not directly stolen the money, he had simply taken the adjusted amount. Security had monitored him for one week, in which time he had taken £70.00. After his dismissal, it was found that his father was a milkman. Stan lived not in Great Portland Street, but in Hoxton, one of London's most depraved areas. Stan did spend most of his ill-gotten gains on clothing. His mohair suits, silk shirts, ties and footwear did all come from Dunn & Co, but this was all a front, that was easily believed by everyone. The personal details that he had submitted when joining Masseys in 1963 had never been checked. Romaine was someone that you would believe without question. It was estimated that he had "skimmed" off over £30,000 during his ten-year stint. Putting that into perspective, his salary over that same period would have been around £8,000. Five months after being escorted from the premises, Stan Romaine was killed by a hit and run driver whilst crossing the road just outside Hoxton Station, he was carrying a Dunn & Co bag containing a new suit, shirt, and tie. At his funeral, that over four hundred people attended, Ruggie was told that Stan had amassed over 350 suits and shirts at his flat overlooking Hoxton

Square. No one was ever charged in respect of his sudden death. He was just thirty years old.

Barbara was doing very well at Cunard and at the end of 1972 she was rewarded with a 50% wage increase.

I still have the "memo" from Cunard in Southampton, it read that they were pleased to inform Ms. Harrison that her salary would increase from £651.00 per annum to £975.00. She was given a new title, that of Assistant Buyer. In addition, they also paid her travelling expenses. She was rich, so I needed to look after her, just in case I became destitute, which I nearly did on several occasions.

In March 73, Slade were at the top with, "Cum feel the noise" and I became 22 years old. The celebrations were nowhere near the level of the previous year. I was seeing a lot less of the other members of our longstanding group of friends. The main reason for this was the fact that we all had girlfriends, the exceptions being brother John and Joe 90. There would be no "famous five" holiday this year. In fact, apart from us accompanying Johnny Skeels on his honeymoon, there would never be another holiday for us boyhood friends again. I was kept busy with football two or three nights per week and on Sunday mornings. I still played the records in the Aberfeldy on Sunday evenings, but the perpetual drinking sessions around various parts of the East End were almost over. I had purchased a car, a Ford Classic Capri, it only cost me £50.00, a far cry from my top of the range 1600E that I had once owned, however I needed a car for when I resumed my stint at Leysdown in May.

I had decided that our next football dance would take place in the summer of 73. I also increased the price of the ticket, it would rise to £7.50, as running three teams was now becoming very costly. I managed to book a hall in Bow that held up to 400 people and had a very modern bar, although we were still allowed to provide our own booze. In addition, Johnny Skeels and Christine were to marry in September, Johnny would be ditching the mattress that he kept in the back of his van.

At the beginning of April, TB called me and asked if I was available to go to Leysdown, as manager, and that he wanted me to start from Saturday the 21st, the day after Good Friday. "Tie a Yellow Ribbon Round the Old Oak Tree" by Tony Orlando was No. 1 at Easter 73. Whilst I did not want to leave Babs, I could not turn down the chance of managing Leysdown again. It transpired that Johnny Young, last year's manager, was no longer in Billy's good books, even though he was his wife's relative. This left the door wide open for my return. I got to choose my staff, once again I would team up with the Captain, Precious, Long John and Alf Alpha. Jimmy Saville had left Masseys to follow his old man's career path as an Arthur Daley replica. Guy had become so obese that he could only manage to get to the shop nearest to his home and that was

A Life Like No Other

on the Isle of Dogs. Barney Rubble had also left Masseys and had joined another, but much smaller East End Bookmaker, Colin D. Sims. I needed to add three replacements.

Finding the three additional staff would prove to be a difficult job. Plenty of blokes asked if they could go, but I needed them to be acceptable, socially, whilst also being trustworthy! When I say trustworthy, this is only in the sense that they would be part of our "inner circle" which mainly meant keeping your mouth shut. After some deliberation, I settled upon Dave "wonky leg" Lewis, so named because he had suffered a horrendous injury whilst playing Rugby. He walked with the aid of a stick, however he was known to be something of a hard man and had the connections to help, should he ever get into trouble that he could not rectify by himself. Whilst he was a partial cripple, he had the looks of Peter Sarstedt, his reason for wanting to go to Leysdown was purely to test his ability to pull birds, of which there were plenty, during the summer season. I figured that Long John and Wonky Leg could hold each other up after drinking sessions. John Smith was the second new addition that agreed to go. John was a very strange bloke. He was twenty-three years old but was living with a woman of fifty-one. He was not what I would call ugly, but she was no oil painting. She was however Scottish and had been brought up in the Gorbals area of Glasgow, widely acknowledged as being one of the toughest places in Europe. John would often turn up for work with cuts and bruises to his face, and whilst he would never openly admit to it, these wounds had almost certainly been inflicted by his girlfriend. She also worked at Masseys and had earned the nickname "swabs", which was a boxing term for the corner man that repaired facial damage during rounds. John Smith had a lisp, and he slurred his words, most of his sentences were illegible, although swabs always seemed to know what he was saying. I had felt sorry for "slur me words" as he was commonly known, and had asked him to join us at Leysdown, simply to help him get out of this unsuitable relationship. He must have been terrified of swabs as he even asked me if she could come as well. I told him straight, no women allowed to work at Leysdown. To my surprise, he did go, I took him in my car, and what he told me during our car journey to the Isle of Sheppey about his situation was, even to me, quite unbelievable. I promised him that I would never tell anyone what he had told me, I never have and whilst I was tempted to write about it, I decided to uphold the promise that I made to him. The third newcomer to the mayhem known as "Masseys Leysdown" would be "slippery" real name Tony Magri. Tony was of Maltese descent. It was rumored that he was related to the famous boxing family of the same name, although he himself never mentioned this. His right eye was slightly higher than his left, sitting almost on his forehead. His nose had been repositioned on his face, several times, by the look of it, which suggested that he may have been a boxer at some stage, albeit a bad one. He had worked at Masseys for over eight years and was known as "slippery" due to his uncanny knack of almost always being in trouble but seemingly able to get himself out of any situation. Tony was recognised as being one of the best counterhands in the firm and was as sharp as anyone that I had met, he could also work out bets in his head. He would be my third settler, whenever needed.

58 - The Honeymoon

Before going back to Leysdown on the 21 st, April 73, I had to arrange an engagement party. I had already booked the venue, The Angel, at 109 High Road, Ilford. The Angel was managed by Den and Angie (I kid you not) they were a married couple that lived in the downstairs of a house that my eldest brother and his wife rented close to West Ham Underground. The Angel was a massive Pub, with a large function room above. Our engagement party took place on Saturday 14th April 73, about 180 guests turned up. My dad did the disco. The food and drink were provided by the pub, and I paid the bill. I have no recollection of how much it was. Although we only provided a buffet for our guests, it was lavish. Waiter and waitress service were provided for both food and drink. Half an hour into the evening, brother John called me over, pointed at a small man holding a tray of champagne glasses and said,

'Look who that is.'

I looked and saw that it was none other than Jack from the café in Bow Road, where John and I had spent most mornings whilst playing truant, seven years previously. Jack asked us to stand exactly where we were, he ambled over to the kitchen and returned with his wife, Millie. Millie was over the moon,

'Oh, my boys,' she said, tears streaming down her cheeks.

'But they are still horrible little bastards,' said Jack.

Millie spent the rest of the evening offering John and me plates and plates of food. We never saw them again. Babs and I were now officially engaged, and I could now sit next to her whenever we were at her parent's house, which was not often as Babs spent most of her time at ours.

Managing the Leysdown shop presented me with the same problems as it had done in previous years. Controlling seven other blokes, all older than myself, all individual, but on the other hand, all very much the same. With this new crew came even more drinking, more hangovers, more late mornings. Some days I would be the only one in the shop at opening times. Thinking back, I was without doubt taken advantage of. I had two cripples, two gays, a bloke whom I could not understand, a Malteser as slippery as an eel and another that laughed like a cartoon dog and continually threw punches at me. I could possibly have been the only "normal" person there. Driving back home twice a week, whilst not far in terms of distance, still presented me with added pressure. Some nights I would not get back until 9.00 pm, I would then only get to

A Life Like No Other

have two hours with Babs before she went home to her parents to get ready for work at Marble Arch the next day.

I took one week's holiday, in July. Babs did the same. We had two goals, firstly to take Babs to visit my relatives in Yorkshire and secondly to prepare for our fourth football dance. I left Alf Alpha in charge at Leysdown. On Sunday 15th July 1973, I drove Babs, for the first time, to Beverley in East Yorkshire, the birthplace of my Mum, and still home to my Yorkshire Nan and several aunts, uncles, and even more cousins. It would be a journey that we would make many, many times during the next fifty odd years. "Rubber Bullets" by 10CC was at No. 1 and we sang along to it as we drove North. Babs was now eighteen years old and past the age of consent, although this made no difference to me, as she was swiftly installed into my Aunt Carol's spare bedroom and I was given a very, uncomfortable two-seater sofa that was about five feet in length, I am six feet tall. Barbara fell in love with Yorkshire, my relatives fell in love with her. Babs maintained a close relationship with my Aunt Carol throughout her entire adult life.

We returned to London on the Thursday before the dance, which was taking place on Saturday 21 st July. We had sold all 400 tickets. We could have sold more. The increased price of £7.50 did not deter anyone. I knew that tickets were changing hands for £15.00, we had created a "black market." We grossed just over £3,000, our costs were slightly more than half of this figure, we were to make £1,400 nett. I considered putting on a dance every month, making it my main source of income, however what transpired on the night made me change my mind. I had hired "bouncers", there were three massive blokes, supplied by my old mate, 'Hardman Ronnie Parish' they were stationed outside the door, suitably attired in penguin suits. Ronnie was there himself, having driven back from Leysdown to take charge. At around 10.00 pm the first of the gate crashers arrived, there were about ten of them and the four hard men were finding it difficult to control them. Another half a dozen then turned up. We were physically stretched in trying to keep them from entering. They seemed to have a bona fide story, saying that one of our players had taken money from them but had not given them any tickets. They had been told just to turn up at the door and they would be let in. The player in question had not mentioned this to me or handed over the money that he had supposedly taken from them. When I confronted the player in question, he simply said that he had no idea about any of this, it was quite apparent that he did. I had to decide, let the sixteen, already drunk, blokes in or not. I decided not to. A mass brawl ensued. The police came, arrests were made. Four blokes were hospitalised. I was told to shut down the event by 11.00 pm, our licence was until 12.30 am. It was to be our fourth and final football dance. The player in question never turned up for pre-season training and I was faced with having to raise funds by other means in subsequent years. Those football dances are still a topic of conversation amongst people that were there, some of whom I have kept in contact with during the intervening years. Great times.

At the end of the season, I returned from Leysdown some £1,500 richer. I had almost stopped gambling completely. I had a wedding to pay for, we had set a date, Saturday 17th August 1974. Firstly, however we had another wedding on our minds, Johnny Skeels and Christine Wilmore were to marry in September 73, but more importantly, Barbara, brother John, plus Brian Ellery (Herbie) Joe 90 and myself would all be accompanying the newlyweds on their Honeymoon. We were all bound for Lloret-del-Mar. The Honeymoon was booked for Saturday 6th October 1973, I of course, arranged the booking, at Sharps Travel Agents. "The Simon Park Orchestra playing "Eye Level" was at No. 1, who remembers that? What utter "crap"! The blokes packed their swimming trunks, shorts, and T-Shirts. The girls packed bikinis, boob tubes and loads of suntan oil. When we arrived, it was colder in Spain than it was in England. Half of Lloret was closed. On our first night, we found, "The Red Lion" English Pub. Johnny Skeels was in his element. Entering the Red Lion meant more to him then entering his new wife. Being with his mates was a definite bonus for Mr. Skeels. For me, I mistakenly thought that once there, I would, for the first time, be sharing Barbara's bed, after all we were engaged to be married. Joe 90 was with Herbie, and I was with brother John. Barbara was right next door, alone. Johnny Skeels and Christine had separate rooms. Barbara was determined to keep me out and she did. What a totally different world we lived in back then. The Red Lion, our home for seven nights, consisted of a snooker table, dart board, two pinball machines, dominoes, cards, and skittles. It also sold Watney's Red Barrel. What more could a red-blooded newlywed bloke have wanted? None of this seemed to bother Christine.

The Hotel that we all stayed in, the name of which, escapes me, was made up of four separate skyscrapers. Each block was identified by its different coloured balconies. There were red, yellow, blue, and green balcony facia's, each block reaching skywards, twenty-two floors to each block. Our room keys had corresponding, colour coded fobs, we were all in the yellow wing. In the pub, on about the third night, brother John, along with Herbie was chatting up a couple of Scottish girls. I think they were arm wrestlers from Peterhead. We all left the Red Lion at the same time, I was being extra nice to Babs, but to no avail. When we reached the Hotel reception brother John and Herbie disappeared with the two Jocks and the rest of us made our way back to our rooms. At around 3.00 am there was a bang on my door. Rather bleary eyed, I stumbled out of bed opened the door and let John in. He snarled at me in his usual joyful way, my head hit the pillow and I was gone. In the morning, I tried to wake John as it was getting near the time that breakfast would be finished. As

A Life Like No Other

he would not wake, I pulled the two sheets from his bed to reveal a blood-soaked bottom sheet.

'What the hell have you done?' I exclaimed.

John looked down the bed and calmly replied,

'God knows, it must have been those birds.'

John had a hole in his side as big as a ten pence piece. The blood, that had been emanating from the wound a few hours ago had congealed. I called the reception, they sent someone with a first aid kit. The would-be nurse announced that John would require stitches as the wound was too big to simply put a plaster over. When I quizzed him about the previous night, John was oblivious as to what had happened to him. We told the police about the nice Scottish ladies and whilst they checked, they could find no trace of the two girls within our hotel. It was concluded that the girls were not staying at our hotel, although they had made it look as though they were. Their motive for the attack on my brother was robbery, although John had no idea if he had been robbed or not. We had knocked on Joe 90's door to find Herbie, but he had not returned. I was extremely worried, as Herbie owed me a tenner! We found him asleep on a sofa outside the lifts on the first floor, he also had no recollection of the previous night's happenings. Later we were to find out that these girls had been operating in Lloret for weeks but had gone undetected. The police told us that they were certain that these girls were spiking the drinks of their prey. We did put a Haggis outside the Red Lion, as bait, but they never returned. Two nights later, John and Herbie were once again chatting to two girls, I kept a close eye on them. These girls were from Bermondsey, South London, a far more sinister place than Peterhead, just not as grey. Well, I need not have worried, as two years later, John and the girl from Bermondsey, Brenda, married. They remain married today, over 40+ years later, and from memory John has never been subjected to the embarrassment of being mugged by a girl again.

59 - August 17th, 1974 – A Day to remember.

The football season 1973/74 had drawn to a close. My Sunday team, Aberfeldy FC had won the premier division of the Corinthian Leage but had lost yet another cup final. My East London representative side had played seven matches and had won them all, scoring 36 goals and conceding just one, which was an own goal by brother John. During that season, we played Leytonstone in a charity match at our home ground, East London Stadium. Leytonstone were the No. 1 "amateur" team in England and had, three weeks previously played Turin, in Italy, in front of 100,000 people. Leytonstone had won that game 1-0 and were proclaimed as Europe's top non-professional football team. Lawrie Leslie, formerly West Ham's No. 1 goalkeeper was their manager. We managed to beat Leytonstone 1-0 in front of 3,500 spectators and raised over £5,000 for Barnardo's.

Second only to beating Leytonstone (sorry Babs) was the fact that on Saturday 17th, Augst 1974, I married my childhood sweetheart. Well, she was a child, and I was a sweetheart. Together Babs and I planned, and executed, the whole of the wedding arrangements. No wedding planners back in the day! We had booked All Saints Church in Poplar for the wedding and the Council Chambers just 100 yards away from the church, for the reception. Some-how we managed to invite 150 guests to the Church and sit-down meal afterwards. A further 100 guests were invited to the buffet in the evening. Babs did not want to buy a wedding dress; she hired one instead. I took her, on no less than five occasions to a massive dress hire shop in Stamford Hill, North London, each time was for a fitting and each time I waited for hours in the car outside. Her idea was to save on the dress and spend the money on our Honeymoon, which I had booked, again using my friends at Sharps, for the day after our wedding. We were to leave for the airport in the early hours after our reception. Our intended destination was to be, Pathos, Cyprus.

The wedding day arrived. "When will I see you again" by the Three Degrees was Top of the Pops. It was the day after my stag night. I was out until 4.30 am. My dad was waiting in the kitchen when I climbed through the window. You see I had no trousers on, the trousers had contained my keys and money. To this day I do not know where I ended up or how I got back to the flat in Blair Street. I did not go to bed. At 8.00 am I was carrying crates of beer up three flights of stairs in the Council Chambers. About half a dozen of us had to get everything in place for the reception, before midday, as that was the time that the caterers needed to begin. The wedding was at 2.00 pm. Our Vicar was David William Randall, he was a regular in the Aberfeldy and used to watch us play football on Sunday mornings. He was banned from performing Sunday Services. Whilst I was working in Hong Kong in 1993, I saw David on the TV. He had, "come out" as being gay and was exposed as never having been ordained. There was talk of all marriages performed by him as having to be annulled. It did not happen, and I remained hitched to Babs. I did wonder if they would annul all funerals overseen by Mr. Randall, but as this meant digging up the dead, I figured it would prove too difficult. We left the church to the sound of a female soloist singing Babs's favourite hymn, Ave Maria. After the photographs had finished, Babs and I climbed into a white Rolls Royce. We drove the 100 yards or so to the Council Chambers and stopped. I leaned forward and asked the driver if he would drive around for fifteen minutes as I wanted to get some value from having to pay a small fortune to rent the car. At the reception, my brother John, the best man, handed me my keys and some money, he told me the trousers might never be found, adding that he would not mention in his speech, exactly what I had been up to on my stag night. I never did find out.

At around 7.00pm the evening guests started to arrive. The proofs of the photographs turned up and were spread out on tables. Guests were invited to order photo's, should they want to. This was a long and laborious part of the evening, something I think no longer exists at wedding receptions. David and Rebecca Sharp, owners of the Travel Agents, arrived. They took me to one side and told me that they had some bad news, it was indeed bad. We were booked to go to Cyprus via a package that Sharps had put together for us. On the morning of our wedding, the package company collapsed, there was no insurance back-up within the industry at that time and to all intents our Honeymoon and money were lost. Before I had time to digest this news and relay it to Babs the Sharps told me that they had managed to book us a holiday in Majorca, not the same as Cyprus they pointed out, but at such short notice it was the best they could do. We would be leaving on the Monday as opposed to that night.

We arrived at Palma Airport late on Monday evening, after a delay at Gatwick of some four hours. We were not best pleased. We were even less pleased when shown to our room, at the supposedly five-star Hotel that had been booked for us. We laid on the bed, as most people seem to do upon arriving in a Hotel, what we saw on the ceiling was disturbing, Babs told me that she was not going to be able to sleep. There were a million ants, climbing the wall on one side of the room, marching across the ceiling, and abseiling down the other side. On the floor, at the bottom of the long line of ants were three or four cockroaches' these hard-shelled pests were being dragged along by an army of the smaller insects. I left the room, descended the four flights of stairs, and presented myself at the reception. I explained my position and asked to be moved to another, "ant free" room. The receptionist went to great lengths to explain to me that all the rooms had ants.

'Oh,' I said, so they are a feature of the Hotel, that's alright then.'

I saw a sign on the desk that informed me that the Thomas Cook representative would be available from 8.00 – 10.00 am on Tuesday morning. I left it at that. I climbed the four flights of stairs back to our room. I assured Babs that I would stay awake all night, to ensure that she was not attacked and carried away by the ant army, adding that I would be 'on the case,' first thing in the morning. She believed me, showered, and went to sleep. I followed a few minutes later.

The following morning, I met with the Thomas Cook rep, I explained that we were on Honeymoon and that our holiday had been a last-minute re-arrangement. The rep was very apologetic and told us that she would be back in the afternoon to give us some news. We had only wanted a decent room. Upon her arrival that afternoon, she informed us that we were going to be moved, out of busy Arenal, to the small resort of Cala Brava. We went along with it. We packed our unpacked luggage and were taken in a taxi to a beautiful Hotel on top of a cliff overlooking a small private beach. This was the five-star accommodation that we should have had in Cyprus. We had a wonderful Honeymoon and I even got to share a bed with Babs. We eventually managed to get to Pathos in 1979, and what an adventure we had!

Upon our return to the UK, we were living with Barbara's parents. They had given us two rooms, which we had decorated, prior to getting married. It was not ideal, but it was a start. In early September, barely three weeks after our wedding, we were visiting some old friend's that lived in Grays, Essex. They themselves had been married just prior to us but already had their own house. As was normal back in those days, my friend and I drove to a Pub, The Bull in Grays, whilst the ladies stayed put and chatted. Prior to leaving I had been thumbing through the local paper and found myself looking at houses for sale. There was an interesting property for sale in Grays, I made a note of the Estate Agent, my mate seemed to know the street upon which the house stood. We arrived at 20 Manor Road, Grays at around 7.30pm, a for sale sign was fixed to a wall at the front of the house. I knocked on the door, a bloke aged about sixty answered,

'I have come to look at the house,' I said.

The man, seemingly a little put out, replied,

'I have not been told anything by the agent.'

Despite his hesitancy, he let us in, and I had a good look around. After raising a few questions, I asked if I could return the following morning with my wife, he agreed.

A Life Like No Other

Babs and I made the twenty-five-mile journey from Poplar to Grays on Saturday morning, after seeing the house we sat in the car outside. We agreed that we would like to buy it. The price in the paper was £9,500, I returned to the house, I offered £9,200 and my offer was accepted, although the vendor pointed out that the agreement was subject to us obtaining a mortgage. I explained that I did not require a mortgage. I asked for the details of his solicitor. I had £9,000 in cash, and cash was not a bad thing in 1974. All this money had come from gambling and other areas of the betting world. I had already arranged a loan of £1,000 in order, that I could buy a new car, the car would now be put on ice. We moved into our first house at the end of October 1974, just seven weeks after first seeing it. Our days of living in Poplar were at an end, although I was still driving there every day to work or manage the three football teams that I was still in charge of. "Gonna make you a Star" by East End legend, "David Essex" was at the top of the charts.

All Saints Church – 17th August 1974 – The Reverend David Randall presiding.
At the altar – Bill Harrison – Barbara Harrison – Me – John Lucas